CW01506450

Dr Nicholas Clements is an honorary research associate in the School of Humanities at the University of Tasmania. Born in rural Tasmania in 1982, he now lives in Launceston. Nick is an avid rock climber and bushwalker whose passion for Tasmania's landscape and history inspired him to write *The Black War*.

the BLACK WAR

FEAR, SEX AND RESISTANCE IN TASMANIA

NICHOLAS CLEMENTS

UQP

First published 2014 by University of Queensland Press
PO Box 6042, St Lucia, Queensland 4067 Australia
Reprinted in 2014 (twice), 2015

www.uqp.com.au
uqp@uqp.uq.edu.au

© Nicholas Clements

This book is copyright. Except for private study, research,
criticism or reviews, as permitted under the Copyright Act,
no part of this book may be reproduced, stored in a retrieval system
or transmitted in any form or by any means without prior
written permission. Enquiries should be made to the publisher.

Cover design by Luke Causby (BlueCork)
Cover image courtesy of Allport Library and Museum of Fine Arts, TAHO.
Typeset in 11.5/16 pt Adobe Garamond Pro by Post Pre-press Group, Brisbane
Printed in Australia by McPherson's Printing Group

Cataloguing-in-Publication Data entry is available
from the National Library of Australia http://catalogue.nla.gov.au/

ISBN 978 0 7022 5006 4 (pbk)
ISBN 978 0 7022 5243 3 (epdf)
ISBN 978 0 7022 5244 0 (ePub)
ISBN 978 0 7022 5245 7 (kindle)

University of Queensland Press uses papers that are natural, renewable and recyclable
products made from wood grown in sustainable forests. The logging and manufacturing
processes conform to the environmental regulations of the country of origin.

For my mother and father

CONTENTS

CONTENTS

FOREWORD

The tragic history of the Tasmanian Aborigines has been one of the most enduring themes of Australian history, the subject of books, articles, theses, novels and films. European fascination with the Tasmanians can be traced back to exploring expeditions that visited the Island before the first permanent settlement in 1803. French expeditions of 1796 and 1802 left engaging accounts of the traditional life of the bands inhabiting the south-east coast on the eve of the British invasion. European interest persisted throughout the 19th century, stimulated by a series of linked misconceptions. The Tasmanians were regarded as the most primitive people in the world, representing the early childhood of the human race, a benchmark from which advancing evolution could be measured. The death of Trugannini in 1876 was widely regarded as an event of global significance. It was thought, quite erroneously, that the Tasmanians were a distinctive race of which she was the last surviving member. Here was the one clearly documented case of the extinction of a whole race of people, an event that appeared to confirm the all-conquering contemporary theory of evolution.

Historians were drawn to the subject as well. Since the 1830s they have investigated the relations between the Island tribes and the British invaders. In every decade since then the tragic story has been retold with varying degrees of originality and artistry; there has been much repetition and retailing of well-worn stories. But there has been quality as well as quantity. Colonial Tasmanians left us a rich historiographical heritage. Particularly notable were the works by John West, James Calder and James Bonwick, published between 1852 and 1870. Many writers continued to be drawn to the subject in the 20th century, and in the early years of the present century Island history became the epicentre for the swirling controversy known as 'the history wars'.

Two traditions of history clashed. The first reflected the common outlook of the first 60 years of the 20th century – the emphasis was on the benign nature of Australian colonisation, which advanced with little conflict, and when it did occur the Aborigines were often to blame. The rapid continent-wide decline of the indigenous population was attributed to introduced diseases rather than to frontier conflict, which it was believed never amounted to a state of warfare. The contending tradition emerged from the work of a generation of revisionist historians writing in the last 25 years of the 20th century. They returned to attitudes that had been common in the 19th century and emphasised the violence inherent in the whole colonial project. They saw frontier conflict as a form of warfare and attempted to provide an account for the consequent loss of life.

Nicholas Clements has written a book that, while reflecting upon the history wars, has transcended their angry contention and has, consequently, brought them to an end. In itself that is a significant achievement. He has also written a book that compares favourably with any other work in the field written in the last 150 years. He has achieved this by great depth of scholarship and by the forensic power of his interpretations, placing many of the controversial questions of the history wars beyond the reach of reasonable doubt.

Clements has reaffirmed the deep seriousness of the Black War and illustrated with abundant evidence the impact of the conflict on black and white alike, and on the whole of Tasmanian society. Perhaps the most striking conclusion is the extraordinary vigour of Aboriginal resistance, which was far more effective than anything of the kind seen on mainland Australia. This can be partly explained by the rugged mountainous terrain, which was ideal for guerrilla warfare, and by the inadequacies of the European muskets. But a major influence on the conflict was the fact that the overwhelming majority of Europeans out on the frontiers of settlement were assigned convicts forced to work in dangerous situations that free labourers would have avoided. They were usually unarmed, on foot and rarely had access to horses.

Nicholas has great empathy for both the beleaguered Aboriginal bands and the hapless convict workers. He is remarkably even-handed, avoiding the partisanship that has characterised and diminished much of previous scholarship. He concentrates instead on the tragedy that engulfed black and white alike; with a compassionate eye he sees the convict workers as unwilling victims of the Imperial project. And that is entirely apt. Nick is an eighth generation Tasmanian, descended from convicts, one of whom arrived in northern Tasmania in 1804 with the first expedition to establish the settlement on the Tamar River. His ancestors lived through and participated in the conflict of the 1820s.

The Black War is an account of a short period in Tasmanian history. But it is an important book for the whole of Australia and for anyone with an interest in our national story.

– Henry Reynolds

PREFACE

I cannot recall ever learning about the Black War when I attended high school in Tasmania in the mid-1990s. I remember vividly the Greeks and the Romans, Captain Cook and the First Fleet, Ned Kelly and Gallipoli, but the frontier conflict that raged across the island of my birth was never discussed. My first real encounter with this event came when I won a scholarship to do my Honours project on Aboriginal representation in Tasmania's colonial newspapers. What I found shocked me. How could an event such as the Black War go so unnoticed? We can be sure that, if it had taken place in the United States, every school child would learn about it, artists and filmmakers would re-create it, and it would be an integral part of the national narrative. The patriotism that Americans are famous for is built upon a curious symbiosis of the good and the bad aspects of their history. Australians, on the other hand, are much more ambivalent about the skeletons in their national closet. The cultural brokers of the last century have led Australians to graze contentedly on a lean historical diet of national triumphs, sporting heroes and rural battlers.

I finished my Honours in 2007, but I was only getting started with the Black War. When Professor Henry Reynolds suggested I expand the project into a PhD, I jumped at the chance. The 'top-down' histories had already been written, but as I surveyed the literature on the war, a gaping hole became apparent: Where were the social histories? No one had yet looked seriously at the attitudes or experiences of the colonists, let alone of the Aborigines. This would be my niche, I thought, but one problem lingered: How was I to weave the vastly different experiences of Aborigines and colonists into one volume?

The answer came to me on a rainy afternoon in 2008, as I sheltered in my one-man tent somewhere in rural Serbia. I had taken a gap year to explore the British archives and vent what remained of my youthful exuberance by riding a motorbike solo around Europe. On this particular day I prepared a modest feast of packet-pasta under the cover of my vestibule, and settled in to begin reading the last of my books: *The Palestine-Israeli conflict: a beginner's guide*. The format immediately caught my attention. Half was written by an Israeli scholar and the other half by a Palestinian scholar. Like most left-leaning students, I was an uncritical Palestinian sympathiser, who had learnt to demonise the oppressive, land-hungry Israelis. But now, reading it from both sides, a basic fact of psychology dawned on me – almost everybody *believes* they are a good person and that their actions are justified. From this angle, the traditional dichotomies of right and wrong, good and evil simply miss the point. Both Israelis and Palestinians are caught up in extraordinary circumstances, and both believe they have God and justice on their side. The book's format raised my consciousness of the issues, and helped me empathise with both sides. What is more, I now saw plainly that moral judgment was unhelpful, and that understanding the conflict meant first understanding the psychology of those involved.

It was late, and I was weary by the time I finished, but I had solved my dilemma – I would write two histories in parallel.

Almost five years after my Serbian epiphany I was awarded my PhD, by which time I had already begun turning it into *The Black War* for the general reader. Unlike the thesis, the book's referencing has been kept to a minimum, so as not to interrupt the flow of the narrative. Those seeking more details, references and engagement with the literature are encouraged to consult the thesis, which can be accessed via the University of Tasmania library website (http://eprints.utas.edu.au/17070/). That work bordered on 200,000 words and included a detailed tally of every violent incident recorded between 1804 and 1842. This book is much smaller – a distillation of the most interesting and important parts of the thesis, swept free of academic cobwebs, and delivered in more sprightly and accessible language. It may shock some, and infuriate or upset others, but whatever else its effects, I hope readers find it as illuminating as I did my beginner's guide. I hope it reminds us that our forebears, black and white, were the same as you and me: imperfect mammals who generally did what they thought was right, or at least, what they felt was necessary.

NOTE ON TERMINOLOGY

Tasmania (see Figure 2, page xviii) was initially named Van Diemen's Land. It was known colloquially as Tasmania from the early 1800s, but was not officially renamed until 1856. I use Tasmania because it is most recognisable. Likewise, the island's frontier conflict was not called the Black War until the mid-1800s, but I use it here because it has been known by this name for over 150 years.

I use 'the interior', 'the east' and 'the frontier' to refer to the greater eastern part of the island north of the Derwent River (See Figure 1A, opposite). In Chapters 7 and 8 I also discuss two minor frontiers, which I call the 'north-west' and 'sea' frontiers. The north-west frontier refers to the greater north-west of the island (see Figure 1B), but especially the lands occupied by the Van Diemen's Land Company. The sea frontier refers to the Bass Strait islands and the northern and eastern coastlines visited by sealers (Figure 1C).

Some of the terminology in *The Black War* is no longer common, or even appropriate. Words like blacks and natives, gin (Aboriginal woman) and half-caste are considered offensive today, but are used here because they were contemporaneous. My intention is authenticity, not offence.

I have also sought to distinguish Aboriginal and European percep-tions by employing different terminology in the alternating white/black sections of each chapter of this book. In the white sections, Aborigines are either blacks or natives – the two most common ways they were referred to by colonists. In the black sections, they are either Tasmanians or Aborigines, and Europeans are referred to as whites or invaders. Aborigines were not united, but all came from the same island, which is why I call them Tasmanians.

Where possible I use the names of individual Aborigines, but I avoid using tribe names, as the records are insufficient. The tribe names made up by colonists are also avoided, as they were just vague labels given to Aborigines seen in certain areas. With the exception of the Mairremmener, I use only a general geographical reference when talking about particular tribes. Aboriginal place names are not used either, as they were poorly recorded and tribe specific. I use modern place names throughout.

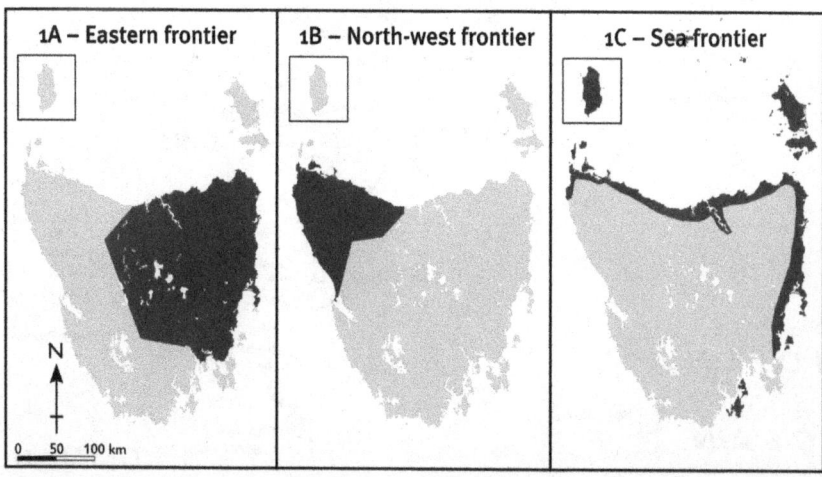

FIGURE 1

Bass Strait

King Island

Flinders Island

Green Island

Funeaux Group

Woody Island

Cape Barren Island ▲ Mt Munro 716 m

Preservation Island

Hunter Island

Cape Grim

Robbins Island

Highfield Point
○ Circular Head

Mount Cameron West

Arthur River

Banks *Strait*
Cape Portland
Ringarooma Bay
Swan Island

Eddystone Point

Burnie ○ ● **Emu Bay**

Hampshire

Stony Head
Port Dalrymple
○ George Town
○ Port Sorell

Tamar River

Ansons River

Peak Hill ▲

▲ Surrey Hills
Black Bluff ▲
1339 m

Forth River

Rubicon River

Pipers Lagoon

South Esk River

North Esk River

Paterson Plains
○ **Launceston**

Ben Lomond

Fingal ● Break O'Day Plains

Dairy Plains
Meander Crk

Norfolk Plains

Macquarie River

South Esk River

St Pauls

Tasmania

Western Tiers

Great Lake

Arthurs Lake

Campbell Town ○

Elizabeth River

Mt Ossa ▲
1617 m

Central Plateau

Shannon River

Ouse River

Lake Sorell

Lake Regents Plain

Lagoon of Islands

Swansea
Great Oyster Bay

Freycinet Peninsula

Pieman River

Mersey River

Penstock Lagoon

Lake Echo

Dee River

Derwent River

▲ Table Mt
Oatlands

York Plain
○ Lower Marshes

Tooms Lake

Eastern Marshes

Macquarie Harbour

Bothwell

Spring Hill

▲ Blue Hills
Lake Tiberias
Colebrook

Quoin Mountain ○
Hollow Tree

▲ Blue Hills

Hamilton

Clyde River

Green Ponds

Prossers Bay
Prossers Plains

Maria Island

Sandspit River

Marion Bay

Gordon River

Jordan River

New Norfolk ○

Richmond ○

○ Pittwater
○ Sorell

Carlton River

Bream Creek
East Bay Neck

Forestier Peninsula

Risdon Cove ○ ● **Hobart**

Mt Wellington 1269 m ▲

Kingston ○

Tasman Peninsula

Huon River

Birchs Bay

Storm Bay

North Bruny

INDIAN OCEAN

Port Davey

D'Entrecasteaux Channel

Partridge Island

South Bruny

TASMAN SEA

Cox Bight

N

0   25   50   75 km

KEY

Mairremmener Territory
(defined by Calder 2010)

FIGURE 2: Tasmania

INTRODUCTION

Eastern Tasmania was the scene of horrific violence between 1824 and 1831. The Black War, as it became known, claimed the lives of well over 200 colonists, and all but annihilated the island's remaining Aborigines (see Figure 3, page 2). It was a small guerrilla war, but one of titanic proportions for the colonists and Aborigines involved. They were settlers gambling everything in the hope of making their fortune; women and children accompanying their husbands and fathers to the other side of the globe; lonely, underpaid soldiers trying to make the most of a year or two's hiatus from their sweltering equatorial posts; convicts hoping to serve out their sentences as painlessly as possible; and people who had inhabited the country since time immemorial, now struggling to negotiate the strangers in their midst. Some of these people were victimisers, but all of them were victims. This book explores their attitudes and experiences during one of the darkest periods in Australia's history.

The Black War in context

The Black War deserves to be considered a conflict of significance. Nowhere else in Australia did so much frontier violence occur in such a small area over such a short period. And this violence was by no means one-sided. Henry Reynolds and Richard Broome are the only historians to make serious Australia-wide casualty estimates for frontier conflict. Extrapolating from regional counts, both suggested a ratio of ten Aborigines killed for every European, though Broome stressed that this was just an average. Ratios, he argued, could be as high as 40 to one in regions such as Gippsland, Victoria, and as low as four to one in Tasmania.[1] In fact, between 1824 and 1831, 219 colonists and 260 Aborigines were reported killed in eastern Tasmania, which implies a ratio of just over one to one (see Figure 3, below).[2] In earlier research I argued that the Aboriginal death toll was probably closer to 600, but this

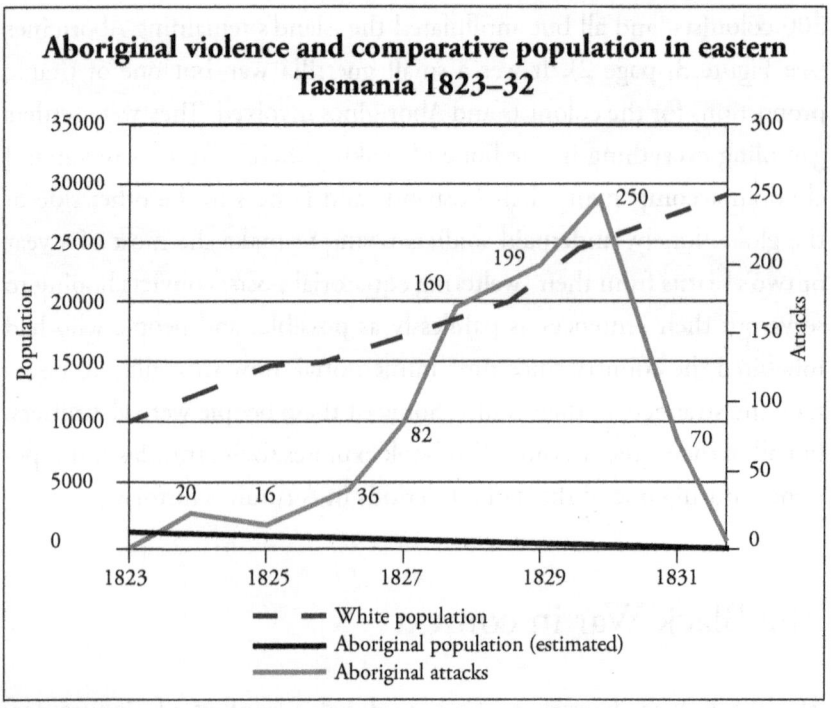

FIGURE 3

still implies a ratio of less than three to one.[3] In other words, the Black War was also the most evenly matched frontier conflict in Australia's history, and the Tasmanians the most effective Aboriginal combatants.

The Tasmanians' effectiveness as guerrilla fighters places them in a similar league to the Māori, despite the latter's fearsome warrior culture, fortifications and guns.[4] During the largest of the New Zealand wars, Te Kooti's War (1868–72), 212 British colonists and Kūpapa (loyalist Māori) were reported killed, compared to 399 anti-government Māori.[5] These casualties are comparable to those suffered in Tasmania. What is more, Te Kooti began his campaign with almost 1000 followers, of whom about 250 were warriors, which is very similar to the initial aggregate strength of the eastern Tasmanians.[6] Such parallels are all the more striking in light of the Māori's relatively sophisticated military technology and organisation.

Historian Mark Finnane has shown that the Black War was an extraordinarily violent conflict, even when using the most conservative casualty figures.[7] In contrast to the World Wars the Black War appears tiny, but this simple comparison is misleading. When it comes to experience, per capita death rates are far more important than absolute death rates. To use the measure most favoured by social scientists, the recorded European death rate in the Black War equated to 15 killed per 10,000 colonists per year, averaged over the eight years of the conflict.[8] This was half the death rate of Australians in World War I – 30 per 10,000 per year, averaged over four years – but much higher than World War II, which on average cost the lives of six out of every 10,000 Australians in each of its six years.[9]

If the European death rate in the Black War was high, the Aboriginal death rate was astronomical. In earlier research I estimated that the eastern Aboriginal population was around 1000 at the war's outset, and that colonists killed about 600.[10] By accepting these figures we arrive at a staggering annual death rate of 1364 per 10,000 per year, again averaged over the eight years of the conflict. Even if we only acknowledge the 260 recorded killings, the reduced Aboriginal death rate of 591 per 10,000 is still extremely high. In fact, it is 11 times higher than average death rates for wars between non-state societies around the world, and 60 times higher than those between state societies.[11] Per capita, then, the Black War was one of the more destructive wars in recorded history.

Since the late 1940s, the tragic fate of the Tasmanians has been the subject of an international debate that has called into question the character of the British Empire and ultimately the Australian nation. It has also become emblematic of racism and greed at its most destructive. In fact, many historians and social commentators have levelled the gravest of all charges against the British in Tasmania. In *The Fatal Shore*, perhaps the most popular history of early Australia, Robert Hughes called it 'the only true genocide in English colonial history'.[12] Accurate or not, this oft repeated and rarely questioned claim has brought Tasmania considerable, if undesirable attention from scholars around the world. In Chapter 3 I bring to bear on this question my findings about colonists' attitudes and experiences, and consider whether that concept of genocide would have been recognisable to its supposed perpetrators.

The history of the history of the Black War

In 1835, Henry Melville published *The History of Van Diemen's Land*, the first in a series of worthy nineteenth-century books to examine the Black War. The most renowned and perceptive of these was John West's 1852 masterpiece, *The History of Tasmania*. West's seminal book was followed by others, such as James Bonwick's *The Last of the Tasmanians* in 1870, and James Calder's *Some Accounts of the Wars, Extirpation, Habits, etc. of the Native Tribes of Tasmania* in 1875. These authors were sympathetic towards the Aborigines, sometimes to the point of compromising their reliability, but their writings, along with the tales of old frontiersmen, kept the memory of the war alive well into the late nineteenth century.

During the first half of the twentieth century, however, the Black War received almost no scholarly or literary attention. This 'silence', as WEH Stanner called it, was broken in Tasmania in 1948 by Clive Turnbull's anthology of government correspondence *Black War: The Extermination of the Tasmanian Aborigines*. Writing in the wake of the Holocaust, amid all the indignation that ghastly episode had inspired, Turnbull was extremely critical of the British government. His book went through several editions, but it was not until the publication of Lyndall Ryan's *The Aboriginal Tasmanians* in 1981 that the war began to attract substantial pockets of attention. Since then, there has been a proliferation of books, theses and articles by scholars such as Lloyd Robson, Brian Plomley, Cassandra Pybus, Henry Reynolds, Ian McFarlane, James Boyce and, most recently, Graeme Calder.[13] The literature on the Black War has almost always been sympathetic to the Aborigines and disparaging of the colonists – at least, that was, until 2002 when Keith Windschuttle published *The Fabrication of Aboriginal History: Volume One, Van Diemen's Land 1803–1847*.

Windschuttle claimed that historians, because of their anti-western and postmodern ideologies, had embellished and even fabricated their evidence to portray Europeans in the worst possible light. This claim possessed a hint of truth. Windschuttle identified a number of errors in past scholarship. However, if exaggerations had crept into the profession, none were so egregious as his own charge of an academic conspiracy to deceive the public about Tasmania's past. The conspirators – the 'orthodox school' as he termed them – certainly agreed the Aborigines had been invaded and often maltreated by the British. Beyond this though, all they had in common was a desire to empathise with the island's vanquished peoples.

Windschuttle was right to point out that, taken too far, this impulse can (and sometimes did) encumber the historian's objectivity. Yet it is equally true that historians who eschew such emotion will neglect two of the most important considerations for reimagining and reconstructing the past: what was it like for people at the time, and what does it mean for us today. Objectivity and empathy are both indispensable to the historian's craft, and need not be incompatible.

While scolding the historical profession, Windschuttle put forward his own version of events, in which he attempted to exculpate the colonists, while painting the Tasmanians as thuggish 'criminals' who essentially brought about their own demise.[14] Their mere existence 'owed more to good fortune than good management', in Windschuttle's eyes.[15] Possibly his boldest claim, however, was that '[t]here was no frontier warfare in Van Diemen's Land'.[16] In hindsight, given the weight of evidence and scholarly consensus against him, it can seem remarkable that Windschuttle was taken so seriously, yet the response to his book in the media and in universities was electric. Even prime minister John Howard weighed in to support Windschuttle's 'patriotic' interpretation of history. It seemed the nation's historical consciousness had awoken from a long slumber.

The furore ignited by Windschuttle raised larger questions regarding Australia's treatment of Aboriginal and immigrant groups. It seemed everyone wanted to stake a claim to their own preferred version of history. Dubbed 'the history wars', these fiery exchanges continue to reverberate. In one sense, the discipline has profited from the greater commitment to empirical rigour and accountability that Windschuttle inspired in his bid to discredit previous scholarship. But the history wars have also had the pernicious effect of further polarising the debate. In the media this has been caricatured as a stand-off between 'black armbands' or 'bleeding hearts' on the one side, and 'white blindfolds' or 'racists' on the other.

Sadly, the main victims of this 'war' are nuance and balance in historical writing and public discourse, at a time when they are needed more than ever. This book attempts to circumvent the ideological stalemate by systematically juxtaposing Aboriginal and colonial perspectives. Alternating white and black perspectives underscore how vastly different these were, though they also reveal some surprising parallels.

A separate but related shortcoming of Black War literature has been its unswerving tendency to examine the conflict from above, with narratives arranged along the well-worn chronology of government responses. There is merit in this framework, but its dominance has been at the expense of other perspectives, namely those of the people involved. Historians, in their preoccupation with questions about the ethics and legality of government policy, have paid little attention to these people, how they perceived their enemies, what it was like for them to live through the war, or how they fought it. Answering these questions from both a European and an Aboriginal perspective is my overarching purpose in writing this book.

Making the dead speak

Examining contact history from Aboriginal perspectives is not without precedent. In 1981, Henry Reynolds published *The Other Side of the Frontier: Aboriginal Resistance to the European Invasion of Australia*, for which he collected fragments of archival and oral evidence from across the country to piece together an overview of Aborigines' experiences. In most areas, a lack of evidence has prevented historians undertaking more focused studies, but in Tasmania, there is a relative wealth of observer reports describing the speech and behaviour of Aborigines.

The most important of these observers was George Augustus Robinson (see Figure 6), who abandoned his family and a successful building business in 1829 in order to fully devote himself to 'the remnant of this much injured race'.[17] Armed with unflinching conviction and determination, he led a party of Aboriginal envoys on an intrepid series of 'friendly missions' between 1830 and 1834 in the hope of conciliating the remaining tribes (see Chapter 6).[18] Robinson's religious zeal was matched only by his moralistic arrogance, yet part of his motivation was an undeniably genuine humanitarian instinct. No European had more impact on the fate of the last Tasmanian tribes, and no one bears more responsibility for the ways they are remembered. His voluminous Tasmanian journals and papers, edited by NJB Plomley in *Friendly Mission* (1966) and *Weep in Silence* (1987), probably constitute the richest single collection of ethnographic material from the colonial period anywhere in Australia. Replete with descriptions of Aboriginal testimony, actions and emotions, Robinson's writings, together with other archival snippets, make it possible to reconstruct a substantial, if incomplete picture of Aboriginal attitudes and experiences.

Historians of the Black War have tended to ignore the colonists' experiences as well. One reason for this is the dearth of surviving first-hand accounts. About 80 per cent of victims were male convicts or ex-convicts. Some of these men were literate, but if they wrote anything about the war, scarcely a word of it has survived. Luckily, there exists a vast trove of letters, diaries, newspapers, police records and reminiscences describing their actions and utterances. By probing these sources it is possible to bring to life the forgotten worlds of the convicts, settlers and soldiers, and rediscover their experiences of the war.

Chapter summary

I begin this book by placing the Black War in its ideological, cultural and historical contexts. This is the task of Chapter 1, which looks at who the colonists and Aborigines were, and how they thought, before surveying the nature of frontier relations in the years leading up to the conflict. The exploration of the war commences in Chapter 2 by examining the attitudes of participants. Here we see that colonial violence was initially motivated by the desire for sex and the thrill of killing, but later by revenge and self-preservation. Aborigines were provoked by insult and encroachment, but they were also motivated by the desire and later the need for food and blankets. In Chapter 3, we investigate the nature of the violence and the tactics employed. Among other things, this chapter reveals that the Black War exhibited an extraordinary solar rhythm, whereby colonists mostly attacked by night, and Aborigines always attacked by day.

Chapter 4 canvases the experiences of Aborigines and colonists, paying special attention to their wartime emotions. The case is made that, on both sides of the frontier, people's lives were profoundly affected by the relentless threat of violence. Fear dominated the colonists' experience; while for the Aborigines, emotions such as anger, despair and sadness were equally salient. Chapter 5 examines the ill-fated 'Black Line', the largest domestic military offensive in Australia's history. This 'Grand Operation' was not only a failure, it was also a horrendous experience for those involved, and a demoralising blow to the colony. What is more, the event had less significance for the Aborigines than previously thought, and probably contributed little to their decisions to surrender. Chapter 6 focuses on the year 1831 and the ways both sides experienced the end of the war. The frontier community was shocked when the surrender of just a few dozen Aborigines brought the war to a close. Their jubilation was in stark contrast to the sombre anguish of the surviving Tasmanians – the last of their people, now all but expunged.

Tasmania's eastern interior was the primary frontier on which the Black War was fought, but there were two other theatres of conflict that demand attention. The stories of the north-west and sea frontiers, although they are not the central focus of this book, are indispensable to its story. For this reason, I have included a concise but probing examination of each in Chapters 7 and 8, respectively.

The north-west frontier shared many characteristics with the conflict in the east, but it also exhibited a number of significant peculiarities that helped to foster an especially grisly brand of violence. Aborigines in this isolated region continued their attacks for more than a decade after the eastern tribes had surrendered, though they ultimately suffered the same fate.

On the sea frontier the sealers of Bass Strait established a system of slavery both by trading with and raiding the coastal tribes of northern and eastern Tasmania. Scores of Aboriginal women and girls were enslaved, and in most cases treated appallingly. Some tribes were literally stripped of all females. The sea frontier is a story of deprivation and predation, cruelty and resistance; yet in an ironic twist, it was also the principal birthplace of Tasmania's mixed descent Aboriginal community.

As this book leads the reader back and forth across the frontier, the line between hero and villain should fade. At its core, *The Black War* is a story about two peoples who just wanted to be free of each other, but were powerless to escape the contingencies of history. The world was shrinking rapidly in the early nineteenth century, and sooner or later Europeans and Aborigines were bound to clash, but it was Tasmania's unique circumstances that turned this encounter into a 'war of extermination'.

CHAPTER ONE

BACKGROUND

White

The peoples of Tasmania and Europe lived very similar hunter-gatherer lifestyles for at least 30,000 years. Then, around 5000 BP, the Neolithic or First Agricultural Revolution began transforming Europe, setting its various tribes on a path of unprecedented political, economic and technological development. Being ignorant of their own humble origins, Europeans assumed a sense of inherent superiority over those peoples who retained hunter-gatherer economies. This intuitive ethnocentrism was nurtured by other motives as well. From the seventeenth century, chattel slavery became one of the most profitable industries in the world, and the enslavement of millions of blacks demanded both natural and moral justification. This task fell to scientists, theologians and philosophers, and the rationalisations they devised left a lasting impression on the European psyche.

European racial thought

The late eighteenth century was the height of the Enlightenment. Europe saw a steep decline in church power, and unprecedented technological and intellectual flourishing. This was also an era of ambitious exploration and imperialism. As the known world rapidly expanded, questions were raised at all levels of society about the nature and significance of newly discovered peoples.

Enlightenment thinkers worked tirelessly to categorise the living world into hierarchical order. The antecedent of this movement was the 'Great Chain of Being', an idea that went back to the ancients, and remained popular well into the nineteenth century. Atop the Chain was the Christian God, followed by Jesus, the angels, humans, animals, and finally non-sentient organisms. Among humans, white European males were superior, followed by white females, Asians, Africans and so on, all the way down to the natives of Tasmania, who were scarcely distinguishable from apes. According to this idea, hierarchical differences were natural and unalterable, so efforts to 'raise up' the lowly were considered futile.

Chain of Being thinking appears to have been prevalent among colonists in Tasmania. In 1827, Land Commissioner Roderic O'Connor referred to the local blacks as 'Ourang Outang's [sic], [a] disgrace it would be to the human race to call them Men'.[1] In 1830, Mrs Prinsep, the wife of a visiting army officer, also claimed they were 'like the Ourang Outang'. She believed they were 'undoubtedly in the lowest possible scale of human nature'.[2] Many such remarks were penned at the height of the war, but even in 1820 a visitor to Hobart observed that '[t]he aborigines of this island are supposed [by locals] to be the most degraded of any known in the world'.[3] Only the well-read grasped the specifics of the Great Chain and other complex theories, but over time an understanding of their basic themes percolated down through society.

The Great Chain of Being had an ambivalent relationship with the ascendant evangelical Protestantism of the late eighteenth century. Evangelicals advocated monogenism, the idea that all humans descended from Adam and Eve. Their preachers insisted that, given the right conditions, people of any race might be 'improved'. Missionaries flocked to

British colonies in the Americas, India, South Africa and the Pacific. In Australia though, the native inhabitants attracted little interest before the 1840s. Missionary resources, it was thought, were best invested in more promising races.

The thinking of frontier colonists was especially influenced by the notion of savagery. More a folk genre than a cogent philosophical concept, savagery was vague enough to sit comfortably with most scientific, philosophical and theological assumptions. It came in two varieties. The 'noble savage' was popularised by the French philosopher Jean-Jacques Rousseau in 1754. Rousseau proposed that social progress led, not to virtue, but 'toward the decrepitness [*sic*] of the species'.[4] Savages had not progressed far from the 'state of nature', according to Rousseau, thus they retained much of the 'purity' and 'nobility' associated with this original state. Rousseau's writings exerted an enormous influence on European thought.

The desire to encounter the noble savage is particularly evident in the writings of the explorers who 'left Europe when the dreams of Rousseau were the toys of the speculative'.[5] By the early nineteenth century, however, the noble savage was being undermined not just by emerging intellectual trends, but also by the disillusioning experiences of explorers and settlers.[6] In fact, the French explorer Julien Crozet reported directly to Rousseau on the 'grotesque' savages he encountered in Tasmania in 1772. To his unflattering description, Rousseau replied despairingly: 'Is it possible that the children of nature can really be so wicked?'[7]

The noble savage rapidly lost its grip on the middle-class imagination from the beginning of the nineteenth century. Its antithesis, the ignoble savage, had always been popular among the less educated working class.[8] These people imbibed their negative views about indigenous peoples from the pulpit, but also from adventure tales such as *Robinson Crusoe* and *Gulliver's Travels*. Respected ethnographer Margaret Hodgen concluded that the majority of Europeans were 'anti-savage, and strongly so'.[9]

Imperialist ideology also played an important role in the tragedy that unfolded in Tasmania. The unparalleled expansion of the British Empire between 1756 and 1815 brought vast swaths of the world's population under its rule. During the same period, the French, Ottoman, Mughal and Safavid empires either fell or waned considerably, leaving Britain as the sole imperial superpower.[10] For these reasons, Britain's imperial policies were increasingly shaped by ideological considerations, the most important of which was legitimacy.[11] The physical, political and to some extent cultural usurpation of so many people demanded justification. Many indigenous peoples were exploited, oppressed and even killed in the process of colonisation, and conscientious Britons needed to rationalise this profitable, but morally ambiguous conduct.

Since Australia was populated by hunter-gatherers, the Colonial Office assumed it was a 'desert and uncultivated' land that could be 'claimed by right of occupancy'.[12] This tradition was first formalised by the English philosopher John Locke, who famously asserted that no man could 'own' land until he had 'mixed his labour with; and joined to it something that is his own'.[13] Together with the pervasive assumption that nomadic peoples had no meaningful attachment to land, this conception of ownership helps explain why colonists were so bewildered by the tenacity of native resistance.[14]

Legalistic defences were strongly reinforced by the biblical injunction to subdue the earth and till the soil. When settlers presented their justifications for appropriating native land in the colonial newspapers, their appeals to international law were invariably laced with religious language. Even those who felt uneasy about such transparently self-serving justifications could not challenge the colonial project without flagrant hypocrisy.[15]

Establishing a right to the land was necessary for settlers' sense of legitimacy, but not always sufficient. It was widely believed that dispossessed peoples should be recompensed with the blessings of civilisation and Christianity. In fact, the increasingly powerful evangelical and humanitarian movements considered it imperative to export Britain's superior customs and religion to the 'barbarous' corners of the globe. Viewed through this lens, colonialism was not only a legal right, but also a moral obligation.

In reality though, there was a fundamental contradiction inherent in the very concept of 'humane colonisation', since colonisation entailed dispossession, which was manifestly inhumane. Humanitarian colonisers were nonetheless convinced that, once Britain's 'superior' laws, customs and beliefs had been imposed, native peoples would thank them.

Of course it was only the conscientious colonisers who felt the need for these justifications. Most of Tasmania's first colonisers were unencumbered by such scruples. Convicts and soldiers were not there by choice, and needed no contrived excuses to soothe their consciences. To them, the blacks, like the landscape and the authorities, were simply dangers to be negotiated. Most felt bereft of rights, and they had no intention of extending any to 'savages'.

Who were the colonists?[16]

There was considerable diversity among Tasmania's early colonists, but those engaged in the Black War can be divided into four main groups: emigrant settlers, soldiers, convicts and ex-convicts. Before examining the roles these people played in the conflict, we must first establish who they were and the circumstances in which they lived.

Emigrant settlers began sailing to the colony in droves after 1820, hungry to exploit the offer of free land and a new start. Most were young, middle-class families, though some men came alone. When Governor George Arthur took office in 1824, he was instructed to provide these wealthier settlers with sizeable grants and a corresponding number of convict servants, which allowed a group of about 200 large landowners to monopolise the island's agricultural economy within just a few years.

Free emigrants were not the only settlers on the Tasmanian frontier. In the first two decades of settlement, convicts could be granted a small parcel of land on completing their sentence. These men became settlers in their own right, and some did well. By the time the war began, however, many were working for the wealthier emigrant settlers, having found it impossible to compete. Those ex-convicts who persisted as small landholders often had no convict servants; others had just one or two. Consequently, these men were almost as likely to encounter natives as those under sentence.

This is in stark contrast to emigrant settlers, who often had dozens of servants and relied on overseers to manage their estates. They spent comparatively little time in exposed situations, often running their operations from Launceston or Hobart. Their servants, on the other hand, were regularly exposed to attacks, and it was these convicts and ex-convicts who comprised the bulk of those killing and being killed by blacks.

The vast majority of convicts were men, transported on sentences of seven years, 14 years, or life (see Figure 4, page 18).[17] Most were assigned to free settlers, for whom they laboured in exchange for their upkeep. About ten per cent earned tickets-of-leave, entitling them to limited probationary freedoms, while approximately four per cent gained conditional pardons, restricting them only from returning home.[18] None were convicted murderers, and few were professional criminals. In fact, most were just young working-class men who had fallen on hard times.[19]

Convicts' lives were tough, both before and after conviction, but while we may pity them, we must not forget the hardening effects of squalor and violence. The archives are replete with testimony affirming the bad character of convicts, and not all of this can be dismissed as class prejudice. The experiences of convictism and frontier life were highly conducive to the callousness that will be described throughout this book. Once sentenced and torn from their families and homes, the life of a convict was characterised by harsh discipline, loneliness and deprivation.

Those sent to Tasmania were repeat offenders and, therefore, even more likely to have been affected by the cruelty of convictism.[20] Many did not have the strength of character to resist the brutalising effects of such an existence.

The military comprised the remainder of the frontier population. In 1829, Tasmania's garrison consisted of nearly 1000 soldiers from the 40th, 57th and 63rd regiments, about half of them distributed throughout the interior.[21] Small detachments of between two and eight men were dispersed widely on the frontier to protect outlying settlers against blacks. This deployment was highly unorthodox, and it left many detachments without the supervision of an officer. While soldiers grumbled about the boredom and privation of their posts, settlers complained of their drunkenness and inefficiency. These men came from the same socioeconomic backgrounds as the convicts – indeed, some convicts were former soldiers – and they were subject to similarly harsh punishments. The convict system and the military both produced hardened and brutalised men; the one major difference was that soldiers were trained to kill.

Very few colonists were interested in learning about the island's native inhabitants, and even fewer were concerned about their welfare. Settlers were concerned with economic prosperity, to the exclusion of most other considerations. Convicts and soldiers were the engines of colonisation, but they were not there by choice, and their interest in the natives rarely went beyond killing them, having sex with them or avoiding them. Theirs was a situation that gave little encouragement to humaneness, and much to inhumaneness. Thus, the colony's demographic and socioeconomic characteristics helped incubate the war.

First contact

On 7 March 1772, French explorers under Marion du Fresne became the first Europeans to encounter the natives of Tasmania. When the

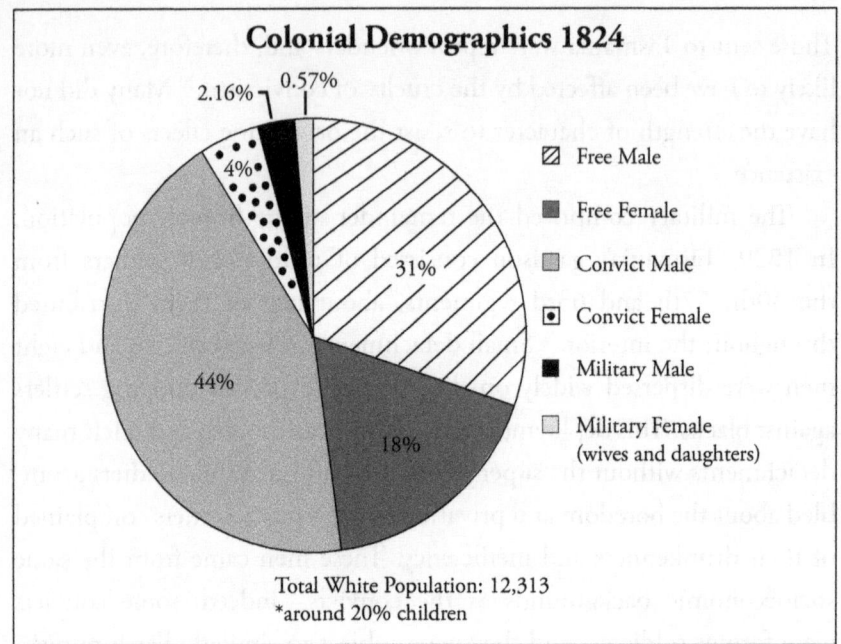

Colonial Demographics 1824

2.16%   0.57%

4%

31%

44%

18%

- ▨ Free Male
- ■ Free Female
- ▨ Convict Male
- ⊡ Convict Female
- ■ Military Male
- ☐ Military Female (wives and daughters)

Total White Population: 12,313
*around 20% children

FIGURE 4

sailors rowed ashore at Marion Bay, neither they nor the tribe poised nervously on the beach could have grasped the full significance of the meeting. Culturally and technologically, there had never been a meeting between such fundamentally different people. As the esteemed biologist and historian Jared Diamond put it, 'no two peoples on earth were less equipped to understand each other'.[22] The historic meeting began on friendly terms, but for reasons the visitors did not understand, it ended with a sailor being speared and several natives killed or wounded.

Thirty-one years passed between du Fresne's departure and the arrival of the first settlers. In that time, seven British and two more French expeditions visited south-eastern Tasmania, most achieving some communication with the natives. These encounters were often tense, but never openly hostile. The explorers were men of science, curious and generally well intentioned towards the island's inhabitants, but the colonists who came after them had different priorities altogether.

Kangaroo economy

The British seized Tasmania on 12 September 1803, in a flurry of paranoia about French interests in the region. The colony was split in two after its first year, with Colonel David Collins assuming command in the south, and Colonel William Paterson in the north. After its initial establishment at Risdon Cove, the southern capital was moved to Hobart in 1804, while the northern colony was administered from Launceston. From the outset the home government effectively abandoned both settlements. Britain was now fully preoccupied fighting Napoleon, so resupplying her most distant and inconsequential outposts became a low priority.

Both colonies were forced to fend for themselves during the early years of settlement (see Figure 12). Collins was heavily dependent on indigenous foods, and Paterson could procure almost nothing else. Hunting was the island's main industry for most of the first decade. Kangaroo meat became the staple food and its fur was widely used to make clothes. As game levels were depleted, hunters were forced to venture further into the interior, facilitating the first significant encounters with the natives. Such men were exposed to considerable danger from the more numerous and powerful blacks, who attacked them on at least two dozen occasions during the first decade of settlement.[23]

This early violence went both ways. Bushrangers were becoming a serious problem by 1808, and several of these well-armed bandits were notorious for their cruelty towards blacks.[24] They were clearly not alone, however. Four government proclamations issued between 1808 and 1813 condemned the killings, rapes and kidnappings of blacks that were apparently common at the time. Although some amicable contact did take place, a clear pattern of occasional, small-scale violence predominates in the accounts of early frontier contact.

Expanding beyond the beachheads

By 1813, the now united colony had become largely self-sufficient. Although hunting remained common, cereal crops, sheep and cattle had replaced marsupials as the staple foods. Intermittent contact with blacks continued as the settlements spread further and further along the lush river valleys radiating from Launceston and Hobart. Soon after his arrival in 1817, Governor Sorell reprimanded those 'in the habit of maliciously and wantonly firing on and destroying, the defenceless NATIVES', and threatened 'to punish any ill-treatment'.[25] Two years later he was forced to issue a similar threat, yet no punishment was ever issued. 'The government disapproved of oppression', as John West pointedly observed, 'but it was either too weak, or too indolent, to visit the guilty'.[26]

Archival records for the second decade of settlement are scarcely better than those documenting the first. Our knowledge comes from official documents, the *Hobart Town Gazette*, and a handful of private letters and journals. There was much hearsay regarding frontier violence between 1813 and 1823, but only about 50 specific incidents were recorded.[27] Again, there was some friendly intercourse, but the evidence indicates that frontier relations continued to be infrequent and mostly hostile. This is unsurprising given that the majority of those making contact with natives were convicts and bushrangers.

Sex and the shortage of women

In 1822, there were six times as many men in the colony as women, and the ratio among the convict population was 16 to one.[28] The military permitted only one soldier in eight (usually the officers) to have their wives and children accompany them on overseas duty.[29] The few available women in the colony were mostly convicts, who could take their pick of men, and generally opted for wealthier, free suitors.[30] For convicts and soldiers this made sexual opportunities – to say nothing of loving relationships – depressingly scarce. Thousands of predominately young men in their sexual prime were forced onto the frontier without any 'acceptable' sexual outlets.

This situation produced its fair share of homosexuality and bestiality, but it also meant that native women were highly coveted.[31] Initially, some frontiersmen were able to trade for sex, but as demand outstripped supply, and as more and more women were taken by force, the relationships necessary for such exchanges broke down. Consequently, rape and abduction became increasingly common.

The link between the gender imbalance and sexual predation did not go unnoticed. One settler writing to the *Tasmanian* went so far as to suggest that the government should release all female convicts into the interior in order to stem the prevalence of 'nameless crime' and 'the aggressions of the Stock keepers upon [the natives'] Wives and Daughters'.[32] West drew the connection more explicitly: 'It would be impossible even to hint [at] the series of facts, which are authenticated to the writer, and which strangely blended ferocity and lust. The sealer, or stockman, who periled his life to accomplish the abduction of a native female, thought that danger but fairly avenged by the destruction of her relatives!'[33]

'Keeping' native children

Colonists also coveted native children. By 1813, Governor Davey was convinced 'the resentment of these poor uncultivated beings has been justly excited by ... the robbery of their children'.[34] Thirty-seven baptisms of native children are recorded between 1810 and 1820, and there were probably others that were not baptised.[35] Governor Sorell echoed Davey's condemnation in 1819, demanding all colonists who acquired their children 'illegitimately' to hand them over to the government, but this was never enforced.[36]

Tasmania's first chaplain, Robert Knopwood, was aware of the prevalence of kidnapping from the outset. In January of 1806, he recorded that some convicts had brought a 'little native girl' into Hobart, but that she promptly 'made her escape out of a window'.[37] In 1814, Knopwood was gaining the trust of a local tribe until '[a] number of children were forcibly taken from them, and they disappeared'.[38] According to the *Colonial Times*, the practice of kidnapping only subsided in the early 1820s, when 'many of the native tribes were suffering severely from some most loathsome coetaneous [skin] disease ... [which] prevents many of the Settlers in the interior from taking into their service infant natives, as has been the case, for the purpose of bringing them up in a civilised manner'.[39]

Colonists stole native children for several reasons. Some entertained genuine, if misguided, civilising intentions. Not far beneath the philanthropic surface, however, was the need for labour. Many native children who were taken under the pretext of being 'civilised' became little more than slaves.[40] In some cases, there were almost certainly sexual reasons for keeping native children. Chapter 8 describes how the Bass Strait sealers regularly took native girls from mainland Tasmania to keep as sex slaves, but paedophilia also occurred elsewhere in the colony.[41] In 1824, for instance, convicts raped two nine-year-old 'half-caste' girls in separate incidents. Likewise, one convict was hanged for raping a four-year-old girl the same year; two more were executed on the same charge in 1828; and in 1830, yet another three convicts swung for gang-raping a magistrate's five-year-old daughter.[42] The *Colonial Advocate* recognised in 1828 that the problem of 'child rape' stemmed from 'the transportation of male convicts without a due proportion of females'.[43] If such men were unable to restrain themselves in the face of certain execution, it stands to reason that native 'orphans' were also preyed upon.

Pre-war encounters

About 1814, one or more groups of blacks began visiting Hobart.[44] By 1822, a tribe known as the 'town mob' was regularly seen on the outskirts of Hobart, attracting some curiosity, but more often pity and disgust. Colonists' attitudes towards these 'fringe-dwellers' are difficult to gauge. One resident complained it was 'disgusting to behold, the state of nudity in which they wander about our streets'.[45] There was even a 'barbarous custom of encouraging the Black people [with rewards of alcohol] to murder or mangle one another ... for the [onlookers'] amusement and gratification'.[46] These 'unsightly prostitutes', 'drunkards' and 'beggars', most of them detribalised orphans or refugees, gave newly arriving colonists their first impression of the island's natives.

Despite their visibility, few references to fringe-dwelling blacks survive, and the so-called wild tribes seem to have attracted scarcely more attention. Settlers were usually too busy establishing themselves to spend time musing over the island's 'degraded blacks'. The occasional spearing was readily explained away as the barbarism of ignorant savages, provoked by unscrupulous convicts. No one seems to have considered the impact of encroachment on the original occupants. It was assumed they would simply 'move on'.[47]

The natives were of greater interest to convicts and free labourers. These frontiersmen, West pointed out, were often stationed 'forty and fifty miles [64–80 km] from their masters' dwellings, were rarely visited, and were under no immediate control'.[48] Some stockmen and sawyers seized on the sexual opportunities presented by this lack of surveillance. The company of a black woman, whether obtained by exchange or by force, was probably one of the few pleasures these men experienced. Eventually though, many frontiersmen found themselves watching their backs – especially those who had incurred the natives' displeasure.

In 1819, Governor Sorell predicted that, 'if the natives were intent upon Destruction ... the Mischief done by them ... would be increased a Hundred Fold'.[49] But as expansion continued, and no major resistance was encountered, the Governor's concerns were abated. When he was recalled in 1824, Sorell did not even mention the natives in his lengthy handover letter to George Arthur.[50] That same year, the *Hobart*

Town Gazette reassured its readers that 'the sable natives of this Colony are the most peaceable creatures in the universe'.[51] This complacency appears to have been ubiquitous. Preoccupied as colonists were in the mid-1820s, with suppressing an unprecedented epidemic of bushranging, scarcely anyone imagined that a much deadlier threat was imminent.

Black

Tasmania was once joined to mainland Australia by land bridges across which humans migrated in several waves before Bass Strait flooded for the last time around 10,000 BP.[52] Sites in both the north and south of the island bear evidence of human occupation extending back at least 34,000 years.[53] Remarkably, Tasmanians never became culturally or linguistically homogenous. Tribes from different areas retained distinct hunting and gathering practices, butchery and cooking methods, stone tools, shelters, watercraft, art, rituals and mythologies.[54] What all Tasmanians had in common, however, was a marked divergence from their mainland ancestors. The most visible of these differences was technological. Tasmanians' toolkits were much simpler than those used by mainland Aborigines. In fact, as they adapted to more favourable conditions, they abandoned unnecessary technologies until they had the simplest toolkits of any modern humans.[55] They were, nonetheless, a spectacularly resilient people, who had evolved rich social and spiritual lives. Understanding something of these ways of living and believing is essential for putting into context the Aboriginal perspectives discussed in this book.

Social structure

The most prominent unit of Tasmanian society was the tribe (see Figure 13). Depending on the carrying capacity of the land, these consisted of

30 to 80 individuals, all sharing a common dialect and migratory pattern.[56] Tribes were comprised of hearth groups of four to ten (generally related) individuals.[57] Hearth groups shared a campfire, and had the capacity to be semi-autonomous with regard to movement and subsistence, though most endeavours appear to have been coordinated at the tribe level.[58]

Two or more tribes occasionally met to trade, socialise, perform ceremonies, arrange marriages, settle disputes, and carry out various other businesses. Tribes occupying contiguous areas and speaking similar dialects were more likely to be allied, but a failure in diplomacy could result in war.[59] These affiliates, as I will call them, do not appear to have been especially tight-knit, but they may have been important for support and communication during the Black War.

Tribal affiliates did not have names, but historian Graeme Calder utilised the term 'Mairremmener' to refer to an affiliate known to colonists as the Oyster Bay and Big River tribes.[60] These were in fact many tribes. They utilised the territory north of the Derwent River, south of the highland lakes, and east of the Dee River to the coast (see Figure 2, page xviii). They were responsible for much of the violence during the Black War, thus it is useful to have a collective term for them, even if they were never fully united.

The tribal leadership structure in Tasmania is poorly understood, but it does not appear to have been particularly hierarchical. The most common observation, exemplified by the Quaker missionary James Backhouse, was that 'the chiefs among these tribes are merely heads of families of extraordinary prowess'.[61] It seems chiefs were not autocratic leaders, but respected patriarchs and warriors looked to in times of turmoil.[62] Naturally, these men played a pivotal role in the Black War.

Territory and movement

Tasmanians were territorial, and certain places appear to have been central to their identities. Linguist John Taylor identified 33 Tasmanian words for 'country', and showed that part of a tribe's name 'was a geographical reference to the location of the[ir] territory'.[63] In 1838, after ten years of experience among the surviving Tasmanians, Robinson asserted that the island 'was divided and sub-divided by the natives into districts, and contained many nations'.[64] A tribe's territory was expansive and often shared with allies, but if venturing into foreign country, access had to be negotiated lest they invite conflict.[65]

Tasmanians knew their country intimately. They were deeply in tune with their surroundings, knowing where to go, when to go there, what to take, how to take it and when to leave it. Tribes were almost always on the move, manipulating the country as they went using sophisticated burning techniques that encouraged the proliferation of game.[66]

Shelter, diet and health

During the summer months most Tasmanians slept in the open air, employing windbreaks where necessary, while in the winter they built huts. On the rugged west and south coasts, tribes constructed large beehive huts that could house up to a dozen people. Eastern tribes, on the other hand, tended to build smaller, less robust structures. Tasmanian food economies were also regionally distinct. When inland, tribes subsisted largely on kangaroo and other marsupial species, but when on the coast, they lived predominantly on shellfish.[67]

Pre-colonial Tasmania appears to have been free of serious endemic diseases. The island's inhabitants were nevertheless susceptible to common ailments, and like most humans at the time, attributed illness to evil spirits, sometimes called '*Raegeowrapper*'.[68] In response, they employed a range of treatments, but the standard panacea was to make deep incisions into the affected area 'to let out the devil'.[69] Through the medium of a shaman, Tasmanians also enlisted the help of good spirits.[70] One colonist observed that '[e]very tribe of the Blacks has a medical man, peculiar to itself, who is consulted in all cases of sickness or accident'.[71] For Aborigines, health was an important concern, indistinguishable from spiritual wellbeing.[72]

Violence

Gender relations in Tasmanian society were strongly patriarchal, and some European observers wrote unfavourably about the mistreatment of women. The early settler George Lloyd emphasised 'the slavish exactions of savage husbands', and claimed that '[h]ard labour is the matrimonial inheritance of the poor gin'.[73] During migrations, women carried everything except the weapons, so the men could hunt. They were also primarily responsible for the collection of shellfish and plant materials, as well as for food preparation, hut construction, and the care of infants. This was a normal and appropriate division of labour to the Tasmanians.

Domestic violence was also normal. French explorer Jacques Labillardière reported that women were 'often victims of the brutality of their tyrants'.[74] He was one of several observers who recorded evidence of domestic violence, and to some extent, it was probably part of most women's lives.[75] However, as Chapter 4 reveals, Tasmanian society generally seems to have been characterised by loving relationships, not just between men and women, but between relatives of all kinds.

Internecine violence was common in most pre-modern tribal societies, and Tasmanian society was no exception.[76] Robinson's Aboriginal envoys gave him more than a dozen accounts of small but fierce clashes between tribes, mostly ambushes or arranged battles.[77] One source of provocation appears to have been trespass, but most violence centred on women.[78] Jealousies or failed marriage agreements could precipitate fights, but there is also evidence that tribes raided their enemies for women.[79] When vendettas got out of hand they could result in generational feuds, though most conflicts appear to have been constrained by a ritualised system of law based on honour and proportional retaliation.[80]

Religion

Tasmanians were animists, who perceived the agency of spirit-beings in all the workings of nature. Like all modern humans, they developed mythologies to make sense of the world around them, though many of the details of their spiritual lives remain obscure. Furthermore, the evidence we have comes to us through an imposing cultural and linguistic barrier. Robinson was the first European to record detailed observations of Aboriginal beliefs, but even these are limited. He never learnt more than a smattering of any of the Tasmanian languages, and he wrote with palpable condescension about their 'childlike superstitions'. What is more, when he began his observations in 1829, Aboriginal society had already collapsed. Still, the surviving evidence allows us to reach some tentative conclusions about the Tasmanians' spiritual world.

Tasmanian creation myths were strikingly similar to the elaborate Dreaming myths of mainland Australia, both having evolved from an earlier common belief system. Woorrady, one of Robinson's most trusted envoys (see Figure 5D), informed him that 'LALLER a small ant first made the natives'.[81] '[O]n his first formation', Woorrady continued, the black man:

> had a tail like a kangaroo and no joints in his knee; that ... he never could lay down and always had to stand up, and was obliged to sleep standing; that [the spirit-being] DROE.MER.DEEN.NE cut off his tail and rubbed grease on the wound and made joints to his knees. He then for the first time sat on the ground and expressed his approbation of the comfort.[82]

However, humans were not Laller's only creation. Woorrady explained that this ant also 'made all the rivers; he cut little streams and thus made big rivers. Said that he made the kangaroo out of the ground and that they run away: he described it by putting his hand on the ground and shewing how they came out and run away'.[83] In Aboriginal mythology, beings were not only made from the earth, but also transformed into it. According to Trugernanna (see Figure 11), the Bruny (then spelt Brune) Islanders believed an ancestor spirit called Moinee 'was hurled from heaven and dwelt on the earth, and died and was turned into a stone and is at Cox Bight, which was his own country. The natives say that there is a large stone standing up which is MOINEE and that he was a native and turned into this stone.'[84]

Tasmanian creation myths also focused strongly on celestial bodies. Robinson observed that his envoys 'spoke on the subject of the stars with great zest'; indeed, 'they have names for the stars and constellations and are aware that they revolve … They call the black spot in the Milky Way or Orion's Belt a stingaree [*sic*] and say the blackfellows are spearing it.'[85] He noted further how they 'described constellations in the heavens as resembling men and women, men fighting, animals, and limbs of men; together with names for the stars'.[86] The Bruny Islanders, for instance, told him 'that the two stars in the Milky Way are two men, and Mars is his foot and the Milky Way his road'.[87]

Tasmanians had creation stories for Animals too. In 1831, for instance, Robinson's envoys explained the creation of the wombat: 'two black men was asleep when a DROEGERDY came at night and scraped fire on them … they caught hold of his leg, and … put him in the ground; and that afterwards they used to catch him and eat him'.[88] Robinson recorded several other Tasmanian creation myths, all with the same Dreaming-like structure and content.[89]

In Indigenous societies, stories of animal creation have often been associated with totemism and totemic law, as have taboos on eating particular animals.[90] In Tasmania, taboos regulated the consumption of certain species, particularly wallabies and kangaroos. These only applied to some people and often only to animals of a particular sex. In 1832, for instance, the Quaker missionary George Washington Walker observed that '[s]ome will eat only the male of a particular species, others only the female, and I am assured by those who know well their habits, that they would rather starve than infringe this rule'. Walker also mentioned a song that described which animals were off-limits to married women.[91] Such observations are supported by Robinson's journals.[92] Taboos were almost certainly connected to the spirit of the forbidden animal, and they may explain why Tasmanians refused to eat introduced species.

All humans were thought to possess spirits. Robinson wrote on a number of occasions of people being possessed by a personal 'devil' or totem spirit. The north-east chief, Mannalargenna (see Figure 5C), spoke constantly of a powerful guiding spirit. Often he was gripped by violent convulsions that he and his terrified onlookers took to be possession experiences, usually resulting in some profound insight.[93] Mannalargenna was a revered shaman, but there is reason to believe all Tasmanians assumed a personal totem spirit. Indeed, they recognised a complex pantheon of spirit-beings associated with humans and animals, good and evil, skyscapes and landscapes, and the forces of nature. This was how Tasmanians perceived the world around them, so it stands to reason that the violent chaos of the war years was experienced as spiritual chaos.

Death

Death was a very important rite of passage in Tasmania. Most tribes cremated their dead, though some were known to impale them upright in hollow trees.[94] There is also evidence that bodies were occasionally entombed in specially made huts, or buried beneath shallow mounds.[95] In all cases, the funerary and mourning processes were highly ritualised. Walker recorded that, 'for those who are removed by death, they are in the habit of setting apart a certain portion of the day to indulge in lamentation; near relatives are said to keep up the practice for months'.[96]

Europeans were fond of asking Tasmanians what they thought happened after death. Responses varied, but most seem to have believed the souls of the deceased went to a distant island – an isle of the dead.[97]

The funerary site was nevertheless a place of great danger. The convict writer Jorgen Jorgenson observed that Tasmanians 'would rather go miles round than pass close to them'.[98] The spirits of the dead inspired great fear, but if treated cautiously, their powers might also be harnessed.[99] Human remains were thought to be especially powerful, and were often carried as charms.[100] A lurking spirit might also be called upon to divine information. When Robinson was trying to discover the whereabouts of the Mairremmener people, Mannalargenna told him 'a dead man's devil that had been put in a tree was walking about and would tell him [their location]'.[101]

Tasmanians took death and the spiritual forces it unleashed very seriously. These things could be managed when death was infrequent, but during the Black War it was all around them. Often they could not even retrieve the bodies of fallen kinsfolk, let alone perform the proper funeral rites. In such cases, a dissatisfied spirit might be considered as dangerous as the white man's guns.

Ritual and ceremony

Rituals were central to Tasmanian cultural life, and served a variety of purposes. Propitiating the spirits was one of these. In one instance, Robinson witnessed men reciting a particular song as they straightened their spears and suspected it was 'to invoke the spirit'.[102] Another type of propitiatory ritual was performed by some of the Aboriginal women enslaved by sealers in Bass Strait. One of them assured Robinson that 'the song was the devil's song and their attitude is a homage paid to the fire spirits ... They say that they sing to please the devil, that the devil tells them to sing plenty. These devotees of the devil are excessive in their devotions.'[103] Some rituals were cloaked in secrecy. Of one in particular, the naturalist Richard Davies wrote in 1846 that they were 'extremely jealous of this ceremony being witnessed by strangers; but I had, upon one occasion, an opportunity of being an ear-witness of it the whole night'.[104]

Tasmanians had strong ceremonial cultures that were intimately related to their ritual lives. They engaged in regular song and dance, which served a variety of functions, from storytelling and entertainment, to healing and mourning.[105] One of the more detailed descriptions of a ceremony comes from the Silesian agriculturalist, Adolphus Schayer, who observed dances performed by Robinson's party:

> The warrior ... gets so worked up that, after a few minutes he can barely speak, and can only utter inarticulate sounds and perform actions accompanied by movements expressing anger and the love of fighting, and in that way he comes to a state of mind which is close to madness. This moment seems to be the specific aim of the whole performance, because it's then that the men rush towards him, and giving vent to frightful screams.[106]

The largest ceremonies were those that occurred at intertribal gatherings. These were held several times a year, and could involve several hundred people.[107] Their full significance is unknown, though it is clear that ceremonies of all sorts were fundamental to Tasmanian cultural life, and they became increasingly difficult to conduct during the Black War.

First impressions

The arrival of a mysterious race of white-skinned men posed enormous challenges to the Tasmanians' worldviews. Their spirit-world contained all sorts of fantastical beings, but nothing like those that were now appearing on their beaches. Tribes undoubtedly spent many evenings around their campfires discussing the new arrivals. Who were they? Where did they come from? Why were they here? Where were their women? What were the wooden islands on which they lived? What was wrong with their skin? What did they eat? What did their words mean? Why did they behave so strangely? And what were all the strange animals and objects they possessed? The Tasmanians never imagined they would be confronted by such questions. They had no precedent for profound cultural difference, and thus no preconceptions of the types engrained in the minds of their visitors.

The Tasmanians' bemusement was evident to the first explorers. When Mara, an 'inquisitive and intelligent' man, took the opportunity to go on board a French frigate, he was overwhelmed by the experience: 'Everything surprised him, stunned him, fascinated him … with each new thing he showed the greatest surprise.'[108] Such wonderment, however, was easily replaced with indignation. The white men's peculiar behaviour often aroused laughter, but their constant infringements of custom led also to distrust and anxiety. 'They observe us closely', wrote the French explorer François Péron in 1802, 'always their suspicions of us are unfavourable.'[109]

There is some evidence that Aborigines believed the white men were returned ancestor spirits.[110] John West asserted that when Tasmanians died, 'they expected to re-appear as white men on an island in the Straits'.[111] Robinson's observations also support this claim, which corresponds with their belief in an isle of the dead. He recorded on several occasions that Tasmanians went to England when they died.[112] In fact, Walter George Arthur, an Aborigine born around 1820, wrote personally of this belief in later life, claiming 'black people died then arose from the dead [and] became white men'.[113]

It must have been an incredible experience to encounter white men for the first time (see Figure 9). Kickertopoller, an east coast man, told Robinson how 'he saw the first ship, that it came to Maria Island, he was a boy at this time and was with his tribe; that in the morning they saw the ship at anchor off Maria Island, that they were all frightened and run [*sic*] away, that it looked like a small island and that they could not tell what it was'.[114] Woorrady, a Bruny Islander, also shared his experience with Robinson: 'the white men when they first came cut [carved] the head of a man on a tree and … Natives call it WRAGEOWRAPPER [devil], and when the children saw it they were frightened and run away.

Said when they saw the first ship coming at sea they were frightened, and said it was WRAGEOWRAPPER.'[115]

Most Tasmanians learnt of the white strangers from the intriguing tales that circulated throughout the island. We do not know what these tales were, but they may not have been entirely negative. For all the misunderstandings that Tasmanians had with the explorers, there was also a great deal of goodwill and gift giving. These white men also had the virtue of leaving. By contrast, those who later appeared on the Derwent and Tamar rivers were just as strange, only not as friendly, and certainly not as temporary.

A different kind of white man

By 1803, the white men and the bizarre items they left behind had undoubtedly taken their place in the Tasmanians' rich storytelling culture. Their relations with the explorers had been mixed, but they may also have had encounters with the sealers who began venturing from Sydney into Bass Strait as early as 1798. If so, it is safe to assume these notoriously cruel and unscrupulous men did not improve the reputation of the whites.[116] Whatever their reasons, south-east tribes came to view the first colonists with ambivalence and suspicion, choosing to stay aloof and monitor them from a safe distance. 'At last plenty of ships [came]', Woorrady told Robinson, 'the natives went to the mountains, went and looked at what the white people did, went and told other natives and they came and looked also.'[117] They knew there was something different about these latest interlopers. Unlike their predecessors, these whites erected large shelters and they also had several women among them, but their most distinguishing feature was that they stayed.

The period around first settlement may also have been a time of sickness for some tribes. There is good evidence that introduced disease took a heavy toll on the people from the Huon River district around this time.[118] Surprisingly though, with the exception of an epidemic of respiratory disease on Bruny Island in 1829, there is no other reliable evidence of introduced sickness among eastern Tasmanians.[119] This does not rule out the possibility of unrecorded epidemics, but it does cast doubt on the idea that disease was a major factor in their demise. Nevertheless, the confusion and despair associated with the initial epidemic in the south must have been tremendous, and the victims most likely drew some connection between the new arrivals and the calamities befalling them.

If Tasmanians considered white men to be ancestor spirits – as it appears many did – it is not surprising that some came to view them as malevolent. In 1829, for instance, Robinson recorded that the word for white man among the Bruny Island people was '*Raege*', a variant of '*Raegeowrapper*' (devil).[120] Later, he and others observed that tribes from the north-west, north and east also referred to whites as evil spirits.[121] This interpretation was probably not universal, but however Tasmanians perceived them, the white strangers were about to profoundly change their lives.

Early violence

The first major affray with the whites took place at Risdon Cove on 3 May 1804. Most of the newcomers now resided on the other side of the Derwent River, but a few had stayed behind. Around midday, a large body of over 100 Tasmanians – men, women and children – advanced on the cove. Their intentions were not clear. One witness thought they were a hunting party, but the white man in charge considered them 'very far from friendly'. He ordered his men to open fire with what must have seemed like thunderous but invisible spears. A carronade was even fired, its echo heard across the Derwent. The Aboriginal death toll is uncertain, but the sources suggest it was probably not much higher than six.[122] In other words, Risdon was probably not the large-scale 'massacre' some have suggested it was. It was certainly not the primary catalyst for the Black

War, as Governor Arthur later concluded, though it would have remained firmly lodged in the memories of local tribes.

After the Risdon affray, the south-eastern tribes appear to have kept their distance. The next wave of violence erupted during the drought of 1806–7. Over a nine-month period, southern tribes killed or wounded several whites. Most of their six recorded attacks originated in competition for game, as evidenced by the confiscation of kills and the spearing of kangaroo dogs.[123] These attacks were measured responses to specific infractions; they were not intended to dislodge the whites. Without the benefit of hindsight, the Tasmanians surely never imagined the overwhelmingly male strangers would multiply as they later did, and thus had no reason to take drastic or indiscriminate action.

Frontier encounters around the northern settlement were similar to those in the south. There were five encounters in 1804 and 1805, three of which were hostile. The next incident, however, was not recorded until 1819.[124] Little is known about life in the north during the intervening years, but hunting and bushranging were prevalent, so presumably there was considerable contact. If the hearsay evidence is to be believed, these encounters were often hostile. In 1810, for instance, John Oxley reported that, '[f]rom the many atrocious cruelties practised on them by the Convict Bush Rangers, they avoid as much as possible the appearance of a White Man; they are however (in consequence no doubt of the treatment they receive) very troublesome to the Solitary Hunter'.[125] As in the south, however, serious conflict in the north was a long time coming.

Interaction

There were probably also many non-violent encounters in the pre-war years. Some Tasmanians approached the newcomers in the hope of conducting trade. Others were simply curious. On the western shores of the Derwent, the early settler George Lloyd recalled that 'the settlers and their sable neighbours lived upon tolerable though very questionable terms of friendship'.[126] Some tribes learnt they could obtain desired goods from particular white men, either as gestures of kindness, or in exchange for sex. They immediately realised the advantages of using glass as a cutting tool.[127] Blankets became sought-after items, as did tea, flour, sugar and tobacco. The most significant import, however, was the dog. Eastern tribes were very quick to master the art of hunting with these novel animals, which considerably altered their economies.[128]

The Tasmanians who had the most contact with whites were those who, for various reasons, became fringe-dwellers around the growing settlements. Some were probably refugees, while others had simply become addicted to alcohol and tobacco. There were also some intact tribes that occasionally visited Hobart and Launceston in the early 1820s. The most notable of these was the tribe of 50 that came into Hobart in November 1824 and the tribe of 64 that visited in October 1825.[129] There was also a tribe reportedly numbering 200 that visited Launceston in January 1825.[130] Given the risks involved in these visits, we must assume the tribes had strong reasons for making them. The desire for introduced goods was clearly important, but they could also have been seeking sanctuary from enemies, treatment for skin disease, or attempting to recover abducted women and children. We can be more certain about why they left, which in most cases was because of mistreatment.[131] Broadly speaking, there was never a golden era of frontier relations. Even during the relative peace of the first two decades, the Tasmanians dealt reluctantly and uneasily with the whites, if they dealt with them at all.

Women and children

Scores of Aboriginal women and girls would be abducted and raped in Tasmania, but in the early years of colonisation, the situation was more complex. Before 1827, some fringe-dwelling tribes prostituted their womenfolk to white men. There were two reasons tribesmen did this: to gain favour and prestige with the powerful white strangers, or to procure dogs and introduced foods. The east coast settler Charles Meredith recalled that 'the blacks were in the habit of forcing their gins to visit the whites in order to obtain what they could from them'.[132] In fact, a number of contemporaries remarked on the prevalence of this behaviour. The assigned convict Thomas McMinn, for instance, claimed:

> Mr McGregor a sawyer, had frequent intercourse with the gins [around Oatlands]. He was accused by my fellow servants of stealing their sugar to bribe the black men to allow their gins to retire with them. Frank Allen, one of Mr Anstey's convict servants was also suspected, and accused of doing the same.[133]

When tribes began to disintegrate, women sometimes made these exchanges on their own initiative.[134] When ostracised or displaced from tribal life, some even chose to live permanently with white men.

Nevertheless, there were soon many more sex-deprived white men on the frontier than there were Tasmanians willing to engage in prostitution. This led to an increasing number of rapes and abductions. Women were usually seized in campfire ambushes, and after being raped were either released, killed or pressed into bondage.[135] There is almost no documentation describing these ordeals from women's perspectives, though we can safely assume their experiences were horrific. Likewise, the families of abducted women suffered terribly from worry and loss. In addition, Aboriginal men felt emasculated, and in some cases betrayed. The settler William Brodribb claimed that, although 'there was a constant [consensual] communication between the stock-keepers and the female Natives', the men 'felt enraged at the stock-keepers taking their wives by force'.[136]

Tasmanian men were nothing if not jealous and vengeful, and they often sought retribution. In April 1819, for instance, the *Hobart Town Gazette* was informed that 'a native woman, supposed to be the wife of a Chief, had been maltreated by two of the stock-keepers; that she escaped after much ill-usage; and that the tribes returned and attacked', leaving the two stock-keepers seriously wounded.[137] The desire for this kind of retribution drew a growing number of tribes into ever-augmenting cycles of bloody revenge.

Kidnapping was another major cause of Aboriginal hostility during the early years of colonisation. In the case of the 'Oyster Bay tribe', West claimed they became belligerent after 'a native had been shot in an expedition to capture some aboriginal children'.[138] Likewise, when children were abducted in the Coal River area in 1810, their kinsfolk responded 'by spearing cattle, and other acts of hostility'.[139] The attitudes of the children are evidenced by the fact that so many of them eventually escaped back to their families. Historian James Calder wrote in 1875 that 'they were as difficult to tame permanently as wolves or wood pigeons are, unless when taken so young as to retain no remembrance of the wild life to which they were born; and there is hardly an instance of their not rejoining their own people on reaching manhood'.[140] This resistance to kidnapping, both by children and their families, is probably a major reason why it declined in the 1820s.

Thunder sticks

One of the most mysterious and troubling aspects of the newcomers was their guns. When fixed with a bayonet, a gun resembled a spear, yet it was never thrown. It made a noise like thunder, a flash like lightning, and at exactly the same time produced a hole in its target – but not always. Robinson was told that, before most Aborigines had glimpsed their first gun, a rumour spread among them of 'weapons that vomited forth thunder and lightening and annihilated their unfortunate race'.[141] Even when the whites had become a familiar presence, their weapons retained an element of wonder. After a year of getting to know Aborigines from Bruny Island and elsewhere, Robinson came to believe they 'attribute[d] magic qualities to firearms'.[142]

Nevertheless, Tasmanians grew savvy at negotiating these baffling weapons. They may not have understood the source of a gun's power, but they soon realised it fired a projectile, then lost its power for around 30 seconds, at which point an advance or retreat could be made. The *Colonial Times* wrote in 1826 that, 'when a person happens unfortunately to get surrounded by a tribe, they will rush in upon him the moment after he discharges his musket, fully aware that, before he can again load and prime his gun, they can close upon him, and thereby put him to death'.[143] Once they understood this, Aborigines often taunted white men to fire.[144] They also recognised that not all guns were the same, and thus needed to be negotiated in different ways. For example, an Aboriginal woman told Robinson that a double-barrelled shotgun was known as 'a "Lowena", a gun that would shoot twice'.[145] It seems guns became less intimidating once Tasmanians understood their limitations.

Untenable coexistence

Initially, Tasmanians seem to have believed there were not enough whites to pose a serious threat, but as West observed, '[t]he rapid colonisation of the island from 1821 to 1824 … [meant that] on every reappearance the natives found some favourite spot surrounded by new enclosures, and no longer theirs'.[146] As the balance of power tipped in the white man's favour, he grew bolder and more dangerous. Every act of violence and betrayal eroded relations further, and once they had broken down entirely, suspicion and miscommunication made them difficult to restore. In 1823, William Parramore observed that '[b]etween the natives of our neighbourhood and the English there is no communication, which, I think, is owing to the barbarous manner in which they are treated by the English'.[147] Indeed, by the middle of the decade, most tribes had ceased all contact with the forbidding strangers.

Despite their general reticence, the Tasmanians' pre-war response to the invaders was by no means passive. Some tribes were openly hostile.

When the Russian explorer Fabian Bellingshausen investigated the situation in 1820, he found that '[t]he natives of Tasmania live in a state of perpetual hostility against the Europeans'.[148] Collectively, Aborigines attacked the strangers at least 57 times during the first two decades of settlement.[149] Although these pre-war incidents constituted only six per cent of the total number of recorded attacks by Aborigines, they were not insignificant to the people who executed them. Assaulting the whites not only suborned the wrath of powerful and dangerous beings, it also undermined any chance for fruitful cooperation, so it was not a decision made lightly. For this reason Tasmanians were cautious in the early years. When they did retaliate, they appear to have followed traditional precepts of proportional justice. But as the invaders multiplied, so too did the Tasmanians' grievances, and by the mid-1820s it was clear that targeted revenge was not having the desired effect. All tribes had made concessions, and none had wanted to go to war with the strangers, but at an alarming pace the war was coming to them.

CHAPTER TWO
ATTITUDES

White

On 8 April 1825, the *Hobart Town Gazette* warned its readers that, if they continued to mistreat the blacks, they 'will scatter blood and conflagration, death and ruin throughout every district in the colony'.[1] At the time, few shared the editor's concern, but from 1825 to 1828, the number of native attacks more than doubled each year (see Figure 3, page 2). As the body count grew, the public's apathy was replaced by panic. By 1828, colonists had no doubt they were fighting a war. But this was not a conventional war, and the enemy could not be combated by conventional means. The blacks were not one people, but rather a number of disparate tribes. They had no home base and no recognisable command structure. No one knew how to find them, much less how to negotiate peace with them. It seemed no one understood their cultures or spoke any of their languages. Even if communication had been possible, the government had no power to redress their grievances. With every colonist that disembarked, and every farm that was established, war became less and less avoidable. Perhaps it was inevitable.

Suppressing the blacks

In their struggle to bring the Black War to a close, colonists only ever had three options before them. One option was removing the natives, voluntarily or by force, to either a reserve or an offshore island. The *Hobart Town Gazette* first suggested this idea on 11 November 1826. The *Colonial Times* concurred: 'We make no pompous display of Philanthropy – we say unequivocally, SELF DEFENCE IS THE FIRST LAW OF NATURE. THE GOVERNMENT MUST REMOVE THE NATIVES – IF NOT, THEY WILL BE HUNTED DOWN LIKE WILD BEASTS, AND DESTROYED!'[2] Despite agreeing on almost nothing else, the fractious colonial press eventually gave its unanimous support to a policy of exile to an offshore island.[3] In the interior, where the difficulties of removal were starkly apparent, there was much less support for the idea, particularly as the war dragged on and colonists felt more strongly than ever that mere removal was more than the 'savages' deserved.

The second option was conciliation and amicable coexistence (see Figure 8)[4]. Early in the war, when most believed black violence was the product of a few rogue leaders, this seemed a reasonable aspiration. The government and some in the press held on to the hope of peaceful coexistence until well after it had ceased to be a realistic option, but on the frontier, it was dismissed from very early on as being utterly impracticable.

The war created a growing tension between pragmatic frontiersmen and humanitarian townsfolk. 'In the interior', wrote John West, 'the blacks were spoken of with intense fear, and detestation: [while] in the capital, even their depredations were questioned, and the subjects of conversation, were rather their sufferings than their crimes.'[5] Those on the frontier grew increasingly impatient with the government's humanitarian stance, and they expressed this unreservedly in letters to government officials and newspapers, as well as in private writings. On 29 July 1828, for instance, a Patersons Plains settler vented in his diary:

'these savages murder about 20 settlers or servants every year and our canting government contents itself with issuing proclamations which might as well be directed to the shark in Bass's Strait'.[6]

In the public sphere, a snapshot of settler opinion can be gleaned from the *Tasmanian* of 26 February 1830. This editor presented several responses to a recent letter published by the Aborigines Committee, which urged 'kindness' rather than violence.[7] 'God help us!', wrote a settler from Bothwell:

> Are the operations of the bush to be regulated by a Committee in Hobar-
> ton. What do they know about it? While the Committee is arguing,
> debating, bandying letters about from place to place, the white inhabitants
> are murdered, dwellings burned to the ground and terror and conster-
> nation spread over the country. The settlers in the country take quite a
> different view of the matter to what do the Gentlemen at Hobarton.

In the same issue, a Clyde Valley settler asserted:

> we in the interior are in the most imminent daily danger of our lives and
> property – of having our houses and barns burnt about our ears in all
> directions, and our families butchered by these savages; and are we to be
> smoothly informed how we are to act, and that, on the defensive, by a few
> comfortably seated Gentlemen in their well-furnished and well-protected
> houses in Hobart-town?

Conciliation was all well and good in theory, but the *Launceston Advertiser* echoed popular opinion when it proposed in July 1829 that the enemy's 'audacity is protected and nourished by our forbearance'.[8]

The third option for ending the war was to exterminate the blacks, an option that grew in popularity with every passing month. In May 1828, the *Colonial Advocate* argued that 'unless the blacks are *exterminated* or *removed*, it is plainly proved; by fatal and sanguinary experience, that all hope of their ceasing their aggressions, is the height of absurdity … *In the name of Heaven is it not high time to resort to strong and decisive measures?*[9]

By 1830, extermination was plainly the most favoured course of action among frontier colonists. One east coast settler believed that 'nothing short of their total destruction will put an end to their outrages'.[10] The *Colonial Times* also felt the colony now had 'no other chance of obtaining peace than [by] the annihilation of the whole race'.[11] Even the *Tasmanian*, whose editor was usually sympathetic towards the natives, declared that they possessed 'something like a determination to destroy all before them, [thus] Extermination seems to be the only remedy'.[12] Colonists were not advocating extermination for its own sake – at least not in public – but as a settler from Jericho put it, 'the only remedy is their total annihilation – to save ourselves a similar fate'.[13]

Rovers and pursuers

Pursuit parties and roving parties were the government's primary martial response to the native problem. Pursuit parties rallied in the wake of an attack to hunt down the culprits. They occasionally 'came up with the natives' and managed to shoot some, but for every success, they experienced dozens of failures. 'In truth', West reflected, 'the pursuit of a party of aborigines, was a very hopeless affair.'[14] There were two main reasons for this. First, when the natives knew they were being pursued, 'their well known caution and cunning' put pursuers at a considerable disadvantage.[15] Second, party members had little incentive to exert themselves. Pursuit parties were mostly comprised of soldiers and convicts, neither of whom had a choice in participating. No doubt their bleak prospects for success also dulled their enthusiasm. Rewards might have sweetened the deal, but they were never offered.

Public attitudes towards pursuit parties were understandably pessimistic, though it was never suggested that native war parties ought *not* be pursued. Despite criticisms of individual parties, there was relatively little disapproval of the system. Whatever their failures, pursuit parties at least gave colonists a sense of agency at a time when many felt powerless. Some pursuers also gained the impression – not always wrong – that, even if they were unable to catch the perpetrators, they at least drove them from the district.[16]

Roving parties, on the other hand, were full-time patrols in search of the blacks. They were of two types, both under the direction of local magistrates. Military parties (as they will be termed here) comprised soldiers and convict field police, while the civilian parties were composed almost entirely of assigned convicts serving on the promise of reduced sentences. Their leaders were 'trustworthy individuals' such as Jorgen Jorgenson, Gilbert Robertson and John Batman, who offered their services in exchange for grants of land.[17] This might have solved the problem of incentive, but for one critical flaw. In almost all cases, rewards were linked to duration of service, rather than the results achieved. Roving parties occasionally executed successful ambushes, but usually only when accompanied by a cooperative native guide. One leader who had 'never been able to fall in with them', maintained that 'there is little probability of meeting with the perpetrators except by mere chance'.[18]

Roving parties received more public criticism than pursuit parties, despite their similarly unimpressive results. A settler writing to the *Hobart Town Courier* rebuked the parties: 'How often do we hear from the parties that they came on the Natives' fires and half cooked opossums, &c., and yet they never saw one Black. For why? They make so much noise by talking and blundering over the dead wood and bark with a heavy tread.'[19] In his evidence to the Aborigines Committee, James Hobbs accused one leader of being 'more employed in looking for grants of land than the Natives'.[20] Confronted with this and other evidence, the Committee recommended the discontinuation of the roving parties in March 1830, citing their tactical ineptitude, meagre results and the problems of finding suitable leaders.[21] But, having conceived of no alternative, Arthur did not heed this recommendation until the following year.

Participants also expressed negative attitudes towards the roving party system. The tormenting hardships and incessant failures drove many to despondency, especially the leaders. In November 1829, Oatlands' police magistrate observed that 'Jorgenson was really insane many days last week [and] Mr Robertson too, is evidently mad'.[22] The latter confessed: 'I do not know what to do, for I have no hopes of their being captured and I have no doubt, but the parties sent out in pursuit of them have [actually] driven them in upon the settled districts ... my mind is so worn out with disappointment, vexation, and anxiety, that I can hardly write common sense.'[23] Faced with similar disappointments the following year, John Batman's neighbour reported that he 'is almost frantic and now gives up all hope of doing any good with them'.[24]

The military roving parties were – at least in the public's eye – no more effective. One settler complained that 'soldiers are quite useless in pursuit of the Natives; they will not exert themselves'.[25] But the men had their own complaints. It was no wonder they 'do not overtake, capture, or kill any of the natives', wrote another settler, since 'out of their own pay they must provide extra bush dress, as well as extra shoes'.[26] Another gripe among soldiers was the withholding of their rum rations while on roving duty.[27] There were, nonetheless, good reasons for this 'infringement of the men's liberties'. Frequent complaints of inebriation and ill-discipline made their way to the Governor's desk. This behaviour was often attributed to fraternisation between soldiers and convicts, and in 1826, the Executive Council reported:

> the Soldiers are continually prone to form acquaintances with the Prisoners, and like them are addicted to the common vice of drinking to the extreme. The spreading of the Military and Field Police in small parties over the face of the settled districts of the Colony, the very circumstance of the vagrant life they must follow, has a tendency to encourage the propensity to association and drinking.[28]

Despite efforts to keep them apart, the war inevitably brought soldiers and convicts together. In a strange inversion of authority, convict field police were sometimes placed in charge of military roving parties. The civil police magistrates were in charge of defending their respective districts, and the field police were their permanent force. Local constables knew the country better than soldiers, who were moved around frequently, but the latter were naturally reluctant to recognise the authority of the former.[29] FGD Brown, who coordinated parties on the east coast, observed that 'the soldier imbibes a natural prejudice against the prisoner who he thinks infinitely below him in the grade of life', while convicts 'think of a private soldier as a private soldier thinks of them'. 'The result', Brown concluded, 'is a jealousy, a general insult on both sides, and finally hatred.'[30]

The ineffectiveness of the roving parties was not due solely to bickering and ill-discipline. Roving expeditions lasted 'for 12 or 18 days at a time', and according to Sergeant Armstrong, 'the men had frequently to march 30 or 40 Miles [48–64 km] in a day'. Roving, which entailed trudging all seasons through trackless swamps, gullies and forests, was as onerous as it was arduous. The men's miseries were amplified, according to Brown, because the rations were 'not enough to support a hearty man on the fatiguing and harrowing duty of "Black Hunting"'.[31]

The painful irony was that, although army rations were insufficient, two weeks' worth were extremely heavy. Some rovers chose to travel lighter in the hope of being fed along the way, but in a number of cases, attitudes towards the parties were so disapproving that settlers refused to feed or house them.[32] There was also the problem that parties 'were very frequently lost in the bush for three to four days together', which introduced a real danger of starvation.[33] Sometimes they were so hungry and exhausted that rovers were 'unable to pursue' the natives, even when they caught sight of them.[34] Fit men with good equipment were pushed to their limits in the backcountry of Tasmania, thus it is no surprise that these ill-clothed, ill-shod and ill-fed rovers took a skulking attitude to their missions.

Killing blacks: motivations and attitudes

Not all colonists were hostile towards the blacks. The urban middle-class in particular displayed a remarkable level of sympathy for 'this much wronged people'. This generally took the form of recognising the injustices inflicted on the natives, calling for conciliation, and excusing their 'outrages' as the natural response of a 'child-like and ignorant race'. Newspaper editors such as Henry Melville and Robert Murray, though their opinions constantly shifted, printed a considerable amount of sympathetic commentary.[35] Government rhetoric also tended to be sympathetic, especially in dispatches to London. Even some frontier settlers expressed compassion for the natives. They could do little to restrain their servants though, and among these men there is no evidence of sympathetic attitudes.

Disinterest in the natives shifted to distrust in the initial years of the war, and thereafter, to hatred and fear. There was an unmistakable rise in the number of their attacks from the mid-1820s, and there appears to have been a comparable rise in the level of violence orchestrated by colonists (see Figure 3, page 2).[36] The main reasons for this were revenge, killing for sport, sexual desire for women and children, and suppression of the native threat. These motives varied in significance as the conflict progressed.

Tasmania's enormous gender imbalance, and the voracious demand for native women it created, was the most important proximate trigger for the Black War. According to Melville, frontiersmen 'thought little or nothing of destroying the men for the sake of carrying to their huts the females of the tribes'.[37] Sex continued to be a central motivation for attacking natives until around 1828, by which time killing the enemy had taken priority over raping them. There is no indication that sexual assaults decreased after this, though they probably became more a 'fringe benefit' of ambushes that had as their primary goal the eradication of a dangerous enemy.

As black violence grew in intensity, so too did the frequency of revenge attacks and pre-emptive strikes by frontiersmen. The *Colonial Times* reported that, 'once in pursuit, with the murder of a Colonist fresh in their memory, the people will kill, destroy, and if possible exterminate every black in the Island'.[38] By December 1827, Roderic O'Connor was convinced that colonists were 'now so exacerbated at the murders that have been committed, that no mercy will be shown when an opportunity offers for retaliation'.[39]

At night it was not easy for ambush parties to distinguish between combatants and noncombatants. '[T]he difficulty of securing the leader without injury to some of his less guilty companions' was first raised by Captain Clark of Bothwell in 1826. However, this fails to fully explain why white violence was so indiscriminate. There is no evidence that colonists ever attempted to distinguish the innocent from the guilty.[40] In view of this, it is both a curious fact and a staggering hypocrisy that colonists complained so stridently about the indiscriminate nature of black violence.

For some frontiersmen the guilt or innocence of their victims was entirely irrelevant. To men 'distinguished for their malicious vigour', the blacks were merely dangerous animals and their attitude to killing them resembled that of a game hunter.[41] As early as 1824, Adam Amos recorded in his diary several occasions on which he or his son went out 'hunting the blacks'.[42] Such practices became far more prevalent as the decade progressed.[43] In 1830, the *Colonial Times* lamented 'the custom that has been almost universal amongst certain Settlers and their servants, whenever the Natives have visited their neighbourhood, to consider the men as wild beasts whom it is praiseworthy to hunt down and destroy, and the women as only fit to be used for the worst purposes'.[44]

James Bonwick claimed that 'on several occasions [he] heard men declare that they thought no more of shooting a Black than bringing down a bird', and that during the war 'it was common enough to hear men talk of the number of black crows they had destroyed'.[45] Hugh

Hull, who had lived in the colony since 1819, recalled 'it was a favourite amusement to hunt the aborigines ... Sometimes they would return without sport; at others they would succeed in killing a woman, or, if lucky, mayhap a man or two.'[46] Undoubtedly, there were those for whom the 'black hunt' elicited all the exhilaration of stalking dangerous and elusive game.

The history of warfare is riddled with instances of men taking a competitive attitude towards killing, but such attitudes have always come easier to those who could dehumanise their enemy. Tasmania's colonists were particularly successful at this. The notion of savagery, which was popular among frontiersmen, sustained an image of the natives as sinister and bestial creatures. They were variously denigrated as 'beasts', 'monsters', 'devils', 'crows', 'reptiles', 'orangutans', 'monkeys' and the like, which no doubt eased the killer's conscience.[47] Robinson found that frontiersmen considered natives 'a bare remove from the brutes'.[48] Similarly, West claimed it was 'the serious conviction of stockmen, that blacks are brutes, only of a more cunning and dangerous order'.[49] In fact, according to John Stokes, who arrived on the *Beagle* in 1836 with Charles Darwin, 'such is the perversion of feeling among a portion of the colonists, that they cannot conceive how anyone can sympathise with the black race as their fellow men. In theory and practice they regard them as wild beasts whom it is lawful to extirpate.'[50]

As the conflict augmented, so too did the perception and portrayal of blacks as a race of faceless, sub-human killers. The devastating effectiveness of their tactics was undeniable, but this was generally explained away as animal instinct.[51] The *Hobart Town Courier*, for instance, asserted that they possessed 'a craft and cunning never exceeded in any of the human race', but only because they possessed 'more savage rage than the hyena or the ravenous wolf'.[52] Indeed, the success of the natives' 'barbarous' and 'cowardly' tactics seems only to have magnified the degree to which they were dehumanised. In a rare wartime letter penned by an assigned convict, Richard Bradstreet wrote to his family in England: 'friends there are some dangerous animals in this country[;] the country is overrun with black men and women who are so wild they kill every white man they see'.[53]

Colonists' attitudes towards killing blacks were rarely reluctant. William Barnes, who had endured the war from its beginning, admitted:

> The depredations committed upon them by the white people have been carried on for many years and has been upon so large a scale the slaughter has been so indiscriminate and attended with such heart rendering [sic] and unheard acts of barbarity that it is impossible to describe them. These acts are never published in the papers, but are recounted by the perpetrators and are made the subject of exultation – when the killing of from two to twenty blacks is spoken of without the least remorse.[54]

Such attitudes were common. When investigating the killing of women and children at Cape Grim, for instance, Robinson interviewed a convict named Chamberlain, who described his role 'with such perfect indifference my blood chilled'.[55]

Not only were many frontiersmen comfortable with killing blacks, some saw themselves as providing a valuable public service. According to the *Colonial Times* of 2 July 1830, 'the shooting of blacks is spoken of as a matter of levity – indeed, it is considered a meritorious service to the State'.[56] Likewise, historian James Fenton spoke after the war to a convict who insisted he had been 'doing a noble service to shoot them down'.[57] The belief was, one settler wrote, that 'the exterminating zeal, of some, may engender the success and safety of others'.[58]

Colonists who held such attitudes were capable of truly ghastly acts of violence. For example, it was not uncommon for colonists to collect trophies from the bodies of their native victims in the form of ears, digits and heads.[59] Hugh Hull, for instance, recalled that 'one European had a pickle tub in which he put the ears of all the blacks he shot'.[60] No less disturbing was the account James Hobbs gave to the Aborigines

Committee of a convict named Carrotts who 'cut off a Native man's head at Oyster Bay, and made his wife hang it round her neck, and carry it as a plaything'.[61] This macabre fascination with severing body parts was also applied to living victims. A 'gentleman' informed Robinson that 'it was a practice with the stock-keepers to get the men into the huts and cut off their penis and testicles with a knife'.[62] The men who perpetrated such deeds were not merely comfortable with killing and mutilating natives – they positively relished it.

The killing of restrained or otherwise defenceless victims also seems to have excited some frontiersmen. According to Robinson, some shepherds were known to 'ravish the [natives'] wives and daughters ... and set up their children as targets to shoot at'.[63] Similarly, Fenton learnt of a gang of bushrangers that 'was in the habit of binding them to trees, and using them as targets for practice'.[64]

Some acts of violence were of an unquestionably pathological nature. William Lawrence, for instance, related 'several horrid atrocities' to Robinson. One case involved a stock-keeper with 'two pistols, one loaded and the other unloaded; he snapped the unloaded one in his mouth, and the black did the same with the loaded one and was shot dead'.[65] Just as there can be little doubt that the details of some of these stories were embellished in transmission, we can be equally sure that many instances of gratuitous violence were never recorded at all.[66]

Deterrents to violence

Sadism, sex, revenge and safety offered powerful motives for violence against blacks, but at this juncture it will be instructive to consider the legal and moral deterrents as well. The legality of killing blacks was never made clear to colonists. Government proclamations initially forbade harming natives, but as the war heated up, settlers demanded the right to defend themselves. In 1826, the government responded by outlining six conditions under which settlers could legitimately treat blacks as 'open enemies'. This permitted military parties to forcibly 'drive off' natives intending 'to attack, rob, or murder the white inhabitants', but the licence of settlers and their servants remained unclear.[67]

In April 1828, the 'Demarcation Proclamation' legalised limited violence against blacks who were found in the settled districts without a government issued pass.[68] One observer rightly ventured that 'a greater piece of absurdity can scarcely be imagined'.[69] No one really knew where the settled districts began or ended, least of all the natives, who had no way of knowing about the Proclamation, or how to acquire a pass.

Once again, colonists were left confused as to the legality of killing. At points the proclamation seemed to offer great scope for using violence, but elsewhere it read:

> Nothing herein contained shall authorise, or be taken to authorise, any set-tler or settlers, stock-keeper or stock-keepers, sealer or sealers, to make use of force (except for necessary self-defence) against any Aboriginal, without the presence and direction of a magistrate, military officer, or other person of respectability, named and deputed to this service by a magistrate.[70]

These orders were superseded in November 1828 by the declaration of martial law. This removed all common law restrictions on killing natives, and might have given colonists the confidence to do so openly, were it not for the Governor's emphatic qualification:

> BUT, I DO, nevertheless, hereby strictly order, enjoin, and command, that the actual use of arms be in no case resorted to, if the Natives can by other means be induced or compelled to retire into the places and portions of this Island herein before excepted from the operation of Martial Law; that bloodshed be checked, as much as possible; that any Tribes which may surrender themselves up, shall be treated with every degree of humanity; and that defenceless women and children be invariably spared.[71]

These were the most important of the government's promulgations, but in total there were dozens, and together they sent mixed messages to colonists. A correspondent to the *Launceston Advertiser* expressed the bewilderment of his fellow colonists, when he demanded to know 'which of the 999 orders relative to them [the natives] is it intended should be obeyed?'[72] Written in legalistic jargon and often contradicting each other, the government's directives were highly confusing to colonists. For example, the Governor frequently rebuked settlers for not suppressing the violence more 'vigorously', while simultaneously demanding greater kindness and forbearance.[73] So, although the law ultimately protected killers, they were understandably hesitant about reporting their actions to the authorities.

In spite of their stern rhetoric, the colonial authorities were loath to indict anyone for killing blacks for fear of inciting public outrage. Even if they had been willing, the odds were stacked in the frontiersmen's favour. A killing first had to be discovered, and the poorly policed frontier made concealing the evidence easy. Then the guilty parties had to be identified, which was also difficult. The only witnesses were those involved, and the people they told were more likely to applaud than report them.

Settlers often knew about the cruelties perpetrated by their servants, but there was not a single recorded case in which they sought to punish or even reprimand their men for such acts. Some years after the war, a man once accustomed to killing natives was asked whether he believed he was 'allowed to murder the natives in cold blood?' He responded: 'Allowed! Nobody was there to see – nobody knew, and nobody cared. It was war to the hilt on both sides.'[74]

The other possible deterrent was moral. Christianity, of course, has an injunction against murder, but a brief glance at history reminds us that professing Christians are certainly capable of committing atrocities. Humans have always read their holy books in self-serving ways, and sections of the Bible provided ample justification for killing heathens, taking their lands and enslaving them. Had Christianity been strong on the Tasmanian frontier, it would have posed no necessary deterrent to killing blacks. But it was not strong. There were scarcely any churches or ministers outside Hobart and Launceston. Sunday was simply a day to get drunk or go hunting. Most frontiersmen were nominally Christian, but religion had little observable influence on their lives.[75]

Social pressure was the only thing likely to have moderated colonists' behaviour. In Britain, sociocultural forces had served as a moral bulwark, but once in Tasmania, these forces and the surveillance that maintained them were largely removed. Away from home, colonists were not concerned that loved ones would discover their ill deeds. Even settlers, while they sought to establish a good standing in the colony, experienced dislocation from the family and community networks that had once patrolled the boundaries of acceptable behaviour. Isolated as they were at the edge of a settlement that was itself at the edge of the known world, colonists experienced few barriers to killing blacks beyond the difficulty of surprising them.

Genocide?

When the Black War comes up in conversation, the question of genocide is never far away. It is one of the most poignant and controversial questions in Australian history. A number of prominent twentieth-century historians and commentators have asserted that the British committed genocide in Tasmania.[76] Indeed, it is often cited as the clearest case of colonial genocide in history,[77] and at first glance, this can seem obvious. After all, colonisation did virtually destroy Tasmania's native population. On closer inspection, however, the question is more complicated, and to appreciate its nuances we must try to step back from the turbulent emotions that such a horrifying tragedy naturally evokes.

One way to approach the question is to ask: Was the government guilty of genocide? Answering this question would involve delving deep into government policy, which is beyond the scope of this book. However, Henry Reynolds has demonstrated convincingly that the government did not intend to destroy the native population. Indeed, it sought desperately to avoid such an outcome, knowing full well that it would 'leave an indelible stain upon the character of the British Government'.[78] Reynolds did not exonerate the government, but he highlighted some important ways in which it did not resemble a genocidal regime.[79]

The question more appropriate to this book is: were the colonists guilty of genocide? Certainly, by 1830, many frontier colonists appear to have accepted the necessity of exterminating the native population. When we also consider that colonists were collectively responsible for killing several hundred natives, the accusation of genocide begins to look damning. Nevertheless, there are some significant points to consider before passing such a weighty judgment.

First, absent from Tasmania were the kinds of dogma that inspired, for example, Ottomans to massacre Armenians in present-day Turkey, Nazis to exterminate Jews throughout Europe, or Hutus to slaughter Tutsis in Rwanda. Those groups were targeted for specifically ideological reasons. Tasmania's natives, on the other hand, were not killed because of their politics, race or religion. As we have seen, colonists considered them racially and culturally inferior, and this no doubt eased their consciences, but they did not kill them *because* of this. Those who participated in the violence did so largely out of revenge and self-preservation. Even those who were motivated by sex or morbid thrillseeking lacked any ideological impetus to exterminate the natives.

Second, and most importantly, genocides are inflicted on defeated, captive or otherwise vulnerable minorities. The Tutsis were not at war with the Hutus in Rwanda, nor were the Jews at war with the Nazis during the Holocaust. These, like all indisputable genocides, were not wars, but centrally coordinated slaughters of helpless noncombatants. In Tasmania, although both sides killed noncombatants, they did so without coordination, and in the context of a war.

Colonists were engaged in a serious conflict against a capable and terrifying enemy. It was not the natives' colour or creed that convinced them of the necessity of extermination; it was the effectiveness of their attacks, and the strength of their resolve. Likewise, many natives also wanted to exterminate the colonists, as the following section reveals, but it is obviously absurd to call their attitudes or actions genocidal. For the same reasons it seems inappropriate to apply the word to colonists.

Moreover, the Black War was fought on an island from which permanent retreat was practically impossible for most colonists. Avenues for negotiation appeared nonexistent, and with every year the enemy became more dangerous. In other words, colonists felt trapped, powerless and terrified, and the natives were in essentially the same predicament. It is surely not surprising that there were people on both sides who believed exterminating the enemy was the only way to restore peace.

So was genocide committed in Tasmania? It depends entirely on what is meant by that word. In 1948, the United Nations Convention on the Prevention and Punishment of the Crime of Genocide defined it as 'acts committed with intent to destroy, in whole or in part, a national, ethnical, racial or religious group'. Read in isolation, this is meaninglessly broad, which is why the UN definition must be understood in the context of the debates that surrounded and continue to surround it.[80] In particular, the feature that primarily distinguishes genocide from war crimes and other crimes against humanity is *dolus specialis*, or specific intent.[81] It would require another book to sufficiently unpack the legal definition of genocide, and consider its application to events in Tasmania, but I will say this: whatever word we use, we must at least acknowledge that the attitudes and circumstances that provoked colonists to kill natives in Tasmania were very different from those typically associated with genocide.

Black

The Tasmanians had learnt much about the white strangers after two decades of sharing the island with them. Insofar as the vast cultural and linguistic differences allowed, some tribes had sustained periods of amicable contact with particular white men.[82] Whether through such contact or by observation and word of mouth, most Aborigines came to understand something of the white man's habits, strengths and weaknesses. Nevertheless, at least some still believed the whites were ancestors returned from the dead. There was no inconsistency in holding this belief and treating whites as fallible real-world actors, since the spirit-world permeated the mundane as well as the mystical. This interpretation of the invaders as reincarnated ancestors seems to have remained powerful well into the 1830s, thus it must have been a change in circumstances, rather than a fundamental perceptual shift, that roused the Tasmanians to war. The change in question was the rising torrent of white men that swept into the interior during the 1820s. This invasion was the ultimate cause of Aboriginal belligerence, and can serve as shorthand for a suite of more proximate causes, which included the desire to evict the invaders, the desire to avenge a variety of insults, and the difficulty of hunting in hostile territory.

Resistance

Aboriginal violence in Tasmania was, at its core, a resistance movement.[83] Simply put, a violent resistance movement means the use of force against an invading or occupying enemy. However, this does not entail that the expulsion of the invaders or occupiers be the *only* objective. In fact, complete expulsion need not even be considered achievable. Many Aborigines certainly attempted to expel the whites, but at some point the surviving tribes realised the hopelessness of that endeavour. In the final days of the war, Robinson found they had given up all hope of expelling the invaders, and they probably felt the imminence of defeat long before that.[84] But the Tasmanians were not the first people in history to press a lost war – particularly when surrender was presumed tantamount to suicide.

The archives are replete with evidence of Aboriginal resistance, and sometimes it is remarkably explicit. Robinson observed that Tasmanians:

> have a tradition amongst them that white men have usurped their territory, have driven them into the forests, have killed their game and thus robbed them of their chief subsistence, have ravished their wives and daughters, have murdered and butchered their fellow countrymen; and are wont whilst brooding over these complicated ills in the dense part of the forest, to goad each other on to acts of bloodshed and revenge for the injuries done to their ancestors and the persecutions offered to themselves through their white enemies.[85]

In fact, Robinson made a number of explicit statements confirming that 'love of liberty is a ruling passion with these people', and that '[p] atriotism is a distinguishing trait in the aboriginal character'. He was emphatic that Aborigines were 'patriots, [and] staunch lovers of their country'.[86] Roving party leader Gilbert Robertson also discovered, from conversations with Umarrah, Jemmy, Kickertopoller and others that 'they consider every injury they can inflict upon the white men as an act of duty and patriotism'. He added that 'they are in reality a shrewd, cunning race having ideas of their natural rights which would astonish most European statesmen'.[87]

In some cases, Tasmanians commanded enough English to shout their grievances at their victims. When a war party killed three men on the Shannon River in 1826, for instance, they screamed at the survivors, 'go away, go away'.[88] Likewise, the tribesmen who set fire to John Sherwin's house in January 1830 retreated to a distance and began yelling, 'go away you white buggers, what business have you here?'[89]

Resistance movements are inherently political. Nothing illustrates this more than the Tasmanians' use of arson and stock killing. Arson was a largely political tactic, whose main purpose was to intimidate and sabotage the white invaders. Stock killing was wholly symbolic in intent. Attacks on stock almost always occurred independent of other violence, and Tasmanians never ate the carcasses. As the Russian explorer Fabian Bellingshausen noted in 1820: 'They often destroy their flocks of sheep, not that they need meat, but solely to inflict material damage on their enemies.'[90] Moreover, as Chapter 3 explains, both arson and stock killing entailed considerable risk to the perpetrator, and thus cannot be dismissed as mindless vandalism.

Revenge

No European understood the Tasmanians' grievances better than Robinson. In 1831, he recorded in his journal that the reason Aborigines 'bear a deadly animosity to the white inhabitants' was because 'there is scarcely one among them but what has some monstrous cruelty to relate'.[91] Robinson observed the same sentiments throughout the island. When the last of the hostile tribes surrendered:

> The chiefs assigned as a reason for their outrages upon the white inhabitants that they and their forefathers had been cruelly abused, that their country had been taken from them, their wives and daughters had been violated and taken away, and that they had experienced a multitude of wrongs from a variety of sources ... They Complain loudly of the injuries done to them and their progenitors by the whites.[92]

A considerable amount of Aboriginal violence was targeted revenge, especially in the early years of the war. Robinson 'heard them boast with much pleasure of the murders they have committed on the whites, and has known them to be revenged on particular persons for inflicting injuries on them'.[93] One Aboriginal woman told him 'that when one [of her brothers] was shot the other attempted to avenge his death and speared the man that shot him'.[94] Sometimes they even knew their victims by name. When tribesmen besieged a hut on the South Esk River in September 1828, they threatened 'the men by name and ... pelted the hut frequently with stones'.[95] The most notorious case was that of James Cupid, who suffered nine spear wounds between 1826 and 1831. According to one settler, the Aborigines had 'long avowed vengeance on Cupid who has been a terror to them'.[96]

Tasmanians reserved a particular hatred for soldiers. Robinson found they possessed 'a rooted antipathy' and 'an unconquerable aversion to soldiers'.[97] Likewise, the Oyster Bay settler George Story recalled that they harboured 'great antipathy to the Redcoats'.[98] This was probably because soldiers were easily recognisable, always armed, and responsible for many acts of frontier violence.[99] The experiences of Robinson's informants explain why they felt this way:

> [Tunnerminnerwait] stated that a soldier stole upon some natives unperceived and shot a woman. The white savage then took out his knife and cut her throat and cut open her belly and then burnt her in the fire. LACK-LAY further stated that on another occasion some soldiers stole upon the natives at their encampment and fired upon them and shot one man and one woman; and an helpless infant belonging to the murdered woman they also killed, by beating it on the head with a stick.[100]

Such treatment did result in several reprisals against soldiers when they could be isolated alone or in pairs, but generally fear seems to have encouraged most Aborigines to take a wide berth of these men in red.[101] Desire for revenge, it seems, did not tempt them to make suicidal attacks on targets beyond their capabilities.

Violence over women

Of all the injuries Aborigines received at the hands of white men, nothing fuelled their thirst for revenge like violence towards women and children. This can seem difficult to square with the role some men played in prostituting their wives, but to them, a woman's virtue was not predicated on her sexual purity. This is not to say that frontier prostitution never contravened traditional customs, or that greed never encouraged men to exploit their womenfolk. It is merely to say that Aborigines' attitudes towards women and sex were very different from those of British middle-class observers.

Much of the war's initial violence probably stemmed from broken or misunderstood prostitution agreements. In 1826, for instance, stockmen at the junction of the Shannon and Ouse rivers bartered 'blankets and sugar' for sex with some local Aboriginal women. This might have been a fair arrangement, had the men not repossessed the women's payment as they departed, provoking their menfolk to attack the stockmen.[102] This sort of behaviour was a major source of the proliferating violence.

The settler Robert Thirkell claimed to have been 'constantly among the natives', and believed that 'any injury sustained by the white people was entirely occasioned by their own ill-usage of the females'.[103] Likewise, George Lloyd observed that 'the thoughtless conduct of the farm-servants, stock-keepers, and others, in their immoralities with the "gins", embittered in the native mind a sense of wrong already unendurable'.[104] Moreover, the white man's use of violence and deception to procure sex was, in Robinson's opinion, 'the principal cause of unfriendly feeling and animosity'.[105]

Robinson observed that an Aboriginal man 'without a female partner is a poor dejected being. When arrived at the years of maturity his tantamount [sic] object is a wife who can provide [for] himself and family'.[106] These hardships, together with the emotional cost of losing their loved ones, goaded men to retaliate. When asked by a stock-keeper 'why they killed white men', a Tasmanian warrior 'who spoke English' replied rhetorically: 'If black man came and took away his *lubra* [wife] and killed his *piccaninnies* [children], would he not kill black man for it?'[107]

Where the location of a captive woman was known, Aborigines sometimes sent in a rescue party. Just such a rescue was attempted in March 1831 at a farm near Ben Lomond. Two Aborigines stole upon the hut and 'attacked the sawyers, hand to hand ... [while a third was] occupied in capturing a native girl who was living with them. The sawyers escaped after receiving several severe wounds.'[108]

When a woman was able to escape and tell her story, the revenge of her menfolk could be ruthless. Mr Thomson's servant was witness to one such case. He testified that, in 1826, 'Dune the bushranger, brought a native woman to our hut; he brought her by force. The same woman was with the tribe of Natives when they attacked and plundered our hut, and she was with the party who threatened us with death on the following day, about which time Scott was killed.'[109]

Often though, the fates of the women are unknown, and the source records only the retaliation. One settler recounted the story of a man who shackled a woman to a log with a bullock-chain and 'was afterwards found speared to death'.[110] The settler Richard Dry recalled an incident in which two convicts at the Western Marshes 'had forced some black women to their hut and that in revenge for this outrage the natives waylaid and killed the two stockmen'.[111] Some Aboriginal testimony was also recorded. When Temina was captured near the South Esk River in 1825 and asked 'why he killed the white men he said the white men wanted to get the women away from his Tribe'.[112] Clearly, the abduction and abuse of women was common, and the ensuing revenge and rescue missions constituted a substantial portion of the violence perpetrated by Tasmanians.

Torture and intimidation

In many of their attacks, Tasmanians displayed intense fury and brutality, often ensuring their victims died slowly and agonisingly. This was an expression of vengefulness as well as a method of intimidation. In February 1830, the *Hobart Town Courier* reported that James McCarty, a convict, was discovered 'almost lifeless, in a most shocking state, having several severe wounds on his head, back and breast, and his little finger nearly beaten off, and even maggots had engendered in several parts of his body ... McCarty was found 18 hours after the attack upon him by the blacks, lying at the back of the big Lagoon, in a state of insensibility'.[113]

Six months earlier, Charles Chadwick testified that Aborigines surrounded his hut on the Jordan River. They demanded he remove his clothes, then mocked and toyed with him until one took a waddy from behind his back and proceeded to beat him viciously. The tribe then left their victim, but soon after one of the men returned, rolled him onto his back and drove a spear through his arm.[114] Robinson recorded similarly cruel practices. On one occasion, an Aboriginal woman described to him 'the manner of torture they adopted towards their fated victims, via breaking their arms or legs or cutting their heads, and when they did not kill they disabled or maimed'.[115]

This is not to say that Aborigines were incapable of mercy.[116] When Montpelliatta's tribe 'attacked Shone's hut and set it on fire, and the woman run out from the flames and begged of them not to kill her. MONTPELLIATTA the chief took her in his arms and carried her away and would not let the rest hurt her.' There was a limit to such magnanimity, however, for in the same attack they decapitated a man, and burnt his body.[117] Torture and mutilation of the dead were not the norm, but they were not uncommon either. Some cases were no doubt vendettas animated by grief and rage, and targeted at particular white men, though many Tasmanians came to harbour a deep-seated hatred towards all white men.

During the late 1820s, the character of Aboriginal violence changed. As the white men grew in number, so too did their attacks, and targeted revenge became increasingly unmanageable. Robinson told the Executive Council in 1831 that 'the Natives can distinguish between stock-keepers and settlers, and attack the latter, although they are conscious of not having received an injury from them'.[118] Some Tasmanians stated as much themselves. Tribesmen attacking huts along the Shannon River in 1827 'repeatedly said they will, sooner or later, murder every *WHITE* man in the Island!!!'[119] Maybe it was the bitterness, the attrition, or the realisation that all whites were contributing to their destruction, but many Tasmanians clearly stopped caring who their victims were.[120]

Resources

During the latter years of the war, as Roderic O'Connor observed, the Tasmanians became 'more anxious to plunder than to murder'.[121] Since a warm fire was also a conspicuous fire, they plundered clothing and blankets as a means of staving off hypothermia. The white man's foods were even more popular. Tasmanians enjoyed the taste of flour, sugar, potatoes and other novel foods, but by the late 1820s they were also essential to their survival. A man captured near the Clyde River in 1830 revealed that 'when the tribe attacked the hut it was in order to obtain food, and such article as the whites had introduced amongst them, and which now instead of being luxuries as formerly, had become necessities, which they could not any other way procure'.[122]

So why did European foods become necessities for the remnant Tasmanians? There is some evidence that white hunters depleted the native game upon which tribes subsisted. The *Hobart Town Courier*, for instance, reported in January 1829 that 'the number of kangaroos killed lately exceeds any thing [*sic*] before known in the island'.[123] Around the same time, an Aboriginal man told Jorgen Jorgenson that when 'I returned to my country I went hunting but did not kill one head of game. The white men make their dogs wander, and kill all the game, and they only want the skins'.[124] There is no doubt that extensive hunting reduced the wallaby and kangaroo populations in many areas, but this was not the main reason Aborigines plundered the white man's food.

Far more important was the danger of hunting in the vicinity of the ever-expanding settlements. At the height of the war, the retired officer

Thomas Marslen recognised that:

> 'their latitude for procuring food by hunting and fishing, becomes more
> and more circumscribed every year, exactly in the same ratio as the farms
> are extended over the island; and in less than the period of one generation
> they will not have a single untenanted spot left. Starve they cannot, there-
> fore it will always be a war of extermination.'[125]

White encroachment eroded the Tasmanians' capacity to move safely
over much of their country, until it became too dangerous to hunt, and
they were forced to adopt a war economy based on plunder.

In December 1830, the *Hobart Town Courier* remarked that it was
'well known' how the 'extension of the settled districts upon their [the
Tasmanians'] usual hunting grounds has either driven them entirely
from them or removed the kangaroo'.[126] Around the same time, the
Launceston Advertiser predicted that 'as the Aborigines find themselves,
more and more hemmed in, and disconcerted in their annual excursions
and means of subsistence, they will be more apt to commit outrages'.[127]

A similar sentiment was expressed by the captured chiefs Umarrah
and Jemmy, who 'said that the several tribes are quite unhappy in their
present situation, from the manner in which their hunting grounds, their
principal means of subsistence, have been circumscribed'.[128] Eventually,
the invasion became unbearably claustrophobic. Following his surrender
in 1831, the chief Montpelliatta stated that 'when the Aborigines left any
place to go hunting elsewhere, and they returned in the course of eight
days, they found a hut erected'.[129] The Tasmanians wanted to attack the
invaders for numerous reasons, but in the end, they *had* to attack them.

CHAPTER THREE
WARFARE

White

Colonists in Tasmania brought one of the world's most ancient peoples to the brink of destruction within a generation. It is difficult to know how many people inhabited the island before the arrival of Europeans, but the estimates of scholars from various fields suggest the eastern population was at least 2000. By the time the war began in 1824, this population had probably halved, and by 1832, it was practically zero. Fewer than 100 eastern natives survived, sent to 'pine away' on the islands of Bass Strait.[1] The role of colonists and their guns in this staggering decline is the subject to which we now turn.

Gin raiding

By the mid-1820s, the 'gin' raid had become an established tactic whereby frontiersmen ambushed native campsites in order to acquire women for sex. Technically, this was not warfare, but it was a systematic form of violence that provided the tactical template used throughout the Black War. A settler told James Fenton that '[i]t was the custom of the sons and servants of the settlers to lie in ambush for "a mob" of native women and girls, and to seize and carry away the younger ones whenever an opportunity offered'.[2] This behaviour was no secret. In 1826, the *Hobart Town Gazette* asserted: 'No one disputes that many, very many, needless acts of cruelty have been committed upon this perhaps originally harmless race ... [in instances where] stock-keepers have pursued and carried off their women'.[3]

The strongest evidence for the prevalence of gin raiding came from the settlers questioned by the Aborigines Committee in 1830. This was a time when hatred of the blacks was at its most intense, and the respondents had every reason to blame them for initiating the conflict; but instead, they convinced the Committee that attacks were 'frequently made by lawless and desperate characters for the purpose of carrying off the Native women and children; attempts which, if resisted, the aggressors did not scruple to accomplish with circumstances of dreadful and unnecessary barbarity'.[4]

If an ambush was successful, the raiders might keep their captive women chained up for a day, a week or longer, depending on the circumstances. Captain Clark told the Aborigines Committee that, in around 1824, 'a stock-keeper belonging to Mr Lord, named Jenkins, seized a native woman and kept her confined for some days in his hut, always chaining her with a bullock chain to his bed post whenever he went abroad'.[5] Similarly, Mr Weeding claimed that, in the Oatlands district, 'the stock-keepers had chained the females to their huts with bullock chains for the purpose of fornication'.[6]

A more explicit example followed the capture of a woman and her six-year-old daughter at Emu Bay by Alexander Goldie and his two companions. 'The woman is in irons', Goldie wrote in a letter to his employer four weeks later:

> I make her wash potatoes for the horses and intend taking her to the hills
> and making her work ... the woman will not speak and is very often sulky.

> She broke her irons once and was very nearly getting away I think she is
> about 20 or 22 years old. I have no doubt she will work. Barras can make
> her do anything.[7]

Later that year the woman was removed to Launceston, though Goldie
retained the little girl until she died in 1830.[8]

Once frontiersmen had finished with their captives, they generally either let them go or killed them, though the latter option was the
safest and probably the most popular. There were many cases in which,
according to the *Colonial Times*, '[t]heir women have been contami-
nated [raped], and then had their throats cut, or been shot'.[9] Sweeping
remarks such as this might be dismissed as exaggeration if it were not for
the many specific examples that confirm them. Captain Donaldson, for
instance, recounted a story to Robinson, told to him by:

> a man at the westward at a remote stock hut [who said] that the natives
> had been shamefully treated: said he had no right to speak well of them
> as they had killed his wife, but he said that he was witness of a barbarous
> transaction, that two stock-keepers kept a black woman and cohabited
> with her for some time, when they afterwards tied her up by the heels and
> left her to perish.[10]

Similarly, the colony's largest landowner, William Effingham Lawrence,
was informed of 'two stock-keepers [who] took a black woman, ravished
her and then bound her on the ground by each hand and foot, stretching
her spreadeagle, and then left her to perish'.[11]

Some years after the war, Fenton recorded the testimony of a convict
who told him of when he and his fellow stockmen used to hunt blacks
around their campfires, adding that: 'Of course we used to spare a young
female occasionally when we got a chance, and kept her for a few days
before we shot her.'[12] The captured escapee John Perry described an
especially graphic case during a police interview in March 1826. Perry

confessed (though later denied) that Jeffries, Russell and himself, who had absconded to the island's north-east:

> fell in with four men [sealers] and a black woman ... after we shot the men, the black woman came to us, and told us they were Boatmen, and were going after Jins we could not understand her sufficiently to make out where the Boat was, after searching the Bodies we left them, and took the black woman to a Lagoon about a quarter of a mile [400 m] off, where all three of us had connexion with her, Jeffries first, then I and afterwards Russell, we then all four dined together off some fat cakes and kangaroo steamer, neither of us had any further connexion with the woman; about three or four o'clock in the afternoon Jeffries said the Blacks were all treacherous that he had been taken by them at Sydney, and shot her through the head with a pistol.[13]

Such behaviour is reminiscent of armies throughout history that have considered the sexual enjoyment of captive women a perquisite of military success.

Official armed parties

Pursuit parties were raised to hunt down natives in the immediate aftermath of their attacks. They usually spent between 12 and 48 hours in the field. In most cases the nearest constable or officer was alerted, who in turn rallied a party from local military detachments and settlers' establishments. Some communities even had a 'prearranged signal' to announce a pursuit and, by 1829, response times were remarkably fast.[14]

When sightings or attacks occurred in populous areas, several parties could be deployed within a matter of hours. In about 1827, following a siege at the Hadspen property of ex-convict, Thomas Beams:

> The neighbours then began to arrive, some on foot others mounted, they had heard the firing and guessed the blacks were attacking the Beams

home. A war party was quickly got together, two of the older men was left to guard the house, powder and swan drop [lead pellets] was served out and fourteen men crossed the ford … [They] searched the hills and gullies, but could not find the blacks, so they sat down and waited for darkness, about 10 o'clock a faint glow was seen in the sky, one of the party took his boots off and borrowed socks from the others tied them to his feet so as not to make a sound and crept away into the darkness, he came back again in about two hours and reported that he had found the blacks in a deep dark gully, there was about a dozen, one of them was sitting on a boulder apparently on the lookout, the party was now divided into four to come in from each side, the signal for attack was the call of a [?], a charge of swan drop was to be fired and then the camp was to be rushed with clubbed muskets, every thing went off as arranged, at 3 A.M. fourteen muskets poured a charge of swan drop into the blacks, the camp was rushed and when daylight came eleven dead blacks was counted, only one got away.[15]

This pursuit was typical in the way it was organised, but atypical insofar as it succeeded.

Roving parties were proactive rather than reactive, scouring the countryside for weeks at a time in the hope of 'capturing or destroying the Natives'.[16] The idea to contract civilians (settlers and convicts) into roving parties was hatched by Governor Arthur and Oatlands' police magistrate, Thomas Anstey. Familiar with the tried and tested methods of the stockmen, Anstey suggested in November 1828 that 'a few parties each consisting of ten or 12 active men, should look for the native fires *at night*'.[17] Desperate to try something, Arthur agreed. By September 1829, Anstey had fitted out seven civilian parties, and four more were added the following year.[18]

Far more numerous were the military roving parties, which patrolled all the major districts. Although soldiers were better trained than their civilian counterparts, their tactics were much the same. It was well understood that the only way to 'come up with the blacks' was to spot their campfires and ambush them in their repose. The Russian explorer Lieutenant EA Berens, who visited Australia in 1829, recorded a telling conversation with 'one of the officers, who served in Van Diemen's Land', who told him 'about the means they use to move the native inhabitants off the colony. Usually such a detachment sets out for the bush, as if to hunt game; on seeing the natives, they surround them and kill them without any regret.'[19]

Hunting natives, however, was more difficult than hunting game. Sergeant Armstrong, who conducted roving missions out of Bothwell, explained to his superiors that every morning 'they had to rise before daylight to get on the top of a Tier by break of day [to look for fires]'.[20] If a campfire could be descried, and the sleeping tribe surrounded, rovers had orders to capture them if possible, but otherwise to 'drive them by force to a safe distance, treating them as open enemies'.[21] In practice, however, capture was rarely an option. Even when it was attempted, the natives usually ran and were thus shot at. More commonly, attackers fired before announcing themselves, so either way, ambushes resulted in lethal violence.

A look at two successful ambushes – one military, one civilian – will help clarify these points. On 6 December 1828, a party of the 40th Regiment, guided by constables Danvers and Holmes, spotted a tribe near Tooms Lake, east of Oatlands. Danvers described how the party 'got near as possible to them that night', and at daybreak, when they attacked:

> the whole of them jumped up immediately and attempted to take up their spears in defence and seeing that, we immediately fired and repeated it, because we saw that they were on the defensive part, they were about twenty in number, and several of whom were killed, only two [a woman and a boy], unfortunately, were taken alive.[22]

Officially, 'several' turned out to be 'ten',[23] but witnessing the soldiers returning triumphantly to Oatlands, Corporal Robert Ayton 'heard many of them boast that they had killed 16 of the natives, one man in particular boasted that he had run his bayonet through two of them, and that they had gathered them into a heap and burned their bodies'.[24] Many soldiers were young men who had never seen combat, so a successful ambush may have been the closest thing to 'victory' they had experienced. Whatever their reasons, the men's boastfulness says volumes about their attitudes.

The following August, a civilian roving party under John Batman came across a large native camp. They crept as close as they could before one man 'struck his musket against that of another party, which immediately alarmed the dogs'. According to Batman's report, the blacks:

> were in the act of running away into the thick scrub, when I ordered the men to fire upon them, which was done, and a rush by the party immediately followed, we only captured that Night one woman and a male child about Two years old, the party was in search of them the remainder of the Night, but without success, the next morning we found one man very badly wounded in his ankle and knee, shortly after we found another 10 buckshot had entered his Body, he was alive but very bad, there was a great number of traces of blood in various directions and learned from those we took that 10 men were wounded in the Body which they gave us to understand were dead or would die, and Two women in the same state had crawled away, besides a number that was shot in the legs … on Friday morning we left the place for my Farm with the two men, woman and child, but found it quite impossible that the Two former could walk, and after trying them by every means in my power, for some time, found I could not get them on. I was obliged therefore to shoot them.[25]

The only major difference between the two attacks was that the 40th Regiment's kill rate was much higher than Batman's, which no doubt reflected their arms training. Tactically, however, the ambushes seem to have been identical. Although neither soldiers nor frontiersmen had been trained to execute such ambushes, the tactics of the gin raiders were well established by the time the roving parties were formed.

There were also important similarities in the ways the attacks were reported. Neither Danvers nor Batman expressed the slightest concern that they might attract censure for firing on masses of sleeping men, women and children. And neither did. The roving parties were the colony's primary defence against the blacks, and Arthur was unwilling to compromise their authority.[26] Indeed, he went so far as to reassure rovers that their rewards would be safe, even if they were 'unavoidably compelled to use violence, and loss of life ensue[d]'.[27]

Vigilantes and the campfire ambush

John West was characteristically perceptive when he observed that, 'if the authorised [roving party] system was attended with a sad sacrifice of native life, no one will question the atrocities committed by commandoes, first formed by stock-keepers, and some settlers, under the influence of anger, and then continued from habit'.[28] The unofficial vigilante parties almost certainly took a greater toll on the native population than the official roving or pursuit parties. Vigilantes used the same tactics as the official parties, but their opportunities were more numerous, and their motives stronger.

If colonists were actively looking for blacks, they ascended the nearest hill at dusk or dawn looking for signs of smoke, but most ambushes were probably spontaneous. Experienced frontiersmen knew that, unlike smoke from a stockman's camp, the natives' smoke ascended in multiple columns.[29] When a sighting was made, the news passed between neighbouring stockmen, and a posse was raised. Communication was difficult once a camp was surrounded, so plans and signals had to be prearranged, and arms and ammunition checked. When night fell, the men made their way to where the smoke had been sighted, looking now for glowing fires, and the characteristic sounds of a native camp. If the camp could be located, the party split up and surrounded it, generally waiting till first light to attack when the targets were visible, but not yet conscious (see Figure 14).[30]

Men's hearts must have raced with fear and excitement in the crucial moments before an ambush, but even as they were poised to attack, success hinged on several factors. For one, the blacks often slept in huts, which made them harder to pick off from a distance, but easier to surprise. Robinson's envoys told him that 'the white men about those parts [the Blue Hills] had killed plenty of the natives, that they used to shoot them in their huts in the winter time'.[31] More importantly though, men had to ensure their weapons would fire. The most common weapon, among both soldiers and civilians, was the Brown-Bess musket. This was a notoriously unreliable and inaccurate weapon, and at 159 centimetres in length and 4.7 kilograms in weight, it was also extremely cumbersome.[32] The ammunition of choice for close-range encounters was grapeshot (lead pellets), but to be effective, the gun needed to be well maintained, and the powder kept dry. The latter was a constant problem in Tasmania's damp climate, particularly if the men had chosen a misty or dewy morning to attack.[33] Furthermore, guns were generally only good for one shot before the targets dispersed. A proficient soldier could fire and reload three times a minute, but few colonists could achieve that sort of speed.[34] There simply was not the time for repeated firing. More commonly, the party rushed the camp following the first shots, and resorted to clubbing or bayoneting their victims.

None of this mattered unless the party could first get close enough to execute the attack, and this was no easy task. Traditionally, native camps consisted of a dozen or more hearths, spread over perhaps a hectare of ground, but by the late 1820s, their camps were much smaller, and usually hidden. Furthermore, if the night was too cold, assailants would be unable to lie in wait until dawn; if the morning was too foggy, they would be unable to see each other or their targets; too bright and the men might be seen; too dark and they might fumble noisily in the bush. A windy night might drown out some of the noise, but it might also alert the natives' dogs to their scent. Indeed, approaching assailants were often given away by barking dogs, and on some occasions they were even mauled.[35] Thus, with so many contingencies, success was far from assured. Most ambush attempts probably failed; it was only their frequency that eventually broke the native resistance.[36]

Campfire ambushes were generally perpetrated by convicts, but they did not always act alone. The son of one of the earliest east coast settlers gave the following account to Fenton, who, having 'no doubt whatever of its truth', recounted the incident as spoken by his informant:

> As soon as evening approached, I mustered our men to watch for the resting-place of the natives on the tiers. We had six muskets in good working order, and a good supply of ammunition, with ball and heavy slugs. The men posted themselves in good positions for making observations; and at last, in the grey twilight, one of them detected a light smoke rising from a gully two miles [3 km] distant. We carefully noted the spot and waited until near midnight, when we all sallied out together in search of our game. We took no dogs with us, lest they might be heard by the watchful dogs of the natives. Keeping the open country we soon reached the tier, and proceeded stealthily along until we stood over the little gully, from whence we then distinctly saw the smoke arising. It was now necessary to move along as quietly as possible; and, by observing every precaution, we succeeded in getting a pretty near view of the lighted fire, with a mob of natives and their dogs fast asleep around it. Having arranged our muskets and pistols for the fray, the former being loaded with heavy charges of slug and grape shot, we all six noiselessly approached to within a few yards of the wretches, when all of a sudden the dogs gave the alarm by raising a great commotion and furious barking. The natives were on their feet like electricity, but they looked stupefied, and never attempted to run. It would have been all the

same if they had, for we had them nearly all under cover of our guns, which we discharged at once, and dropped some eight or ten like crows. Then there was a jolly scramble to make off, but we dropped a few more as they bolted away into the scrub. Our night's sport made a dozen less natives, whom we left there to rot, and we sent away several wounded.[37]

Even when settlers did not personally participate in ambushes, many condoned, if not encouraged their assigned servants in the practice. Large landowners like George Hobler could raise a substantial party from among their own servants. After one of his splitters was speared, Hobler 'armed four men who I hope will get sight of their night fire and slaughter them as they lie around it'.[38] Nor did he express any disapproval when he discovered 'it was arranged among [his neighbour's] stock-keepers that if the natives made their appearance in that quarter they were to muster a strong party and endeavour to surprise them around at their fires after night'.[39] Settler complicity of this sort seems to have increased in the later years of the war, when the economic and psychological toll of black violence was at its most taxing.

The effectiveness of the campfire ambush as a means of expunging the native threat was widely recognised. A settler writing to the *Tasmanian* in 1828 was certain about what needed to be done:

From experience (and I have for several years been among cattle and stock-keepers in the interior, and seen and know more of the savages than I think necessary to state at this time) I venture to assert that, to the stock-keepers, the Colony will at length owe its relief from the depredations of the Black Natives – None know so well as stock-keepers, how to track them by their fires, and come upon them when asleep. This knowledge, melancholy as has been the effect, is not less true.[40]

Vigilantes, like the roving and pursuit parties that emulated them, realised the only way to counter the 'excessive cunning of the natives' was to attack them at their most vulnerable – when they were asleep. The government considered it beneath British honour to slaughter families as they slept, thus it never became the official policy. In practice, however, the authorities turned a blind eye. The blacks had to be stopped, and although the campfire ambush was not the most 'honourable' mode of warfare, it was certainly the most effective.

Black

> They can subsist on roots and small animals and they know the passes and are well acquainted with the topography of the country. They will travel over rocky ground where no traces are to be seen, and it is only owing to their incautious conduct and their going to huts that the white people have at any time met with them. Their mode of attack is by surreption. They lay in ambush for some time before they make their attack, a sudden and unperceived invasion, or by surprising. Their warfare is that of a predatory nature.
>
> *George Augustus Robinson, journal 14 December 1831*

Contemporaries describing Aboriginal modes of warfare used words like 'system', 'skill' and 'cunning' with mantra-like repetition. Usually they expressed a mix of both admiration and frustration. 'You can not think how cunning the black devils are', wrote one exasperated, but obviously impressed, east coast settler.[41] Likewise, the *Colonial Times* admitted the Aborigines 'evinced a degree of craft and cunning which shews, that although savage, they are not of that inferior order of beings which we have so often been told'.[42] The abundance of such remarks underscores the adroitness and effectiveness of the Tasmanians' guerrilla tactics. Although they ultimately lost the war, their resistance against a technologically and numerically superior enemy was nothing short of extraordinary.

Warrior culture

The Tasmanians were warrior peoples who celebrated martial prowess. Around the campfire, Robinson and his party were regularly entertained by stories of wartime exploits, assassinations and raids. Bravery, skill and honour were central themes animated by the raconteur. In describing to Robinson how his tribe 'track out the PYE.DARE.RER.ME and kill them and take their women to Brune', Woorrady 'appeared animated. He considered them as great achievements and honourable to his nation.'[43] On another occasion:

> One of the aborigines belonging to the north coast was entertaining me and the other natives with a relation of the exploits of his tribe with the Swanport. He said the two nations had met to fight and that the Swanport, apprehensive of their own prowess, had resolved the night previous to the battle to go away, which was assented to with the exception of two fine young men who most positively refused, declaring they would await the result of the forthcoming morn, considering it would stamp an indelible disgrace on their nation should they decline this combat.

The following morning the two warriors met their fates in 'a shower of spears', with the victorious tribe 'exalting in the bloody deed'.[44]

The veneration of war heroes was common. Robinson observed that Mannalargenna (see Figure 5C) 'was universally admitted by all the native tribes who knew him as being the most able and successful warrior of all the aborigines'.[45] The chief was said to have evinced 'astonishing skill in battle' and 'undaunted courage'. Mannalargenna was widely 'considered invincible', and Robinson received 'accounts from himself and others of his exploits in war, in which all the natives agree'.[46] Even the feared chief Umarrah 'was frightened of him and begged for mercy'.[47]

Before the white invasion, internecine conflicts were probably the most dangerous and dramatic events in Tasmanians' lives, thus it was central to their games, art, stories, songs and dances.[48] Robinson observed that their 'dances related the hunting of kangaroo or some battle or an amorous story'.[49] In one such dance, '[t]he motion of the body is the shifting attitude to avoid the spear in fighting; sometimes they call out "the spear is coming"'.[50] In July 1831, Robinson witnessed a typical performance:

> Tonight WOORRADY entertained us with a relation of the exploits of his nation and neighbouring nations or allies ... Said that the BRAYHE-LUKEQUONNE natives spear plenty of his and neighbouring tribes, that they stop behind trees and when they see a native by himself they go and spear him. When the natives relate those exploits they do it by singing it, accompanying the same with different gestures corresponding with the circumstances of the story – the manner of fighting, the blows given, where inflicted and how, whether by spear, waddy or stones, or wrestling, or cutting with sharp stones, pointing to the parts of the wounded. WOOR-RADY is very animated in his relation of the circumstances of his nation, and having a good voice it is peculiarly interesting to attend to him.[51]

This same culture was speedily adapted to the conflict with the whites. In 1831, Robinson observed that 'the circumstances of their plundering expeditions on the whites would often engage their conversation', and 'the most popular of their songs were those in which they recounted their attacks on and their fights with the whites'.[52] In one instance, he described a 'horse dance', in which a tribesman was 'chased by a man on horseback with a long whip, and of his out-running the horse'.[53] On another occasion, he discovered that one of their songs was 'a relation of circumstances relating to the white people, of their seeing a bullock cart going along the Port Dalrymple road heavy loaded with flour, and also of their robbing a hut and taking away muskets, making damper and their concealing the muskets. The song is popular with all the eastern tribes.'[54] Thus, the Tasmanians' warrior culture persisted during the white invasion, expanding to incorporate the new threat.

Arming for war

The Tasmanians used three types of weapon: stones, spears and waddies. Stones were only occasionally used against the whites, either in ambushing them from a high position, or in bludgeoning them once disabled.[55] Their spears were made from several types of timber, and varied in length from 1.25 to 4.9 metres, depending on their purpose.[56] George Washington Walker remarked that the 'natives are very dexterous in the use of these weapons ... They throw them with such force and skill, at from fifty to one hundred yards [45–90 m], as rarely to fail in transfixing the object of their aim.'[57] Spears were very effective at killing game, but without barbs or stone tips, a peripheral spear wound was usually not fatal to humans. For this reason, many white victims were bludgeoned to death with waddies. About 60 centimetres long with a bulbous end, waddies could be used as a club or throwing stick.[58] Robinson observed that Aborigines were 'remarkably dextrous in using this missile and seldom fail to hit their object'.[59]

At the height of the war, tribes required great quantities of spears and waddies. While fleeing an ambush on the Macquarie River in 1828, one tribe abandoned 29 waddies and 52 spears.[60] At Prossers Plains the following year, another tribe left behind 49 spears and over 100 waddies in the confusion of an ambush.[61] In the aftermath of such attacks, tribes needed to re-arm as quickly as possible, but good timber and sufficient time was not always available. Tribes overcame this by stockpiling spears in hidden caches. On the Freycinet Peninsula in 1831, for instance, 'twelve spears [were found] concealed under a rock', and Robinson observed this practice on several occasions.[62] Using these reserve arsenals, tribes were able to re-arm quickly after an ambush, and avoid long diversions to procure timber.

It is a testament to the efficiency of spears and waddies that Tasmanians never converted to using firearms. This was not a problem of access or competence. They regularly plundered muskets, and many knew how to operate and maintain them.[63] They simply recognised that, for fighting a guerrilla war in the Tasmanian environment, their weapons were more appropriate than the white man's.

Tactics

Thomas Anstey of Oatlands proclaimed in March 1830 that '[t]he Natives, during the last 12 months, have coined a spirit of enterprise and hardihood beyond that of any former year. The murders, in this District, have been less numerous, but the burnings of houses, corn [wheat] stacks, fences have greatly increased. The Natives are becom[ing] bolder and the Whites more timid.'[64] Anstey was not the only contemporary to observe increased boldness and system in the Tasmanians' tactics during the latter half of the war. According to the *Tasmanian* of 18 April 1828, they exhibited 'an extent of design and arrangement, that makes savages exceedingly dangerous'.[65] The same year, the *Hobart Town Courier* asserted that 'the natives have formed a systematic organised plan for carrying on a war of extermination against the white inhabitants of the colony'.[66] In 1830, the *Colonial Times* also had to concede that 'the attacks and depredations of the Aborigines ... assume a regular and alarming consistency, and evince ... a cunning and superiority of tactic which would not disgrace even some of the greatest military characters'.[67]

Such observations were not merely excuses for failing to suppress the Aboriginal threat. As the conflict progressed, Tasmanians refined their modes of warfare to better exploit the invaders' weaknesses. 'The black assailant', wrote James Calder, 'never fought till he knew he had his opponents at a disadvantage to themselves. He waited and watched for his opportunity for hours, and often for days, for he knew nothing of the value of time, and when the proper moment arrived he attacked the solitary hut of the stock-keeper with irresistible numbers.'[68]

Reconnaissance was crucial. Even before settlement, French anthropologist François Péron observed of the Maria Island people that 'they surround themselves with sentries in advanced positions who, from the atops of hills and even high in very tall trees, keep a watch on all that takes place'.[69] Years later, at the height of the war, whites had a constant sense of being watched, and their suspicions were often right. Aborigines learnt to stalk the whites and assail them at their most vulnerable. An army captain reported to the Governor in February 1830 that 'the knowledge the natives have of the defenceless state of the house is astonishing as they have invariably made their attacks on the departure of the means of defence'.[70] Following a fatal attack at Spring Hill the same year, an Aboriginal woman divulged to Robinson 'the whole of their plans and schemes'. She explained how 'a party of them had for three days kept watch unseen on one of the rocky hills close to the cottage, intending to wait there until Hooper went out to work without his gun'.[71] This classic guerrilla tactic was evident throughout the island, and almost certainly pre-colonial in origin.

Aborigines planned their attacks in almost every instance. This was most apparent in the decoying strategies they employed. In the summer of 1827–28, a tribe in the Bothwell district began 'to decoy them [their white victims] by lighting fires at a short distance, & to take the opportunity of them being absent to carry off all they could find'.[72] 'No one can conjecture how crafty and subtle they act in the bush', wrote a settler in 1830, 'they even made the fire and smoke in the bush to entice people from the buildings in order that they might plunder.'[73]

Another method of decoying whites was to send in a few men to make a dummy attack, and while they were being pursued, another party would assail the unguarded hut. In July 1830, for instance:

> a tribe of the Natives came down upon the men in the Employ of Lieutenant Betts at the Big Lagoon (Lake Tiberias) … they however were enabled to take to their heels, and made the best of their way towards the adjoining stock-hut … all the arms and men were procured, and then listened back in order to fall in with the depredators, but on their coming to the place,

not a sign of them was perceptible, they had decamped taking away every thing moveable along with them, the men then again returned to Mr. Stokell's, and to their astonishment, found that in their absence, which had only been for a few minutes, the same depredations had been committed upon them, with the addition that the Natives had attempted to set fire to the hut.[74]

A similar diversion was used during an attack on a hut at Norfolk Plains the same year, but on this occasion a third party was also 'employed slaughtering [over 100] sheep which were speared and beaten to death with waddies'.[75]

In the earlier phases of the war, before all trust had dissolved, Tasmanians would occasionally conduct attacks under the guise of friendship:

> by sending some of their people, sometimes women, sometimes unarmed men, who have approached huts with apparently the most friendly disposition, and have succeeded in engaging the attention of the inmates, or in alluring some of them to a distance, and thus enabling their armed confederates to fall suddenly upon their unsuspecting victims and destroy them.[76]

Another tactic, according to James Hobbs, involved having 'the women visit the stock-huts as spies, and then the men attack them'.[77] Deprived as they were of sexual opportunities, white men often took great risks to have sex with Aboriginal women. Some Tasmanians exploited this by sending women to huts for the purpose of decoying the occupants, or gathering intelligence. In December 1827, for instance, 'two black females came to Mr. Talbot's, evidently sent as spies by a horde to which they belonged. They had scarcely left the house, when two of Mr Talbot's servants were attacked by about 150 [warriors].'[78] Indeed, they experimented with various forms of artifice. When an Aboriginal girl was caught snooping around an east coast property in March 1828, it was observed that she 'did not appear to make much exertion to effect her escape'. The girl then:

> with seeming reluctance promised to shew where the natives were encamped; having to make some preparation the men were delayed until day-light when they proceeded under her guidance; they had not been long gone when one of the children perceived some of their warriors laying in ambush in the opposite direction to that where the black girl was conducting the party.[79]

Aside from their involvement as decoys, women almost never took part in attacks. In June 1829, a northern correspondent claimed it was the Aborigines' 'custom to leave their women and children in a place of security, and for about 20 of the ablest and most dexterous of the men to go out on their excursions to rob and murder'.[80] In 1824, for instance, several Aboriginal women who had been captured by George Meredith's men, confessed that during a recent killing, they and their children 'were stationed on the adjoining Hill, while the men attacked the Hut'.[81] This was no doubt a stressful time for the women, who were reported to have chanted to a 'good spirit' for the safe return of their men.[82]

War parties generally comprised between ten and 20 men. When they encountered armed resistance the party often laid siege to the hut in an effort to intimidate, overpower or immolate the defenders (see Figure 15). For example, Robinson recorded an incident in which a tribe of Aborigines 'burnt the soldiers' hut to the ground and piled up the stones for a battery, from behind which they kept throwing fire at the hut and also stones, and calling in English, "Fire at me, you white". The women and the chief stood off in front and the chief kept giving directions how they ought to act. They were all round the hut behind stumps.'[83] Sometimes these sieges could last all day. At the Lagoon of Islands in 1828, a 'party of blacks attacked Mr Allardyce's stock hut ... for more than six hours, until they at last thought fit to withdraw'.[84] Likewise,

John Allen was besieged later that year by 'blacks numbering 13–18', keeping them at bay 'for over eight hours'.[85]

When plans went smoothly, sieges were unnecessary. Swift, hit-and-run ambushes were the safest and most efficient mode of attacking. Typically, a war party would approach their victims with stealth, secure their weapons if they were lying nearby, and spear them while their guard was down.[86] For example, 'at Mr Scott's [in 1830] the attack was so sudden that the men were speared before they had any idea of a native even being near'.[87] The same year, near Pittwater, Thomas Pratt 'suddenly received a blow on the head from a waddy. The poor man immediately looked round, and perceived several blacks close behind him – he ran down the hill in front of the hut, when a native that was behind a log suddenly jumped up and threw a spear at him, which penetrated his back and reached his heart – he died instantly'.[88] Surprise was paramount, and it was the Tasmanians' forte. According to Calder, 'hundreds are the instances of their surrounding dwellings in perfect swarms without their exciting the smallest suspicion of their being at hand'.[89]

Crucial to the success of these attacks was capable leadership. In times of conflict, warriors of outstanding bravery and skill ascended to commanding roles. During the Black War, the weight of responsibility on these men's shoulders was immense. They were often observed coordinating attacks. In March 1828, one such leader, 'his hair thickly smeared with red ochre, was discovered crawling on his hands and knees, and directing about forty others to surround the hut'.[90] Similarly, when a hut on the South Esk River was attacked the same year, the warriors were 'under the control of a chief, who by words and gestures guided their movements'.[91] The best remembered of these chiefs included Tongerlongerter (see Figure 5B), Montpelliatta, Umarrah, Kickertopoller and Mannalargenna (see Figure 5C). Under such men, the Tasmanians adapted and honed their guerrilla tactics to meet the changing exigencies of the war.

By the end of the 1820s, fewer than a dozen tribes remained on the eastern front, and these were coming under increasing pressure from armed parties. Once a district was attacked, it was not unknown for ten pursuit parties to be raised. In response, a number of tribes found it prudent to divide their forces, attack at different points simultaneously, regroup and then disperse before a pursuit could be coordinated. On 13 March 1829, for instance, a tribe launched no less than five attacks on properties just outside Launceston. Collecting accounts that day from two people directly involved, George Hobler recorded with exasperation that there were '4 murdered [a] child missing – and ten speared within about three hours'.[92] He also noticed that the war parties were not encumbered by the booty plundered from the other properties, which further suggests a divide and attack strategy.

Bothwell's police magistrate observed in August 1830 that 'the blacks divide themselves into small parties and attack different places at once widely apart, and then meet again, at some given place'.[93] The strategy of this particular tribe was explained by 'Jack the Black native attached to Allison's party', who confirmed that they 'now divided into ten or a dozen small mobs, the better to effect their purposes'.[94] In all known cases, these divide and attack missions were conducted from a central meeting point. According to an east coast settler, 'the main body, women and children, are left some distance, from three to six miles [5–10 km], in the Hills, while the detachments, as it were, go out in various directions hunting and doing mischief'.[95]

Tasmanians preferred attacks on dwellings because these were both more controllable and more lucrative, but they also attacked many travellers. Carts, which were often laden with food, were attacked on at least two dozen occasions.[96] Attacks on mounted men, though infrequent, demonstrated the Tasmanians' growing boldness.[97] On 29 July 1828, Hobler noted in his diary that 'their knowledge of firearms, horses &c makes them now very formidable – a few years ago they fled from a horse, now they waylay horsemen and spear them'.[98] Earlier that year,

William Walker 'was attacked (although on horseback) by the blacks at Quoin Mount, about four miles [6 km] from Capt Wood's, and together with the horse, most barbarously murdered'.[99] The testimony of the man's master, John Franks, was recorded in the *Colonial Advocate*: 'they displayed a degree of discipline which was admirable, and according to Mr. Franks, "*manoeuvred in the most beautiful style*", in order to surround him; but he providentially escaped by the speed of his horse, although the animal was dreadfully wounded'.[100] Nevertheless, in open country mounted men were extremely dangerous, and the Tasmanians soon developed a cautious respect for them.

Most Aboriginal attacks involved assaults on persons or attempts to plunder food and blankets, but as noted in Chapter 2, sabotage was also in their repertoire. They attacked domestic animals at least 42 times during the war.[101] Oxen and horses were only occasionally targeted, as they tended to be closely supervised.[102] Most attacks were on sheep and cattle, which roamed from pasture to pasture under the often inattentive care of convict stockmen.[103] Over the course of the war, Tasmanians speared thousands of sheep and cattle. It was not uncommon for them to destroy over 100 sheep at a time.[104] Remarkably though, few Aborigines were ever observed in the act of spearing stock, and none were reported killed, which suggests some of them kept a close eye on the stockmen while their comrades undertook the slaughter.

Arson was the other main form of sabotage practised by Tasmanians. They used this tactic on at least 41 occasions during the war.[105] When their intent was intimidation or sabotage, Tasmanians simply set alight huts, barns or crops when the whites were absent, or after they had been killed.[106] Other times they employed arson to disperse besieged inhabitants. In these cases they either placed firebrands around the base of the dwelling, or hurled them onto its roof. William Clark of Bothwell described an instance in which an Aborigine 'leaped a four rail fence, set fire to the building, and was off again with incredible speed, one of his comrades standing on the opposite side of the house to direct his movements by signal'.[107] Only around five per cent of their attacks involved arson, which is probably reflective of how risky it was. Campfire ambushes had revealed time and again the penalty for giving away one's position with fire.

The Tasmanians' resistance was remarkably protracted and effective, in the face of tremendous odds. In hindsight though, they inflicted much less harm on the invaders than they might have. By never attacking at night or in the rain, they significantly constrained their military opportunities. More importantly, however, they never used sabotage systematically. A genuinely systematic attempt to kill settlers' stock and burn their homes and crops would have been disastrous for the colony. So why did Tasmanians not do just that? They no doubt understood that the strangers valued their dwellings, their possessions, and the animals they constantly followed around, but the importance of these things to sustaining the invasion seems largely to have eluded them. Had they fully appreciated and exploited these vulnerabilities, they would have gained a powerful advantage over their adversaries.

Internecine violence and cooperation

The prevalence of internecine violence in Tasmanian society is difficult to gauge. For all its significance, pre-contact warfare was obviously not large-scale enough to jeopardise the island's population. Beyond this we can know little, though it is possible that colonisation amplified existing tensions. Certainly these ancient feuds did not cease with the arrival of the white man. Gilbert Robertson discovered from conversations with Kickertopoller, Umarrah and others, that the Mairremmener 'are hostile to the northern tribes' and that 'many have been killed by the Port Dalrymple Natives'.[108] This probably reflected a long-standing rivalry; as did the conflict described by George Town's police magistrate, who was informed in 1830 that 'several tribes of eastern natives assemble together every year in summer, and move off west to collect red ochre to dress their hair; which they find at a waterfall in the western mountains; and in the fights which occur at these times with the western natives many on both sides are killed'.[109]

The best documented internecine conflict from the war period occurred in 1830. On 19 October that year, ten men and two women from the greater north-east sought sanctuary at John Batman's property at the base of Ben Lomond.[110] The same day, Batman's neighbour wrote to the Governor stating that the chief, Mannalargenna, 'seems very much incensed against the Oyster Bay tribe headed by Mimoune … who he calls a bloody rogue'.[111] At the same time, a letter appeared in the *Tasmanian* from someone present at Batman's. It appeared these 12 were the only survivors of their people, the rest had apparently been 'killed off by the Oyster Bay Tribe … They have many spear wounds all over them, which they received in their battles with Numarrow, and two of them have lost an eye each.'[112] One of their adversaries, a Mairremmener man named Ronekeenarener, had been captured the same month, and confirmed that his tribe had 'fought the Stony Creek tribe and killed a great number'.[113]

This may not have been the only internecine battle that took place in 1830. On 1 November, the five men and two women who surrendered to Robinson at Ansons River told him 'they had recently returned from fighting with the natives of the lakes and that they had killed three of that people and the rest fled'.[114] These were the last open hostilities between eastern tribes, though tensions remained long after they surrendered.

The reasons for the persistence of internecine conflicts are not entirely clear, but colonisation seems to have contributed in at least two ways. First, much of the recorded internecine conflict was over women, at a time when sealers and frontiersmen were commonly abducting and killing them.[115] Violent competition for women was a traditional feature of Tasmanian society, and wartime shortages no doubt exacerbated this pattern. The second possibility was, as Melville put it, that conflict erupted when Aborigines were 'forced to trespass on each other's hunting grounds, being driven from their own by the white population'.[116] When traditional enemies were pushed together there is every reason to expect that pre-existing animosities and wartime stresses militated against friendly accommodation.

Despite these problems, the desire to resist a common enemy appears to have promoted some cooperation between tribes. In November 1828, five captive Aborigines told Gilbert Robertson, the roving party leader, that they had recently attended a gathering of four east coast tribes at the Eastern Marshes. This congress, they said, had two objectives:

> First – to capture wives for the Oyster Bay and Stony Creek tribes who had lost nearly all their women and – secondly – to repel an invasion by the Port Dalrymple … [who trespassed on] the hunting ground of the swan-port tribe … [however] for some cause they have met without committing any act of Hostility and the four tribes I think have made some sort of treaty by which the Swan Port tribe have given all the others [permission] to hunt on their grounds – From whence each tribe sends small parties to rob and hinder the inhabitants of the remote huts – I am informed that they are now on their way to Fight the Big River tribe for the purpose of compelling them to give up their hunting ground for the common good and make common cause in carrying on their warfare against the white inhabitants.[117]

It was probably no coincidence that 12 months later Robertson learnt 'from the natives who had been captured by Mr Bateman [sic] that a general meeting of the tribes was to be held near the Big Lake'.[118]

George Hobler, in his diary for 6 October 1830, also suggested that some tribes were uniting to resist the white invasion: 'one fellow taken a short time ago who could speak a little English said that the different tribes had leagued together sinking their own disputes and determined to exterminate the whites if possible'.[119] Still, tribal differences were often deeply entrenched, and efforts to settle them were not always successful. Wowaree, a northern tribesman, told Robinson that:

> the Port Sorell natives frequently travelled to Circular Head, Cape Grim and Mount Cameron [West] and fought with the wild natives. Said their object in going to their country was not for hostile purposes but to make friends with them and to induce them to visit their country and to aid them in robbing and committing aggressions upon the whites, but the wild or West Point natives would not make friends but fought with them. Several were killed on those occasions on both sides.[120]

Clearly some tribes went to considerable lengths to negotiate alliances in the final years of the war, but they were being destroyed too quickly for an effective pan-Aboriginal resistance to take root. By the end of the 1820s, the boundary between contrived tactical alliances and desperate coalescing was vague. All the tribes that surrendered to Robinson in the 1830s were conglomerates – tribes that had disintegrated and re-formed with other remnants – but by that stage they were far more focused on survival than on resistance.

CHAPTER FOUR

EXPERIENCE

White

On the afternoon of 10 June 1830, Mr Daniels, Captain Wood's overseer at Regent Plain, returned from having lunch with his wife and newborn twins to begin ploughing a nearby field. Shortly after, however, Daniels and his convict co-worker:

> observed the door of the hut was open, this circumstance excited suspicion as it was Mary Daniels' custom to keep the door of the hut bolted on the inside when the men were absent. They accordingly left their work and the husband first reached the hut. A few yards from the door he found his wife and two children lying covered with blood, he called the other man to his assistance and they removed the bodies into the hut, Mary Daniels and one of the infants died in about half an hour, the other infant in about six or seven hours after.[1]

This incident was followed 11 days later by the spearing of Mrs Langford at Green Ponds, in which the blacks also killed her 14-year-old daughter and wounded her son, John (whom they killed the following year).[2] To a colony now awash with reports of violence, these were just two more 'outrages', but to Mr Daniels, Mr Langford, and the hundreds like them who lost friends and family in the war, the effect was far more profound.

The Black War triggered a host of powerful emotions. In the eastern interior, at least 219 colonists were speared, bludgeoned or burnt to death by blacks.[3] Most of these people left behind friends or family, whose grief could be powerful and debilitating. Nevertheless, the prevalence of grief should not be overstated. At least three out of four victims were male convicts or ex-convicts, most of whom had no spouse or family in the colony. Some of these men certainly developed strong, even romantic bonds with their fellow servants, though their deaths often appeared to evoke more anger than sadness.

Native violence enraged many colonists to boiling point. After presiding over yet another coronial inquest into the death of an assigned servant, a police magistrate 'declared that if his family was attacked, he would kill as many as he could of the murdering incendiaries, and affix their bodies to trees, as he would those of any other ravenous animal'.[4] John West noted that attacks on frontiersmen frequently 'provoke[d] their fellow servants to rage' and seeded a craving for revenge.[5] What is more, the objects of colonists' anger were often beyond their grasp, which left them feeling intensely frustrated. It is palpably evident from settlers' writings that they also felt frustrated at the government's failure to protect them, and at their inability to protect themselves.

However, insofar as the written record is our guide, fear dominated all other emotions. There were, of course, reasons why expressions of fear, and the actions of fearful people predominated in official correspondence and newspaper commentary. Colonists publicising news of an attack in their neighbourhood sought to draw government assistance by emphasising locals' fearfulness. Yet, private correspondents and diarists also emphasised fear, and they had little reason to exaggerate this emotion. What is more, emotions like grief and rage only affected some people, some of the time, whereas virtually everybody on the frontier was afraid, all the time. Even if other emotions were underemphasised in the historical sources, there is no reason to doubt the ubiquity of fear.

A sinister new threat

The Black War was not the first time colonists had faced a domestic enemy. From the earliest years of settlement, bushrangers had plagued the interior, sacking properties, and committing occasional murders.[6] But by 1826, Arthur had sent the vast majority to the gallows, and most colonists believed the interior was now safe for settlement. They could not have been more wrong. The *Colonial Times* observed in 1827 that, 'no sooner had bushranging ... become extinct, than another no less terrible evil has broken out'.[7] With shocking speed, the natives appeared to transform from 'the most harmless race of people in the world' into the colonists' 'most bloodthirsty enemies'.[8]

In 1827, William Bryan penned a letter to his local police magistrate only hours after escaping his burning house, exclaiming: 'I have been in houses attacked by white savages [bushrangers] and I put it most solemnly to you, that the system and fury of these Black Monsters exceeded anything I have yet encountered, the house on fire and these furies dancing outside made me imagine I had been suddenly transported to the infernal regions'.[9] The same year, Roderic O'Connor sympathised with the Governor: 'It is deplorable and must be most distressing to His Excellency's mind after having completely given a death-blow to Bushranging that a set of wild Savages should immediately spring up, and commit such numerous massacres, as to alarm all castes of Persons, much more than all the Bushrangers that have ever appeared.'[10] The blacks, with their deadly guerrilla tactics and uncanny elusiveness, were not only more dangerous than the bushrangers, they were also much more frightening.

Economic fear

Financial loss from theft and destruction of property was a constant threat to settlers. In March 1828, for instance, after John Allen had his house and haystacks burnt by the natives, he was forced to ask the government for succour in rebuilding, and 'slept on a sheet of bark for several months'.[11] Likewise, in February 1830, natives burnt 'Mr HOWELL'S premises and property ... The family are now living under a break-wind, without a single article except what they then wore.'[12]

There were no insurance companies in early Tasmania.[13] Most settlers invested all they had in their colonial ventures, and risked ruin if their crops and buildings were burnt, or their stock destroyed. James Hobbs was completely burnt out by blacks in May 1830, after which he lamented, 'it is nothing less than having to commence again as a new settler'.[14] Surviving meant establishing oneself rapidly with minimum setbacks, and from an economic perspective, the Black War produced a maelstrom of setbacks.

Widespread stock killing by natives was a costly burden on many settlers. In a letter to the *Colonial Advocate* in 1828, one settler claimed that the frequency with which sheep and cattle were speared rendered it 'useless to attempt to keep stock. It is better to drive the stock into town, and sell it for any price, than allow it to be made the prey of this accursed race!'[15] In the case of sheep, the acceleration of spearings coincided with a five-fold increase of the colony's wool exports between 1827 and 1830.[16] Such attacks could be especially costly to settlers engaged in the painstaking development of bloodlines. In fact, Arthur later estimated the native threat had doubled the cost of raising sheep.[17] On at least a dozen occasions, horses and oxen were also speared, sometimes several at a time.[18] The high cost and utility of these animals meant their loss constituted an enormous setback to settlers. Neverthless, the heavy toll that natives took on settlers' stock was dwarfed only by the toll settlers feared they *might* take. All were aware of their vulnerability to stock killing, and it weighed heavy on their minds.[19]

The greatest threat to settlers' economic security, however, was arson. Between 1824 and 1831, blacks incinerated no less than three dozen huts and houses.[20] But, again, colonists were terrified of the devastation they *might* inflict, not just on buildings, but on crops. The livelihood of most settlers was conditional on secure grain and fodder harvests to ensure cash flow, animal feed and subsistence. Cereal crops were the colony's primary source of food, but their flammability in storage also made them its Achilles heel, and colonists were acutely aware of this.[21] In February 1830, for instance, Bothwell's police magistrate informed the Governor that '[s]erious apprehensions are entertained by the settlers that the natives having resorted to destruction by fire will also burn up their crops'.[22] Although no tribe ever fully exploited the potential of arson, the fear that they would was entirely reasonable.

A small number of settlers went so far as to contemplate abandoning the colony. James Ross, editor of the *Hobart Town Courier*, declared in November 1830 that, '[i]f the outrages of the Blacks be not put down … we must abandon the island, we must look for safety only to our ships that will carry us to another shore'.[23] In a letter to his sister the previous month, chief civil auditor George Boyes observed 'that unless means are devised to making them prisoner … or, otherwise exterminating the race, the country must be abandoned'.[24] More judicious commentators dismissed these concerns as hyperbolic, yet they were not wholly absurd.[25] Boyes especially, understood all too well the colony's reliance on locally grown crops, and thus its vulnerability to an organised campaign of arson. Had the natives burnt crops and dwellings more systematically, the consequences would have been catastrophic, and the short-term viability of the colony might have been seriously compromised.

Stock killing and arson were also troubling for their resemblance to 'hamstringing', rick burning and other forms of vandalism employed by disaffected rural labourers in Britain and Ireland.[26] They inspired dread among landowners, not just because of the losses they incurred, but also because of the frustration and uneasiness that stemmed from being unable to prevent the attacks or identify and apprehend the assailants. The natives' use of sabotage was no less political than its British and Irish equivalent, and the parallels were unmistakable. Thus, such tactics hit an already frayed nerve among settlers.

Concern for others

Another type of fear felt by colonists resulted from the thought of what the blacks might do to their loved ones. This was not mere paranoia. During the war, almost everyone on the frontier lost someone they knew. On 9 October 1828, for instance, having unsuccessfully attempted to prevent an attack on a neighbour's hut, Patrick Gough was returning home when he:

> was met by his eldest daughter Mary, covered with blood, calling upon her father to hasten home as the natives had killed her mother and sisters. Gough saw his wife about half a mile [800 m] from the hut sitting on the ground, resting her back against the fence, with her infant child in her lap. The poor woman said – 'My dear Gough, it is all over with me, I am killed by the natives.' … [He found] his infant daughter Alicia lying breathless in front of the door with her arms extended … On entering the hut he found Anne Geary lying stretched on the floor, and on being removed to a sofa she vomited quantities of blood; she died about two hours after, and about midnight Alicia Gough, not more than four years of age, breathed her last. Gough's youngest child, an infant 13 months old, had received several contusions, but of a slighter character.[27]

Mrs Gough, who died in agony 19 days later, told of how 'she fell on her knees to the natives and said, "Spare the lives of my *picanninies*"; and that one of the black natives replied in good English, "No you white bitch we'll kill you all'".[28] This incident was widely reported in the press, and sent a wave of outrage and fear through the colony. Patrick Gough tried to move on with his two surviving daughters, but 11 months later, the blacks burnt his house to the ground.[29] Not everyone suffered as greatly, but most experienced some kind of loss.

Stories like this understandably generated great apprehension on the frontier, particularly among families. With the knowledge of so many horrific attacks seared into their minds, men leaving their families for work were constantly anxious about their safety. Natives in Tasmania never once raped a white woman, but this did little to calm fears.[30] Women and children undoubtedly harboured similar fears for the safety of their fathers, husbands, brothers and sons. Constant worry tormented anyone separated from their loved ones during the Black War.

Personal fear

Fear for one's own life tended to trump all other concerns. Such fear could range from gentle uneasiness to paralysing terror. What sort of fear they felt, and how strongly they felt it, hinged on a number of factors. Those who had participated in ambushing blacks, for instance, had added reason to fear their attacks. Another factor was the time of day. It was well known that the blacks never attacked at night, so colonists could sleep soundly no matter how dangerous their situation. This dependable nocturnal respite – possibly unique in the history of modern guerrilla warfare – was a welcome relief, but as soon as the sun rose again, colonists returned to looking over their shoulders. Other important factors included the topography and foliage a person was surrounded by, and the amount of protection they could rely on in the form of dogs, firearms, companions, police or soldiers. The type of work a person did also impacted on their vulnerability and, thus, their level of fear. Those most at risk were rural labourers, who were required to perform strenuous, attention-demanding tasks in exposed locations. These men comprised 87 per cent of all white casualties.[31]

Probably the most important determinant of fear was a person's past experiences, especially their own personal encounters with blacks, and the history of attacks in their area. Colonists realised that some districts attracted more violence than others. They also noticed that, because of factors such as weather, day length and migratory patterns, the natives attacked more at certain times of the year than at others. They made, for instance, comparatively few attacks in early summer and early winter, but in the spring and early autumn, people in many districts had to be on high alert.[32]

Some of the attacks that colonists lived through were truly terrifying. At Great Swanport, the body of James Stanton was found with 'the head beaten in with waddies: the nails of the fingers were separated from the quicks apparently with a knife, the fleshy part of the outside of the hands was cut off, the eyebrows were cut off and the bones of the eyebrows beaten down to the eyes. The whole of the teeth were beaten out of the head and the body otherwise much mangled.' This was awful enough for those who discovered his corpse, but Stanton's master, Lieutenant Hawkins, had to watch the horror unfold from his besieged hut before the blacks turned their attention to him, 'calling upon the dead man by name and laughing about it'.[33]

In 1830, at the farm now abandoned by Patrick Gough, Thomas Peters and his family experienced a different, but no less terrifying, kind of attack. While he was:

> absent a short distance from his house, three black natives … speared two of Mr Peters' daughters, both young women about 14 and 16 years old – the youngest was speared [fatally] in the chest, the other through the palm of the hand. Mr Peters hearing one of his daughters crying most bitterly, hastened with a loaded musket in his hand to the house, where he found the youngest lying at the sill of the door, bleeding.

During this time, Peters and his wounded daughters were shadowed by a warrior 'upwards of six feet [183 cm] high, much resembling a Chief, having his head, face, and hair ornamented with red ochre'. Peters kept his musket near, but was careful to preserve his one and only shot, 'fearing that he might miss fire'.[34] Eventually, the blacks left, unable to finish off their victims, but the ordeal frightened Peters and his surviving daughter off their farm.[35]

The following year, a soldier described an unexpected visit by a stockman who had just escaped an attack at Regents Plains: 'It was a quarter of an hour before he could speak from fright, and the other men abused him and asked if he was mad. At length he spoke and stammered out that there was 50 natives and that he supposed they had killed the other man.'[36] West may have captured the horror of these experiences better than anyone, when he wrote:

> Death, by the hands of a savage, is indeed invested with the darkest terrors: it was rarely instantaneous – it was often the effect of protracted torment, and of repeated blows: often, after a long pursuit, in which hope might occasionally gleam for a moment, to render death to the exhausted fugitive more distinct and terrible … the dying man would be roused by infernal shouts, and there would swim before him brandished clubs, and horrid visages distorted with demoniac rage. Such were the recollections of some who recovered; and such, we may be assured, were the emotions of many that died.[37]

Hundreds of people survived clashes with the natives, many of whom were scarred for life, both physically and psychologically. In 1830, for instance, after surviving a quadruple spearing at her Carlton River property, Judith Pearce 'became, from fright and terror, insane and sent to the Lunatic asylum at New Norfolk'.[38] It was as much a war of the mind as it was of spears and muskets.

In some regions the situation became so alarming that whole families were forced to temporarily or even permanently abandon their farms.

Many settlers insisted they would be forced off their grants if protection was not immediately forthcoming. In 1830, Lieutenant Torlesse reported that 'we all now feel too fearful of them [the natives] being near us, that we never move without a gun'. The fear, he confessed, 'is quite paralysing', and he pleaded to 'exchange my grant at the Hollow Tree for one near Hamilton, Mrs Torlesse being in a very uneasy state of mind, our lives are daily in jeopardy'.[39] Likewise, Paul Minnitt beseeched the Governor for protection after his farm at the foot of the Western Tiers was attacked twice in 1831: 'My late neighbour Bonnolly was driven with his family from his farm and I am much afraid that the same will be my case.'[40]

Many colonists refused to remain in the path of the blacks a moment longer. Mr Kirby, for instance, 'was obliged to abandon [his] hut in consequence of the attack of the natives ... [and] said he would not live at Mr Parker's farm on any account, that the natives were always about there and that it was dangerous for the people living there to leave their hut unless accompanied by two or three other men'.[41] The Blue Hills east of Oatlands was a particularly dangerous area. In May 1830, 'Pennington and his Wife and child fled [the district] to Hobarton', barely escaping with their lives.[42] Robinson observed in 1831 that 'many people' who had once lived in the Blue Hills 'were driven away by the natives'.[43] A similar exodus occurred following several attacks in the Green Ponds district in October 1828. According to the *Hobart Town Courier*, '[t]he wives and children of the settlers around are flocking in to the more populous part of this district, and an uninhabited house is taken as a sort of temporary place of security, there being none in the bush, till some check is put to this horrible havoc in human life'.[44] But few settlers possessed either the time or the money to start over again somewhere safer, so most had no choice but to endure the threat.[45] Moreover, those who suffered the greatest danger – the convicts – had no farms to leave.

Black spectres

The island's grapevine comprised a vibrant network of formal and informal communication channels. Even colonists who had not yet encountered hostile natives knew full well what was in store for them if they did. Tales of attacks were circulated via written correspondence and the press, but more commonly by word of mouth. The stories could be unnerving in the extreme. In December 1826, near Pipers Lagoon, a stock-keeper 'was literally beat to a mummy! His throat cut and his lower extremities cut off!! Indeed he was cut to atoms.'[46] Similarly, at Quoin Mountain, the body of an assigned servant was discovered 'most dreadfully lacerated, eight spears had entered the breast, the head was literally bashed to pieces, the flesh of the upper lip entirely knocked off, and in every respect presenting a most appalling spectacle'.[47] Printed in the newspapers for all to see, these accounts were typical of the stories people on the frontier were hearing every day, often with the violence and gore exaggerated by rumour.

The blacks also inspired great dread among travellers. The island's roads were often no more than rough and narrow tracks, rendering travel a slow and unnerving affair. John Young and Robert Graves were 'certain we were amongst the natives' when travelling through the Clyde district in 1829, 'as his [Graves'] horse would not proceed'. Their fears were confirmed that afternoon when they learnt that a woman had been speared to death nearby.[48]

At the height of the war, most carts moved with an armed escort, but this could abate the traveller's apprehension only so much.[49] Robinson observed that some travellers, 'under the excitement of fear', were prone to hallucinations, 'taking black stumps for black men'.[50] Even the sounds of the bush could inspire dread, as it did for a member of Henry Hellyer's survey team in 1826: 'Byrne went to the Dismal [Creek] for water & heard the Native coo on the other side. He came back frightened to death.' On investigation, 'Byrne's Natives turned out to be a musical tree', yet even Hellyer admitted he could not shake the feeling that 'they are watching us and are not far off'.[51]

The mere knowledge that blacks were out there could cause the traveller's hair to stand on end. In March 1830, while travelling through St Peters Pass, Mrs Prinsep and her companions became apprehensive that the 'natives, who are easily concealed in these dark woods, [would] dart out upon the unconscious traveller'.[52] Riding through the heart of tribal country, she recalled that 'the stories we had heard of the savage aborigines, came in full force upon our minds, and some of our party were fearful of meeting them in the dark hollows of the wild woods'.[53]

In contrast to the bushrangers before them, the blacks took on an aura of dread all their own. As the reports grew more horrifying, colonists evolved a new way of conceptualising the once 'pitiable savage'. By the late 1820s, the natives' sudden and brutal attacks, combined with their ability to 'vanish like spectres', had generated an image of them as magical, even demonic.[54] To colonists, the blacks were a mysterious race that seemed to lurk almost ghost-like in the wilderness. Their intimidating 'war paint' and chilling 'war-whoop' only added to the effect. As the editor of the *Launceston Advertiser* described it: 'They daily exhibit such demoniac delight in the successful accomplishment of their diabolical purposes, and develop such a skill and watchfulness in following up their purposes, that must ... fill the breasts of all the out-settlers and stock-keepers with fear and dread.'[55] The *Colonial Times* referred to them as 'Satan like', while 'the colonists', according to one observer, 'believe them sorcerers'.[56] Even Thomas Anstey felt that '[t]he disposition of the native appears to me to come closer to the cold malignity of a wicked spirit than to the frailty and passion of a man'.[57] Over the course of the war, this mystique became a common feature of colonists' racial thought. The blacks were, as one settler later called them, 'the shadows of a hideous dream'.[58]

Protection

Fear of black violence generated a number of responses among colonists. Some sought to deal with the problem proactively by hunting the enemy at night, but in the short-term this only incited more violence. There were also constant calls for increased military protection, which were progressively heeded. By 1830, almost half of the colony's military force had been deployed throughout the interior.[59] Still, none of this seemed to quell the violence, so the government fell back on its original policy of encouraging 'vigilant self-defence' by settlers.

The first thing many settlers did was to secure their houses and stock-huts. This could include laying turf on the roof to protect against fire,[60] or building fortifications around the house. In 1830, the *Launceston Advertiser* issued advice on how to build 'a high fence made of logs placed upright two or more feet [60 cm+] in the ground and eight to ten feet [240–300 cm] high' to protect premises from 'the violence, the malice, and the watchful cunning of the Aboriginal tribes'.[61] A similar precaution was employed in the Bothwell district (see Figure 7),[62] where 'buildings including a stone dwelling, cottages, barns, etc. … were enclosed within a high brick and stone wall to keep out blacks and bushrangers'.[63] Although not all settlers could afford to fortify their dwellings, most ensured they at least had firing holes built into them.[64] Fear, then, not only pervaded the atmosphere, but also left its mark on the built landscape.

These protections must have been reassuring for women who were left at home during the day. Often, women (or solitary men) would stock up on supplies and lock themselves inside until they were again in protective company.[65] Some settlers took the further measure of arming their wives and children, and training them to defend themselves.[66] But when the enemy was known to be lurking, some women begged their menfolk not to leave.[67] Labourers, on the other hand, were forced to spend their days outdoors, but as the danger from blacks increased many insisted on having guard dogs present at all times. 'My chaps refuse to go without dogs to warn them of the natives hovering round', wrote one settler, 'and my shepherds must have watch dogs chained by their huts.'[68] Another reported that, in the Shannon River valley, '[n]o person dare go any distance from his home without arms and his faithful companion the dog, the latter to give notice at the approach of those savages'.[69] When a tax was placed on dog ownership in an attempt to reduce numbers, the public outcry was intense. The primary objection was expressed in a petition by the 'Inhabitants of the Clyde', which stated that 'in so many instances our dogs have been the means of saving so many valuable lives and property' from the 'daily atrocities' of the natives.[70]

Another precaution was to work in pairs or groups. Putting extra men on a job was costly, but it was widely believed that the blacks hesitated to attack multiple opponents.[71] Bothwell's police magistrate, Michael Vicary, observed that 'in those parts most frequented by the aborigines the servants are fearful of going out simply and in some instances have positively refused to go out alone'.[72] In the north, Malcolm Smith's overseer demanded he 'send another man up as soon as you can as we dare not move out now alone'.[73] George Hobler ensured his sawyers worked in threes because 'it is a dangerous place for the native[s], and if surprised two can scarcely protect themselves'.[74] This strategy worked to an extent, but with the increasing boldness of the enemy, it could also result in more victims.

Firearms were the best security against hostile natives. From 1828, most servants flatly refused to work in exposed locations unless armed. William Clark complained that 'our servants will not go about their ordinary occupation without arms'.[75] Robinson noted of such men that they 'are very much afraid of the natives and cannot venture the shortest distance without firearms'.[76] This demand presented a unique dilemma to a colony that had just put down a severe bushranging outbreak. At best, arming convicts threatened to undermine the carefully negotiated power dynamics of the master/servant relationship, and at worst, to facilitate another wave of escapee violence. Nevertheless, the demands of convicts were so powerful and understandable, that settlers generally yielded.

Some servants flatly refused to go out, despite the threat of severe penalties. In 1824, following the killing of a co-worker and their own narrow escape, a group of shepherds from York Plains deserted their flocks for the safety of Hobart. 'Such is the fear they entertain', reported the *Hobart Town Gazette*, 'that nothing can persuade them to return to their abandoned occupation.'[77] Similarly, in 1828, a settler on the Elizabeth River lamented: 'I cannot prevail on my shepherds to leave home, and if the present state of things continues, I must give up farming.'[78] The district's magistrate confirmed that 'the stock-keepers in a great many instances refuse to attend their charge and express a determination to persist in the refusal while exposed to such sudden attacks'.[79] Strikes of this type occurred throughout the interior and, at the height of the war, threatened to cripple the colony's economy.

The threat of black violence put masters in a difficult position, because the refusal of servants to work under such conditions was at once reasonable and wholly unacceptable. It was never suggested that protesting servants were simply malingering, but some certainly exploited the situation in other ways. There is evidence that convicts occasionally tried to frame blacks for their own robberies, arson attacks, stock killings and even murders.[80] Nevertheless, the potential for scapegoating to over-inflate the record of native violence was probably cancelled out by the unrecorded or wrongly attributed attacks.[81] The vast majority of black violence appears to have been just that – black violence – and the schemers were as frightened as the next person.

A fear not forgotten

Nothing highlights the terror of the war years more than the sanity that returned once it was over. Following the surrender of the last hostile blacks in December 1831, the change in the interior was instant and dramatic. In 1833, Robinson noted in his journal:

When the hostile blacks were out and whilst I was perambulating the country in quest of them, there was not a man to be seen without a musket. No carts were to be seen with out the driver carrying a musket, sawyers and woodcutters of every description, shepherds and herdsmen, were all armed and never went abroad without those weapons. Every hut and every farmer's domicile had [more] the appearance of a fortress than the peaceful habitation of a rural settlement. Now it is vice versa. If you meet a solitary individual in the most secluded part of the forest he is without firearms. The herdsmen and stockmen follow their occupations without the least dread, the woodcutter and others retire to the forest without the least apprehension of danger. There is now no occasion for a hut keeper or companion to the shepherd: instead of three men one is sufficient. The shepherd locks the door and pursues his avocation with confidence.[82]

Although he was prone to an inflated sense of his own importance, there is no reason to doubt Robinson's observation here. It was testified to by many, including the settler Henry Stoney, who recollected that, after the surrender, 'a complete change took place in the island; the remote stock stations were again resorted to, and guns were no longer carried between the handles of the plough.'[83]

But it was the pseudonymous author of several letters to the *Colonial Times* who described the state of alarm most vividly. Writing in 1835, he recalled the gripping terror of frontier life:

when the blacks with indiscriminate and savage ferociousness committed the most daring murders and depredations, sparing neither women nor infants – when no one ventured to plough his fields, gathering in his harvest, or walking a few yards from his own door, without firearms in his hands – when mothers turned pale, and the children screamed at the least rustling noise – these I say were the horrors we experienced in the interior.[84]

Black

> It is very usual for a number of aborigines, when assembled by their fire-
> side under the open canopy of heaven, to recount the sufferings of their
> ancestors, to dilate upon their present afflictions and to consult upon the
> best means of being released from their cruel and bloodthirsty foes.

George Augustus Robinson, journal 23 November 1829

By the time Robinson wrote these words, the remaining Tasmanians
must have found it difficult to see from where their release would come.
As the war drew on and their numbers plummeted, the hopelessness
of their situation must have become increasingly apparent. Mere existence had become a trial, in which hunger, cold and maddening skin
infections ground away relentlessly at their will to resist. Yet they had
no choice but to go on. They still had to eat and sleep. They still had to
launch attacks and defend against ambushes. They still had to deal with
the dead and wounded, despite moving rapidly through the territories of
both black and white enemies. And they still had to cope with the ever-
present trauma of loss and fear.

Experience of white violence

Aborigines possessed extraordinary 'keen-sightedness', and were rarely
caught off guard in daylight hours, but when the sun went down, the
tables of vulnerability turned against them. Hundreds were ultimately
shot because of the need to light campfires. Smoke was the flag that
repeatedly gave away their location, and yet, fires were indispensable for
three reasons. First, there was the need to cook the meat and damper
upon which they largely subsisted. The second reason was warmth.
Traditionally, Tasmanians insulated their bodies with a mixture of animal
fat and ochre, but as movement became increasingly dangerous, access

to both ingredients was restricted.[85] Even when fat and ochre could be procured, it was generally insufficient to guard against night temperatures, which regularly plummeted below zero. Blankets offered some protection from the cold, but unlike fat, they were useless once wet, and keeping anything dry in the island's climate was difficult unless it could be dried over a fire.

The third reason Aborigines needed campfires was their fear of the dark – or more specifically, the evil spirit they believed lurked in the dark.[86] Woorrady told Robinson that this fiend was 'like a black man only very big and ugly, and that he travels like the wind, that he comes and watches the natives all night and before daylight comes he goes away like swift wind'.[87] A number of contemporaries reported that Tasmanians held this belief, and were consequently afraid to move at night.[88] The strength of this aversion is further evidenced by their unwillingness to launch night attacks, despite the tactical advantages this might have gained them.

Despite their fear of nocturnal spectres, Tasmanians did move at night under some circumstances. An Oyster Bay settler claimed 'the natives will not from motives of superstition move after night, but … I have known several circumstances of their travelling … in the dark if closely pursued'.[89] Jorgen Jorgenson also concluded they 'were always fearful of travelling in the night, they never did so, until they were pressed hard by the parties in pursuit of them'.[90] In such cases, the fleeing tribes must have been doubly terrified.

If the Tasmanians' fear of spirits in the night was mere superstition, their fear of muskets in the night was not. A campfire's illumination made it difficult to see what was beyond, so for signs of danger they listened. Still, it could be hard to differentiate between the scurrying of nocturnal life and the cracking of a twig under a white man's foot. Robinson's journals provide several eyewitness accounts of these ambushes from Aborigines themselves. Survivors of one ambush told Robinson that, after their tribe killed three people along the Shannon River in 1830:

a party of white people followed them and came upon them at night and fired in among them and killed one woman and one man. The woman was shot dead, but the man walked a short distance to a thicket and dropped down dead. This woman [one of his companions] informed me [she] belonged to them and was with them at the fire when they were attacked. Said the white people had watched and waited till they made their fire and then came and fired in among them.[91]

An even more graphic account was given by the one-armed chief, Tongerlongerter (see Figure 5B), who told Robinson:

he was with his tribe in the neighbourhood of the Den Hill and that there was men cutting wood. The men were frightened and run [sic] away. At night they came back with plenty of white men (it was moonlight), and they looked and saw our fires. Then they shot at us, shot my arm, killed two men and three women. The women they beat on the head and killed them; they then burnt them in the fire.[92]

Tongerlongerter then recounted another instance, in which the white men 'came near to them at night; then stopped till morning and that when it was little day light came and fired at them. Took away his wife, also DROMETEHENNER. This was near the Lakes. On this occasion they shot DROMETEHENNER's husband through the head.'[93]

Experience taught the Tasmanians never to expect quarter from an ambush party, so they invariably fled at the first sign of an attack. Choosing where to run must have been terrifying, when in any direction the darkness might conceal a musket. A number of immediate challenges presented themselves to those who managed to escape. They first had to find one another and get to a safe location. In many cases they also had to care for wounded kinsfolk who were forced to remain silent in the face of horrific wounds. What is more, their fires and blankets had been abandoned, so hypothermia could pose a serious threat. The following day, an urgent need for fire, blankets, food and spears pressed survivors into action, despite having witnessed their loved ones killed or abducted only hours before.

For those who lived through these attacks the psychological impact could be immense. This was especially true of children, many of whom, according to Robinson, 'witnessed the massacre of their parents and their relations carried away into captivity'.[94] In a letter to the editor of the *Tasmanian*, 'AN EYE WITNESS' stated that, when John Danvers' party, accompanied by the adolescent guide Mungo:

> came to the spot where Mr Bateman [John Batman] had on a former occasion been compelled to kill some of the blacks ... Mungo well recollected the spot and the deed; he was instantly seized with a shivering, and from that moment refused all food: he was soon reduced to extremity and the party had to carry him from day to day, until ... he arrived on Thursday last bearing the near resemblance of a skeleton.[95]

There was probably no eastern Tasmanian who had not suffered a campfire ambush by 1830, so sooner or later the emotions that overwhelmed Mungo were felt by all.

Defensive tactics

Daring attacks are those posterity remembers, but no less important to any fighting force are their defensive tactics. We have already seen that campfire smoke frequently gave away the Tasmanians' position to their enemies. One option was to have no fire at all, eat uncooked food, and use blankets and dogs to keep warm, but this was generally not practicable.[96] As a compromise, Robinson observed that Tasmanians managed 'with small fires, the smoke of which is scarcely perceptible. They will collect the small dry sticks for this purpose.'[97]

They also learnt to make their camps in discreet places. One settler claimed that '[t]heir rendezvous are always very difficult to access, – and they generally choose a spot for their nocturnal resting place, which will command a view of the approaches'.[98] In choosing their campsites, Tasmanians were aiming to obstruct not just their assailants' visibility, but also their access. In 1830, the *Launceston Advertiser* reported on a pursuit in which the party located 'their fires at night but in such a scrubby place that they could not approach them undiscovered; in fact one of the men says they could not find the way to their fires through it'.[99]

The use of decoy fires was another effective strategy. In November 1828, a roving party that ambushed a tribe near the Eastern Marshes was 'quite dismayed' to find a decoy fire burning 90 metres from the main encampment.[100] A similar decoy was described in 1830, when an ambush party discovered a tribe that had secreted itself 'in a deep scrubby ravine' and kindled a fire well away from the main body.[101] In this case, the tribe also used sentinels, a common precaution when travelling through enemy territory. In fact, Gilbert Robertson claimed Tasmanians 'always keep regular sentries'.[102] One party, as they approached a sleeping tribe, was certain of success until 'two blacks watching on the hills on both sides of the gulley [*sic*], gave the alarm, and the tribe fled'.[103] Spiritual means of protection were also available. Robinson's envoys told him 'that the devil comes and tells them when the white men are coming'.[104] Tasmanians no doubt found this belief consoling, but they also possessed a more practical warning system.

Tribes throughout the interior were generally accompanied by dogs, and these animals saved many lives by barking at intruders, and buying tribes the precious seconds needed to escape.[105] The consequences of ignoring such warnings could be fatal. Robinson was told that, before one ambush, the 'dogs barked but the natives paid no attention, when immediately after they were fired upon'.[106]

Tasmanians were far less vulnerable during the day. In fact, they appear to have been rather self-assured in daylight hours. It was their renowned ability to 'baffle all pursuit' that gave them this confidence.

Robinson found they 'ridiculed the idea of white men following them in the woods and many amusing stories have since been told connected therewith'.[107] He recognised that they had 'the greatest confidence in themselves, and when pursued will, contrary to the general notion of the whites, secrete themselves and allow their pursuers to pass them, and then go in a contrary direction; and as a proof of their confidence they walk deliberately away with heavy loads of flour in the face of their crime'.[108]

Another tactic was to throw pursuers off their track with fire. In January 1830, for instance, John Batman and his party were pursuing a tribe that 'set fire to the bush before us every 2, or 3 miles [3–5 km] … to lead me in the wrong direction'.[109] Indeed, Tasmanians used a range of strategies in eluding pursuers, and their success rate, even when hemmed in, astonished their enemy.[110]

Movement

By 1829, the interior was crawling with armed parties. In the vicinity of Bothwell, for instance, there were 'no less than twelve parties scouring the country'.[111] Skilled as the Tasmanians were at evading these parties, it was taxing to be harried so incessantly. In search of respite, many tribes began resorting, even in winter, to the remoter and less hospitable regions of the island. In 1830, for instance, Henry Hellyer discovered a tribe occupying the snowy Vale of Belvoir in winter.[112] Similarly, in 1831, Robinson's envoys told him the remaining hostile Aborigines had taken refuge 'in the obscure recess of the forest or fastness of the hills between the rugged tiers'.[113]

The Central Plateau, despite being exposed and resource-scarce, became an important sanctuary during the latter part of the war. Its extreme climate posed enormous challenges to anyone attempting to survive there in the winter months, but the threat of armed parties was great enough for some tribes to justify the risk and torment. For example, Bothwell's police magistrate observed in 1830 that a small tribe remained in the highlands of the upper Shannon, 'notwithstanding the severe winter'.[114] Nevertheless, sustained refuge in such places was impossible. Dangerous as it was, Aborigines were forced to spend much of their time in and around the sprawling invaded districts.

The best country for hunting was also the best for farming, and over the course of the 1820s, the whites came to occupy almost all of it. Roaming flocks and herds meant that stockmen ventured far and wide, and with constantly prowling roving parties, places of safety in the low country all but disappeared. Traditionally, Tasmanian tribes had followed regular migratory routes via rich hunting grounds, plentiful stretches of coastline and culturally significant sites. In fact, one east coast settler asserted that the timing and direction of these migrations was 'so well known as to enable anyone to describe it'.[115]

Naturally, colonists sought to exploit this knowledge, but the Tasmanians realised this and adapted. During the winter, for instance, they had traditionally moved less and encamped longer, but the white man soon learnt this was 'the best season for pursuing them'.[116] Consequently, many tribes began to stay mobile year round, often forging new and inconspicuous tracks parallel to their traditional routes.[117] One settler noted that 'the Blacks avoid, as much as they possibly can, taking the Hills, – always keeping about the gullies, and rivers, where there is much scrub and stunted undergrowth'.[118] Robinson's envoys added that they 'never stopped on the plains where the white people stayed'.[119] This meant the most congenial camping spots had to be abandoned for less conspicuous ones, and these tended to be deficient in the usual sources of food, water and comfort. It seems, however, that some tribes found ways around this. For example, when a pursuit party surprised a tribe near Cockatoo Valley in 1828, they 'found several glass bottles full of water with strings tied round their necks'.[120] Other tribes learnt to store their plundered flour in discreet underground caches.[121] Indeed, Tasmanians readily altered or abandoned their age-old customs in response to white invasion, often in quite creative ways.

In addition to changing their migratory patterns, the Tasmanians were also forced to move faster. One settler recalled that 'the rapid movements of the blacks was remarkable, 40 or 50 miles [64–80 km] a day must have been travelled by them at the height of the war'.[122] Moving at such speeds gave them an extraordinary advantage, but this came at a cost. John West claimed that 'individuals of the tribes were often left behind. It was the custom to fix small pieces of stick at short distances, to assist the stragglers in rejoining their main body.'[123] Other tribes notched trees for the same purpose, but often the sick, elderly and wounded could not keep up.[124]

Men and women with gunshot wounds or amputations endured unimaginable suffering in order to keep pace. The bodies of those few who survived the war were covered in scars. Robinson observed among the Mairremmener people who surrendered to him in 1831, that 'there was scarcely one among them – man, woman, or child, but had been wounded by the whites'.[125] Years later, on Flinders Island, he again remarked in his journal on the prevalence of gunshot wounds, going so far as to say that 'there is not an aborigine on the settlement nor an aborigine that has been at the settlement but what bears marks of violence perpetrated upon them by the depraved whites. Some have musket balls now lodged in them such as Adolphus … Some of the natives have slugs in their bodies and others contusions, all inflicted by the whites.'[126] Although some of these wounds were no doubt received in internecine combat, the scar left by a 19 millimetre slug is difficult to mistake. These projectiles inflicted terrible wounds, shattering bones, rupturing vital organs and causing massive internal haemorrhaging. Seriously wounded victims had to be left behind; any other course would place the whole tribe in jeopardy.

The same difficulty presented itself with the sick and elderly. They too struggled to maintain the pace of wartime movement, and were sometimes abandoned out of necessity.[127] From the absence of old, ill or recently wounded people among the tribes encountered late in the war, it would appear that this expedient was not uncommon. Sources also suggest that infanticide was resorted to.[128] Before 1824, there is some evidence of tribes committing infanticide in extreme circumstances,[129] so it is no surprise that reports of the practice increased during the most desperate years of the war. Treasury clerk Henry Emmett later wrote:

> the settlers noticed the marked decrease of children: this arose from the policy of the tribes, who finding themselves hard pressed, and who feared the betrayal of their haunts from the cry of their little ones, resolved upon themselves the destruction of their children. Mothers were known to murder their own babes, rather than have them fall into the hands of their implacable enemies.[130]

West was probably right when he asserted that '[i]nfanticide was not common; although, in the latter days, when harassed by daily conflict, the practice, was not unknown'.[131] Although this may have been seen as a form of euthanasia, taking the life of a loved one must have been a wrenching ordeal.

Wartime relationships and emotions

The Tasmanians were highly emotional people. After living with them for seven years, Robinson reflected in his journal: 'Never shall I forget the unsophisticated, the sincere and warm affection of those interesting people.'[132] Rarely were these emotions more evident than when friends and family, torn apart by war, were reunited. In September 1829, eleven captives were escorted to the Richmond jail where three of their relatives had for some time been imprisoned. A local correspondent observed that:

> immediately on their coming in sight of the newly arrived party, the cry of welcome was evinced, and on coming near each other the feeling portrayed on either side would have done honour to the most civilised – the

two women long confined clasped to their arms children and grandchildren each shedding floods of tears of joy. The mutual happiness displayed in the countenances of these poor savage people beggars all description, the mothers overwhelmed in transport in having found their children, and the children in having recovered a parent.[133]

The angst of being separated from loved ones weighed heavily on the minds of Tasmanians. Robinson noted in 1831 that when one of his female envoys 'saw the tracks of her brother she wept much. I asked what she did that for, when WOORRADY said because she MOUNER. CADDY.NOTE.TE, loved him. They have strong natural affections, especially for those who are related to them.'[134]

The feelings of loss and powerlessness were even more profound when loved ones fell into the hands of the enemy. A Mairremmener woman stated that when she was captured and jailed with four others at Launceston, their kinfolk made smoke signals in the surrounding hills to reassure them.[135] Indeed, the desire to be reunited with those who had been imprisoned or exiled probably influenced the decision of some tribes to surrender.

A particularly warm bond existed between parents and their children. This bond could go violently awry if daughters rejected their parents' wishes in marital matters,[136] but for the most part, Tasmanians were firm, guiding and loving parents. There are numerous references to filial affection, particularly in Robinson's journals and the writings of the French explorers.[137] In January 1830, Robinson appealed to the Governor on behalf of a woman who:

has been, and still is, in considerable grief respecting her offspring a lad about 14 years of age, who is at the present time attached to Jorgen Jorgenson's [roving] party ... The generality of parents entertain a strong natural feeling towards their offspring, and ... deplore the loss of a child, with the same degree of anguish that is experienced in civilised life.[138]

Men were also remarkably tender and attentive parents. In 1830, for instance, a South Esk River settler relayed the anxious request of a 'Chief' who had surrendered himself two days before: 'The native boy now with Mr Batman is son to the chief [Mannalargenna], his name is Trelabuenea, his father is most anxious to see him as also the other lad whom Mr Batman took and who I believe is with Mr Robinson, his mother and father are both here and most anxious for the return of the parties to see them.'

When Mannalargenna finally got to see his son, who had been taken from him in an ambush 14 months earlier, he 'took him in his arms kissed him and carried him about all day'.[139] The strength of these bonds was in direct proportion to the pain parents must have endured on seeing their children killed or captured, or when forced in desperation to sacrifice them so that others might survive.

Children were spared none of the war's horrors. They quickly developed a healthy fear of the white man. According to Robinson, 'the natives when they wanted to quiet their children, told them that the NUM LAGGER, i.e. the white man, come, which always was sufficient to quiet the children. Hence the name of white man infuses into the minds of these poor creatures the same terror.'[140] There are no surviving accounts from children's perspectives, but given their immaturity and vulnerability, it is reasonable to assume their experiences were even more terrifying and confusing than their parents'. Many of them had never known a stable existence, having been hunted by the white man for as long as they could remember. The long marches and cold nights pushed them to their physical limits, but it was above all the constant loss of friends and relatives that suffused their young lives with sadness and instability.

Relationships between men and women were central to Aborigines' experiences of the war. As noted in Chapter 1, women bore a disproportionately heavy labour burden, were sometimes sexually exploited, and experienced varying levels of domestic violence. However, it does not follow that Aboriginal women lived in perennial terror and misery, or that their relationships were loveless. Violence was an accepted part of life for all Tasmanians, and not inconsistent with a loving relationship. This is not to excuse domestic violence, which is always detestable; it is simply to contextualise it. Almost all recorded spousal violence resulted from possessiveness, suggesting passion rather than disregard. 'As husbands they seem regardful of their wives', wrote Robinson, but this 'often amounts to jealousy.'[141]

There is no evidence that women resented the burdens placed on them, or that domestic violence negated spousal affections. Women were unwavering in their care and affection towards their husbands. When Penenebope became delirious with fever at Macquarie Harbour in 1833, Robinson noted that his wife, Temgorerer, 'accompanied him and watched him with the greatest tenderness'.[142] And the compassion went both ways. During the same outbreak of disease, Robinson observed that 'wives were most assiduous in their attention upon the husbands, so likewise the husbands upon their wives'.[143] George Washington Walker observed similar behaviour on Flinders Island in 1832: 'Pellonnymyna was suddenly seized with an attack of illness and became unable to support herself. The faithful lover was at her side. Seizing her in his arms he bore her to a place of safety, and during her indisposition, which was tedious, he nursed her with the greatest attention, and most affectionate assiduity.'[144]

Many Tasmanians witnessed their loved ones killed, wounded, raped or abducted by white men, and the resulting anguish probably dominated their experience of the war. For obvious reasons, there is little record of how Aborigines responded in the immediate aftermath of the white man's predatory raids; nor are there any illuminating accounts of how women and girls felt as they were being abducted or gang-raped. The closest we have are the reminiscences of Trugernanna (see Figure 11):

We were camped close to Partridge Island when I was a little girl, when a
vessel came to anchor without our knowledge of it, a boat came on shore,

and some of the men attacked our camp. We all ran away, but one of them caught my mother, and stabbed her with a knife, and killed her. My father grieved much about her death, and used to make a fire at night by himself, when my mother would come to him. I had a sister named Moorina; she was taken away by a sealing boat. I used to go to Birch's Bay; there was a party of men cutting timber for the Government there, the overseer was Mr. Munro; while I was there two young men of my tribe came for me … two of the sawyers said they would take us in a boat to Bruny Island, which we agreed to. When we got about half-way across the Channel, they murdered the two natives, and threw them overboard, but one of them held me.[145]

This account reveals little emotion; however, given the abundance of evidence attesting to the Tasmanians' emotionality, the psychological agony suffered by Trugernanna (see Figure 11) and hundreds like her can be confidently inferred.

Descriptions of Aborigines grieving are common. When death struck, the relatives of the deceased were generally inconsolable, such as when disease tore through the Bruny Island population in 1829. Robinson observed that '[t]he gentle feelings of our natives are almost borne down with agonising sympathy'.[146] Likewise, the doctor on Flinders Island, Arthur Walsh, exclaimed: 'The poignancy of sorrow expressed by them on the death of their friends (which has been often truly painful to me to witness) cannot be surpassed among any class of people.'[147] But, although grief was inevitable, its severity could be mitigated if traditional funerary practices were observed.

Some of the significance of funerary and mourning practices was captured by the missionary James Backhouse when he witnessed the following ritual: 'The ashes of the dead were collected in a piece of Kangaroo-skin, and every morning, before sunrise, till they were consumed, a portion of them was smeared over the faces of the survivors, and a death song sung, with great emotion, tears clearing away lines among the ashes.'[148] As Chapter 1 observes, these rituals were immensely important to Tasmanians, who did all they could to retrieve the bodies of their fallen comrades, but this was often too dangerous.[149] The wartime death of a loved one was wrenching enough, but when families and friends could not conduct the proper funerary rites to ensure the soul's transmigration, they often had to fear the dead man's disturbed spirit, as well as the white men who killed him.

Desperation

As the war dragged on the violence increased and the Aboriginal population plummeted. This meant the involvement of surviving Tasmanians increased exponentially, while at the same time, the number of white men grew by several thousand each year (see Figure 3, page 2). By 1830, there were almost 100 white men in eastern Tasmania to every Aborigine. The latter were being overwhelmed on all sides, and hunted unrelentingly by armed parties, even into the remoter areas that had once provided sanctuary.

The result of this 'harassing life', West explained, was that 'parents and children had been divided, and families had been broken up in melancholy confusion: indeed, they had ceased to be tribes, and became what they were called – mobs of natives, composed often of hereditary enemies. Infanticide and distress, rapid flight, and all the casualties of a protracted conflict, threatened them with weedy destruction.'[150] They lived more or less constantly on the run. By day they moved fast, keeping to the thick bush, hunting and raiding where they could, and watching and listening constantly for armed parties. This frequently entailed travelling through rough country, suffering aching and lacerated feet, exhaustion and long periods of hunger. At night, they had to fear not just the fiends of their imaginations, but also the white men who sought any opportunity to ambush them. Robinson observed 'they were much afraid' when having to camp in the vicinity of armed parties.[151] Under such circumstances, it is easy to see how their nerves would become frayed.

Harried as they were, Tasmanians found sleep hard to come by, and the resulting weariness must have been detrimental to their mood and functioning. Cold, hunger and anxiety were all obtrusive to their slumber, but for staving off sleep there was probably nothing that rivalled the unremitting torment of the 'native pox'. This unidentified skin infection produced scabby pustules that could cover the entire body, and eventually seems to have afflicted almost every tribe on the island. After contracting it himself, Robinson declared that he 'would sooner face a thousand hostile natives than have this horrid infection'. It caused him to lament the plight of the Aborigines who had 'no means of relief except by bursting the skin. I have seen these poor creatures in the greatest torment and scratching themselves as if they would tear the flesh, the blood trickling down their naked bodies.'[152] We can only imagine how this grotesque infection magnified the misery of the Tasmanians' wartime ordeal.

The war all but destroyed the Tasmanians' political and cultural networks. In 1829, for instance, Jorgenson noted that the 'grand corroboree' held each November on the plains north-west of the Ouse River was cancelled 'for fear of being surprised'.[153] Many smaller ceremonies and dances were probably also cancelled on account of the noise and distraction they created, or because there was no one left to perform them. Alternatively, they may simply not have been in the mood. Either way, this cultural disruption must have caused them great distress.

Despite the onslaught of tragedies that Tasmanians suffered during the Black War, their conduct was not merely a series of survival responses. In addition to their myriad defensive concerns, most also appear to have been committed to pressing offensive campaigns against the white invaders, which consumed vast swaths of their time and energy. Thus, although they endeavoured to stay safe, warm and fed, they were also driven by feelings of hatred and injustice. In the end though, the cost of fighting a guerrilla war against insurmountable odds was more than they could bear.

CHAPTER FIVE

THE BLACK LINE

White

> [N]otwithstanding the clamour and urgent appeals which are now made
> to me for the adoption of harsh measures, I cannot divest myself of the
> consideration that all aggression originated with the white inhabitants,
> and that therefore much ought to be endured in return before the blacks
> are treated as an open and accredited enemy by the government.[1]

Arthur to Goderich, 10 January 1828

But how much was too much? Before the spring of 1830, the blacks had
killed or wounded at least 417 colonists, and plundered or destroyed
thousands of pounds worth of property.[2] Demands for 'decisive action'
were growing louder. Governor Arthur, who had long resisted the use of
force, both because of his genuine sympathy for the natives and because
he feared rebuke from London, finally capitulated to public pressure. On
9 September 1830, he enjoined the whole community to 'come forward
and zealously unite their best energies with those of the Government in
making such a general and simultaneous effort as the occasion demands'.[3]
It was to be a mass mobilisation of all able-bodied men to defend the

colony – a *levée en masse*. This was a truly immense and desperate operation, but as Arthur put it, the blacks had 'become so formidable, that
the strongest possible united effort of the Community is necessary to
subdue them'.[4]

Operation overview

The Black Line comprised some 2200 men, of whom approximately 550
were soldiers, 440 were free men, 800 were assigned convicts and 400
were ticket-of-leave convicts.[5] Settlers were encouraged to join in person,
and to contribute assigned servants. The selected assignees, along with all
ticket-of-leave men, were compelled to participate, though the latter had
the option of providing a substitute. Police magistrates arranged their local
forces into parties of ten, each led by a settler and a guide. Although Arthur
maintained overall control, Major Sholto Douglas of the 63rd Regiment
was entrusted with the immediate command of the forces. These were
divided into three divisions. Captain Donaldson led his division of just
over 300 men from Launceston and Norfolk Plains up over the Central
Plateau. Captain Wentworth, with parties stretching from Lake Echo to
New Norfolk, led his division eastward. The third division, commanded
by Douglas himself, pushed south from positions along the St Pauls River.
Before advancing on 7 October, the three divisions formed a staggered
front over 300 kilometres long (Figure 16, line AAA).

Initially, the parties were too widely spaced to form a linked cordon,
so they embarked on a series of scouring missions through the natives'
'most likely haunts'. By 12 October, Douglas' and Wentworth's forces
linked up, creating what was intended to be an unbroken line from Great
Swanport, east to Table Mountain, and south to the Derwent (Figure
16, line CCC and DDD). Donaldson maintained a safety net between
Lake Echo and Lake Sorell until 25 October, when he moved his force
south to reinforce the main line. The whole force advanced sporadically
towards East Bay Neck, until it was disbanded on 26 November.

Despite the line's scale and complexity, the survey and commissariat departments were given only a month to plan and organise it. This allowed insufficient time to make all the arrangements, let alone to reconnoitre the terrain. Furthermore, the best maps of the day were incomplete and inaccurate, and the infrastructure necessary to ensure efficient provisioning and communication was all but nonexistent.

None of these difficulties seemed to dampen the ardour of the community. With every native 'outrage', support for conciliation waned, and it was now widely believed that force was the only alternative. In Oatlands, Thomas Anstey remarked: 'The whole country is now convinced of the wisdom of Coll. Arthur's plan.'[6] Even the anti-government newspapers enjoined their readers to rally to the cause. Enthusiasm was not always accompanied by optimism, but virtually everyone agreed that something had to be done. According to the *Hobart Town Courier*, the native problem had become 'the important crisis on which the future rise or fall of this beautiful colony is to be determined'.[7]

Motivations

A week before the parties began moving out, blacks killed three of Major Gray's servants on the South Esk River, and grievously wounded a fourth.[8] The *Colonial Times* reported that 'the men in question were at work at a little distance from their hut, when the Natives rushed on them, and beat them to death with their waddies. They afterwards disfigured them in a most shocking manner, cutting the heads off of three of them, and placing them between their legs.'[9] The last detail may or may not have been true, but it made the desired impression. Rancour against 'these barbarous savages' was raised to a fever pitch, but this was not the only reason men volunteered.

Twenty-one year old Henry Emmett, a clerk in the Colonial Treasury Office, evinced great excitement at the prospect of 'seeing the whole county'.[10] On 1 October 1830, he and his party, consisting of his brother, two other free men, five ticket-of-leave men and three of his own servants, assembled at 6 am in the courtyard of the Hobart post office, along with 110 other men:

> a large number of persons assembled including the merchants, Public Officers and others, to witness our departure for the scene of the intended operations, all appearing most anxious in the work before them. At 7 o'clock the Governor and his staff appeared, entered the centre of the square, and addressed us in a most feeling speech of upwards of an hour's duration, giving us an outline of our intended duties, everything being done in Military style. At the conclusion of his speech His Excellency spoke to me in the most friendly manner, thanking me for what I had undertaken. He also requested me to take charge of 30 more men as far as New Norfolk.[11]

This was clearly a proud moment for Emmett. Although he came from a respectable family, the young man had achieved nothing of note himself, and had no military experience; now he was commanding 40 men at the personal behest of the Governor, marching off to defend the colony. It was well known that several parties had recently been rewarded and extolled for capturing or killing blacks, so Emmett and the other leaders no doubt recognised the line as an opportunity for personal advancement.

Robert Lawrence, the 23-year-old son of the colony's wealthiest landowner, shared Emmett's sentiment. Throughout the campaign Lawrence, who was also a party leader, went to extraordinary pains to appear zealous and competent in the eyes of officialdom. However, it was 21-year-old George Lloyd who best described this emotion: 'our hearts [were] fluttering with hope and excitement, at the prospect of distinguishing ourselves by the capture of even one of the dreaded savages'.[12]

Volunteers certainly found the social recognition alluring, but they were a small minority of the total force. Most of the men who comprised the Black Line were not there by choice, and this all but precluded their chances of gaining prestige. Although some convicts were initially seduced by the novelty of the campaign and the chance to kill blacks, anyone familiar with the ruggedness of the interior would have found enthusiasm difficult to muster. The possibility of pardons or reduced sentences might have offered some encouragement, but Arthur made it clear that, even if a party was successful, 'no individual is to expect any specific reward'.[13]

The reluctance of ticket-of-leave men to participate is far better evidenced, since many took the option of hiring a substitute. Little is known about how substitutes were paid, but given that the campaign was expected to last at least a month, it was probably substantial. Their willingness to make these costly trade-offs suggests many ticket-of-leave men had strong reasons to avoid serving. Most subsisted on a financial knife-edge, and would have been loath to leave their employment for any length of time. As convicts, they were probably also unenthused about making additional sacrifices for a penal colony founded on their suffering. What is more, there was no shortage of free men ready to exploit their reluctance. Given the option of volunteering without remuneration, or taking part as a paid substitute, many chose the latter. About half of all free participants served as substitutes.[14]

Soldiers' participation was also involuntary, but although they may not have been thrilled at the prospect, there is reason to believe their experiences of the line were not as bad as their comrades under sentence. The line punctuated the boredom of military life, but, more importantly, it gave soldiers a chance to display their authority and expertise to settlers who outranked them in society, and to convicts who could effectively outrank them in the roving parties. As noted earlier, soldiers and convicts tended to despise each other, which may help explain the undisciplined behaviour of convicts during the campaign, while reports indicate that soldiers were generally well conducted.

Setting out

Before it became a harrowing ordeal, the Black Line was quite the party. Enormous excitement surrounded the event, particularly in the major towns. 'Large posting bills was stuck up calling upon all settlers and their servants to volunteer', and in the days leading up to the campaign, Launceston and Hobart became hives of activity.[15] Writing to his wife on the eve of the line's departure, Robinson remarked: 'We are all bustle in this [northern] part of the island. Nothing is heard or thought of but the blacks.'[16] In Launceston, the local newspaper described the scene: 'all day this flourishing little town was full of bustle … The parting from friends and acquaintances sometimes led to an extra glass, but excepting here and there, a married man forced from his home his wife and family [to join the campaign], we saw none but joyous faces, and as far as we could judge, and willing hearts.'[17]

The men made the most of the festivities, much to the ire of their leaders, who had to control them. On the morning they marched out of Launceston, four of Lawrence's eight ticket-of-leave men 'gave me the slip' – probably still drunk – and by the end of the day he had lost another.[18] When his depleted party arrived at Norfolk Plains he found his two commanding officers embroiled in a bitter squabble over where to assemble, and most of the day was squandered in the bedlam that ensued.

The next day, with the sheepish return of his missing ticket-of-leave men, Lawrence proceeded south with the rest of Donaldson's force to scale the imposing Great Western Tiers. He and his men spent the night of 7 October bracing gale-force winds and snow as they huddled together halfway up the escarpment. The following evening, Lawrence recorded in his diary that his party had 'made a very bad ascent, having to crawl on our hands and knees, in some places, and to assist one another over the craggy rocks'.[19] Once atop the plateau, the blacks would have to wait. As the snow again began falling, shelters were frantically erected by

300 shivering men, who must have been wondering what they had let themselves in for.[20]

In the south the situation was equally chaotic. Emmett and his men encountered an intriguing scene as they marched out of town: 'It was quite pitiful to observe the sad state of the poor women and children who followed a considerable way sobbing with their aprons to their eyes, and others with plates of foods and mugs of tea, as if it was to be the last meal we should ever partake of, or that we should never need them again.'[21] After leaving the women behind:

> a fresh trouble commenced this being to get the men past the public houses. The day had been extremely warm and we were all very tired. I stopped for a short time on the road side and allowed some beer to be brought down, but I would not suffer the men to enter the inn, fearing I might lose some of them, though they tried and begged to be permitted to do so. I was determined however, not to grant such permission.[22]

Despite this vigilance, a ticket-of-leave man named Paddy managed to sneak away to the Black Snake Inn, though he turned up two days later, begging forgiveness. Unfortunately for Emmett, the pandemonium of this first day compared mildly to what lay ahead.

Life on the line

Once atop the Central Plateau, Lawrence's division had four days to reach their rendezvous point at Lake Sorell. Although they were supposed to be advancing in unison, the parties had scarcely any idea of their own location, let alone the location of others. Lawrence, for instance, led his party to the outskirts of Bothwell before realising his mistake and beginning the 30 kilometre hike back. Eventually he made it to Lake Sorell, but he was too late. Captain Donaldson had already left to establish a line of posts between Lake Sorell and Lake Echo.[23] On 15 October,

Lawrence was directed to take up a position not far from Lake Sorell, only to find the next day that 'the Sergeant had been playing a trick upon me, having directed me to a station on a high hill, out of the line'.[24]

To make matters worse, Lawrence's men were beginning to protest against the operation, and 'quarrel with one another at a great rate'.[25] Lawrence admitted on 17 October that '[t]he novelty of this campaign is past, and consequently, no longer gives to it that attraction which it at first had'. Adding to his woes, 'Poor Ford has a severe scrophulous attack in the leg; he is scarcely able to walk; and Mr Thornberry has a severe attack of laziness.'[26] Even Lawrence, when ordered on a 'scouring' mission to search the country about the Ouse River on 22 October, lamented: 'I was so dreadfully fatigued that I was quite unable to accomplish such a journey, being like some of the men scarcely able to stand.'[27]

The exhaustion felt by men on the line was not because the government had been frugal in rationing them. They were entitled to '3 oz. [85 g] of sugar, ½ oz. [14 g] tea, 2 lb. [907 g] flour, and 1½ lb. [680 g] of meat' per day, and after much complaining, 113 g tobacco, 14 g soap and 14 g salt were added.[28] At almost 5700 calories, this should have been, if not ideal, at least sufficient to sustain them.[29] The problem was accessing these rations, and Lawrence soon realised that 'many will suffer materially from want of food during this campaign'.[30] There were 30 depots scattered throughout the zone of operations, but they were rarely close and convenient. George Lloyd's provisioning party got lost attempting to find one of these depots and he and his men went 'not tasting food for [a] full 60 hours'.[31] Another party got so lost they 'were four days without provisions … [such that the leader] was obliged to eat the sheep skin straps of his knapsack'.[32]

Even when the ration depots could be found, there was no guarantee they would actually contain rations. Unprecedented rains flooded rivers and turned the already dismal roads into impassable bogs, which made transporting supplies extremely difficult.[33] Major Douglas informed the Governor on 25 October that most parties were not receiving their rations, and what they did receive was so rotten it made them sick.[34] The same was true in Wentworth's division, where Emmett claimed the rations 'made us all very unwell'.[35] On the Plateau, Donaldson's division was equally disgusted by the food. Having received only rancid meat, Lawrence was forced against orders to send his men kangaroo hunting. The situation was so bad by 3 November that an entire section of Douglas' division refused to move until supplied with adequate provisions.[36] By this stage, it seems, the blacks were fading as a priority.

Weather conditions compounded the men's miseries. A correspondent to the *Colonial Times* reported that, from the outset, 'the weather in many parts of the country was more severe than had been experienced at any time during the past winter. It was exceedingly cold, accompanied with squalls of wind, rain, and hail.'[37] According to Lloyd, '[t]he rain fell in torrents during many hours of each day and night for the first fortnight; and rendered travelling through dripping scrubs, flooded creeks, and deep marshes, almost impracticable. When the time for the general halt came round, wet blankets, and soaked gray cotton horse-rugs, afforded but a sorry prospect for a refreshing night's repose.'[38] James Bonwick interviewed 'a veteran shepherd, who had been a guide [on the line]', and reported on some of the hardships encountered by this man and his party: 'Torn by the scrub, hungry and wet, their camp was most miserable. Without tents, the men had to pass an inclement night on that bleak hill, around the fire, or stowed away in the hollows of trees.'[39]

The forces' only relief from the elements came when they stopped long enough to erect makeshift huts. 'The plan of these huts varied according to the taste of the proprietor', Robinson observed when he came the way of the line in January 1831, 'some had verandahs in front with seats, others large porches; some had bark tables; some was thatched with grass; some was in the form of a semicircle.'[40] Lawrence was especially proud of his hut: 'a very comfortable one it is; indeed it is quite a mansion, built of stone, and roofed with stringy-bark'.[41] These huts were sanctuaries against the wild weather and scrub, but outside, the men suffered dreadfully from exposure. Most participants wore cotton garments, but these offered little protection against the weather, and were no match against the scrub, which left them 'almost destitute of clothing'.[42]

The men's loudest complaints were about shoes. Although they were heavily laden with equipment and provisions, many participants wore poor-quality shoes that failed within the first fortnight.[43] In the third week of the campaign, Captain Donaldson complained that 'a great proportion' of his men were barefooted, and by November serious protests were erupting.[44] On 12 November, Captain Mahon warned Major Douglas that his men were shoeless and threatening to desert unless appropriate footwear was immediately issued. Mahon lamented that 'I have myself worn out two new pairs of strong Boots since I left Oatlands. And in a few more days I shall I fear be as naked as the men.'[45] Commissariat officers supplied 2340 pairs of shoes, but most did not reach the men until near the end of the campaign.[46]

By mid-October, Douglas' and Wentworth's divisions had linked up (see Figure 16, lines CCC and DDD), from whence a tight cordon was to be maintained as the parties advanced towards the Tasman Peninsula. During the day, the men were ordered to advance parallel to each other at even distances, and to scour the country as they went. At night, sentries were to patrol back and forth between their party's campfires.[47] This was all in vain though. Vast swamps, impenetrable scrub and rugged mountains all militated against an effective cordon. 'The line was very soon broken', Emmett recalled, 'indeed it could not have been otherwise, even with double the number of men we could not have done so in consequence of many obstacles in the way of a given progress, gullies, and rocky hills were continually met with, rendering the task an utter impossibility.'[48]

The gaps in the line were large and numerous, and reports began filtering back of groups of natives slipping through in several places. Then, after receiving a report on 25 October of a tribe trapped within the cordon,[49] Arthur halted the forces in a 50 kilometre arc from Sorell to Prossers Bay (see Figure 16, line HHH). For more than three weeks the force stayed in this position. A participant writing to the *Colonial Times* described their strategy for maintaining the cordon:

> every leader has nine men placed under him, and he has three differ-ent huts for these nine men and himself, each but at about every 150 yards [137 m] apart, containing three of the men. When under marching orders, or expecting any rush, then one man stations himself at 50 yards [45 m], and another at 100 yards [90 m] from the hut – thus the lines are at present concentrated, so that each man is only 50 yards from his next companion. The watches are very tedious, each individual having to perform eight hours duty as sentry in the course of the day and night. The rapid manner in which the watch-word passes along the line is really astonishing; indeed, the passing of the word 'all's well,' and a message, and sometimes a letter to the next sentry, to be forwarded to the next, *ad infinitum*, is our only amusement when on duty.[50]

At night the scene was impressive. According to Emmett, '[s]ix fires were kept up by each party all night, one in front of each tent, and three others 50 yards [45 m] in front … It was an exceedingly pretty sight to see the fires for miles, especially on the tops of hills, and many of the sentries watchcrys coming down the line at intervals helped the effect.'[51] In order to maintain so many fires, the parties were occupied almost full-time in gathering firewood, and the longer the line remained halted the scarcer dry timber became. Emmett recalled that, for those not on sentry duty, 'there was plenty of work all day collecting firewood for the night fires'. Robinson's description of the site a year later is insightful:

> The road through which we travelled this day was where the Line had been formed … Hundreds of thousands of trees had been stripped of their bark and cut down to make fires. The trees were stuck with bullets. On one

hill a brush fence had been erected as *chevaux de frise* [a spiked wooden barricade] against the aborigines. The ground was torn up by the trafficking of carts, horses, bullocks &c in conveying supplies. Shoes of a light description, worn out, was strewed about. It had all the appearance of a great assemblage of persons having met, and vast destruction was effected among the trees of the forest. Stripped of their covering they were left to droop and die, a monument of a well intended but ill-devised plan. Nature had been completely dismantled.[52]

By November the men were sick from the food, frozen from the wind and rain, and bored senseless from the endless patrolling and gathering of firewood. Worst of all, no one knew what the plan was. The men were given no forecast of operations, because none existed. The Governor developed his strategy according to incoming intelligence, and although there was no shortage of reports, sifting fact from fiction proved difficult. The very structure of the operation made it an engine of rumour. All manner of reports wound their way along the line, some genuine, some invented, but each distorted as they were shouted along.

On 7 November, Lawrence recorded a typical incident of confusion. When a soldier saw what he thought to be blacks in the darkness around him 'he fired, & yelled Look out the Blacks … [and ordered] the men to "keep up the fires in front of the Line", for the purpose of obtaining a greater light. This order was misunderstood and was converted by one of the sentries in to "keep up the firing down the Line"'.[53] On another occasion Lawrence wrote of 'a report flying about the Line, that we are to move to the North-eastern extremities of the Island shortly'.[54] Initially, he believed it, but like most of these rumours, it proved to be false.

The most bizarre report was of white men leading the natives, which first appeared on 13 October 1830. The *Hobart Town Courier* urged caution: 'Misguided as they doubtless are by white miscreants … they are no more to be trusted than ought to be a wild beast, a lion or tiger.'[55] Men on the line supposedly found shoe prints at native campsites, or heard from others who had, but it was the colourful tale of a convict named Thomas Savage that really propelled the myth. On 16 October, Savage reported having been kidnapped the night before by natives led by a bushranger named Brown. Somehow Governor Arthur believed the story, for which a special edition of the *Hobart Town Courier* was printed.[56] That same day, on the Plateau, Lawrence heard that the Governor had himself 'fallen in with a large party of Natives … headed by two White men'.[57] There is no good evidence that colonists ever fought alongside blacks, but the idea persisted because many found it difficult to believe the island's 'ignorant savages' were capable of managing such effective resistance themselves.

The most common reports were of attempts by blacks to penetrate the line. These had an unnerving effect on the men, and meant that they had to fear not just the blacks, but also their trigger-happy comrades. There were dozens of reported sightings; most were probably inventions or mistakes, but they all had to be treated seriously, especially as no one knew how many blacks they were facing. Although some were known to have escaped, it was generally believed, at least until mid-November, that a number of blacks remained within the cordon. To promote vigilance, Arthur actively recirculated the reports he received of sightings and encounters, but by now, nothing could salvage the men's enthusiasm.

The home front

In Hobart and Launceston, civilians took over guarding the jails, ports and public buildings, thereby freeing up the military.[58] Serving in the town guard was, for some, a less strenuous and more visible way of aiding the cause. The presence of civilian guards in Hobart proved quite the novelty until they were dismissed (with great indignation) when fresh troops arrived in late October. In Launceston, the volunteers served until 1 December, by which time they had gained a reputation for 'inefficiency', 'dissention' and overzealously guarding the drinking establishments.[59] But although they were the subjects of much conversation, the intrigue of the town guards failed to distract the community from the gravity of the events unfolding in the interior.

The inhabitants of Launceston and Hobart read the newspapers with intense interest, and were, according to Colonial Secretary John Burnett, 'on the tip-toe for intelligence from the "seat of war"'.[60] Melville recalled that, 'during the months of September, October, and November ... the black war, and nothing but the black war, was the subject of general attention'.[61] Great intrigue surrounded the line, as did sincere concern. Burnett observed that every citizen of Hobart 'seems to take the greatest interest in, and to feel the most intense anxiety respecting the present operation'.[62]

In the interior, colonists were more concerned with their own safety. With so many men and guns sequestered in the line, those left at home rightly feared that the natives would exploit this weakness. In November, for instance, a party of natives attacked the hut of Mrs Field, whose husband was away on the line. The blacks 'broke the legs of one of his [Mr Field's] dogs with a waddy', yet she succeeded in 'repulsing' her assailants by taking up arms and disguising herself in men's clothing (not the first time she had employed such artifice).[63] This was one of at least 50 attacks reported during the campaign, which together created an atmosphere of intense trepidation on the home front.

The end of the line

As the operation entered its fifth week the languishing forces became restless. 'During the delay', Emmett recalled, 'we could not make out what was the intention of the Governor, and were, of course, quite ignorant of his movements.'[64] The tedium was broken when the call went out for volunteers to scour the area inside the line. Emmett, Lawrence and Lloyd volunteered to lead three of the 40 scouring parties. These seven-man parties were to reconnoitre the country between the cordon and the

Tasman Peninsula, but what some thought would be a welcome break, turned out to be the most gruelling duty of the campaign.

Even the fittest and most energetic volunteers had their breaking points and, in mid-November, as he wandered lost somewhere in the rugged south-east, Lawrence reached his:

> I am now quite tired of this business; there is very little chance apparently of success, and a report has just arrived up the Line, which if correct will make it quite useless to proceed further, viz. That the Natives have been traced through the Line in two different places. Hard work, without hope is distressing. The men are all disgusted, and grumbling; they have become so ill tempered that it is almost impossible to manage them except by compulsion. I do not wish to punish, for allowances must be made for the long succession of hard privations which they have endured.[65]

The experience of Lawrence and his party was not unique. When the campaign began, most men assumed they would be home by the end of the month.[66] On 31 October, Arthur assured them 'the final & decisive movement ... [would] commence tomorrow', but a fortnight later they had barely moved.[67] By 16 November, when the line finally lurched forward, party leaders were expressing 'a great deal of impatience',[68] and the men, Emmett recalled, 'were tired of the monotony of the line'.[69]

In addition to the horrendous conditions, there was hay to cut, crops to harvest and lambing sheep to tend.[70] 'Many of the men are now losing two or three guineas per week', Lawrence wrote regretfully; but of greater concern to some was the safety of their families and property.[71] From the moment the campaign got underway, reports of attacks on the home front raced up and down the line, and whether or not they were true, they had a devastating effect on morale.

A significant number of men chose to desert. Lloyd remembered how 'the discomfort experienced in travelling amidst heavy rains by day, and lying upon the damp earth, unsheltered from the chilly dews of night, soon sufficed to rid the ranks of scores of these thin-skinned heroes'.[72] Thomas Faro and his party, who trudged back to Launceston in early November, were among those Lloyd was referring to, but Faro defended his actions in the *Launceston Advertiser*: 'Great complaints are made by his party of wearing their clothes to pieces, and worse yet, the skin of their feet, the flesh from their backs, together with a frequent want of provisions, and that for three days at one time.'[73] Faro and his men were not alone. On 30 October, Robert Foster's party deserted and Douglas feared that within a week the rest of his division would follow.[74] By 3 November, Donaldson's parties had begun to desert as well, and the following week the *Hobart Town Courier* lamented that 'daily desertions are taking place'.[75]

As the prospect of success faded, the Governor's correspondence developed undertones of embarrassment and guilt at having detained the volunteers so long. Realising he could not keep them much longer, Arthur ordered a series of movements towards East Bay Neck on 17 November. This 'final push' advanced over some of the most difficult country the men had yet encountered, intending to rendezvous with the scouring parties who had set out two days earlier. The cordon rapidly disintegrated, as gaps opened up so large the linesmen missed the scouring parties. Lawrence conceded: 'If a hundred and fifty men have passed through [unseen, the line] can no longer be of any use.'[76] Dismayed, he and his party marched for Sorell, where they were permitted to return home early.

Back on the line, things only got worse.[77] The final week of the campaign saw it fall apart with apathy and disorganisation, but no official rebuke was forthcoming. The men had endured great hardships, and Arthur saw no point compounding their disappointment. Only a small number of parties even bothered to push through to the Peninsula. In the last days, most either gave up and turned back, or veered straight for Sorell where they were rationed and sent home. There were no celebrations.

Objectives and results

Government Order no. 10 stated emphatically that 'the object in view is not to injure or destroy the unhappy savages ... but to capture [them]'. Frontier colonists generally ignored the government's injunctions, because in practice they were unenforceable, but during the line operation, they knew the interior would be full of military and civil authority figures, including the Governor himself. Initially, it seems no one knew how seriously to take the Governor on this occasion. The *Colonial Times* confessed:

> we ourselves really do not understand, nor have we been able to meet with
> any who could explain to us, whether the sword or the Bible is meant to be
> the means of instructing the Aborigines in their relative duty to ourselves.
> In other words ... are the numerous parties which are soon to scour the
> interior, to destroy or save these misguided creatures? Whatever may be
> the intentions of the Government, we are fully convinced, that most of
> those who are now preparing for the interior are not aware of the manner
> in which the Government expects them to act.[78]

The *Launceston Advertiser* was resolute about which it had to be. Even if 20,000 soldiers were employed, the editor mused, 'they would not capture all the blacks in seven years – that is to say, if they were bound to catch them alive'.[79]

How indeed were the parties to merely 'capture' the blacks? Again, the *Launceston Advertiser*'s satire is insightful:

> drive all the Blacks in that division up in one corner; and mind, men, do
> not shoot or hurt one, but catch them all alive, oh and be very careful you
> don't hurt them, and if they should attempt to run away from you, tell
> them to stop or you will certainly shoot, and the bare words will arrest
> them, only you must first learn them the language in which it is spoken.[80]

The following week the editor laid bare his true opinion: 'To capture them will be very difficult, but to visit them with condign punishment, will not only be easier of performance, but will far better satisfy the friends and relatives of the fallen.'[81] This seems to have reflected the general attitude in Launceston, where according to one witness, 'nothing was heard or thought of [other] than shooting the natives'.[82]

In Hobart, the atmosphere was little different. The *Colonial Times* reported that 'more than a few are now burning with impatience to signalize themselves, and to immortalise their names by the trophies they mean to bring home'.[83] The meaning of 'trophies' had been revealed three weeks earlier, when it was reported that 'one of the humane ticket-of-leave men who are about being sent into the bush, in search of the Aborigines, congratulates himself that … he can at any time obtain five guineas for each scull [*sic*] of the blacks, with which he expects to return loaded'.[84]

Exterminationist sentiment was certainly common among frontier convicts, but it was not exclusive to them. On 22 September 1830, 400 of Hobart's respectable inhabitants assembled in the courthouse to discuss the establishment of a town guard, but it quickly turned into a debate about the object of the operation. One-time Attorney-General, Joseph Gellibrand, felt certain that colonists were 'about to enter upon a war of extermination, for such I apprehend is the intended object of the present operations'.[85] Gellibrand decried such an outcome, but most believed it was now necessary. Dr Adam Turnbull insisted that '[t]he war must be a war of extermination … the present warfare of the stock-keepers is infinitely more one of extermination than the present one will be'. Even Solicitor-General Alfred Stephen declared: 'If you cannot [capture them] … I say boldly and broadly, exterminate!'[86] Notwithstanding the bombast of the town meeting, it remained to be seen whether the forces were really willing to kill blacks against official orders.

Lawrence's experience appears to have been typical. On 8 October, he and his party 'saw a fire' and 'arranged to sneak upon them before morning'. What followed began as a textbook campfire ambush:

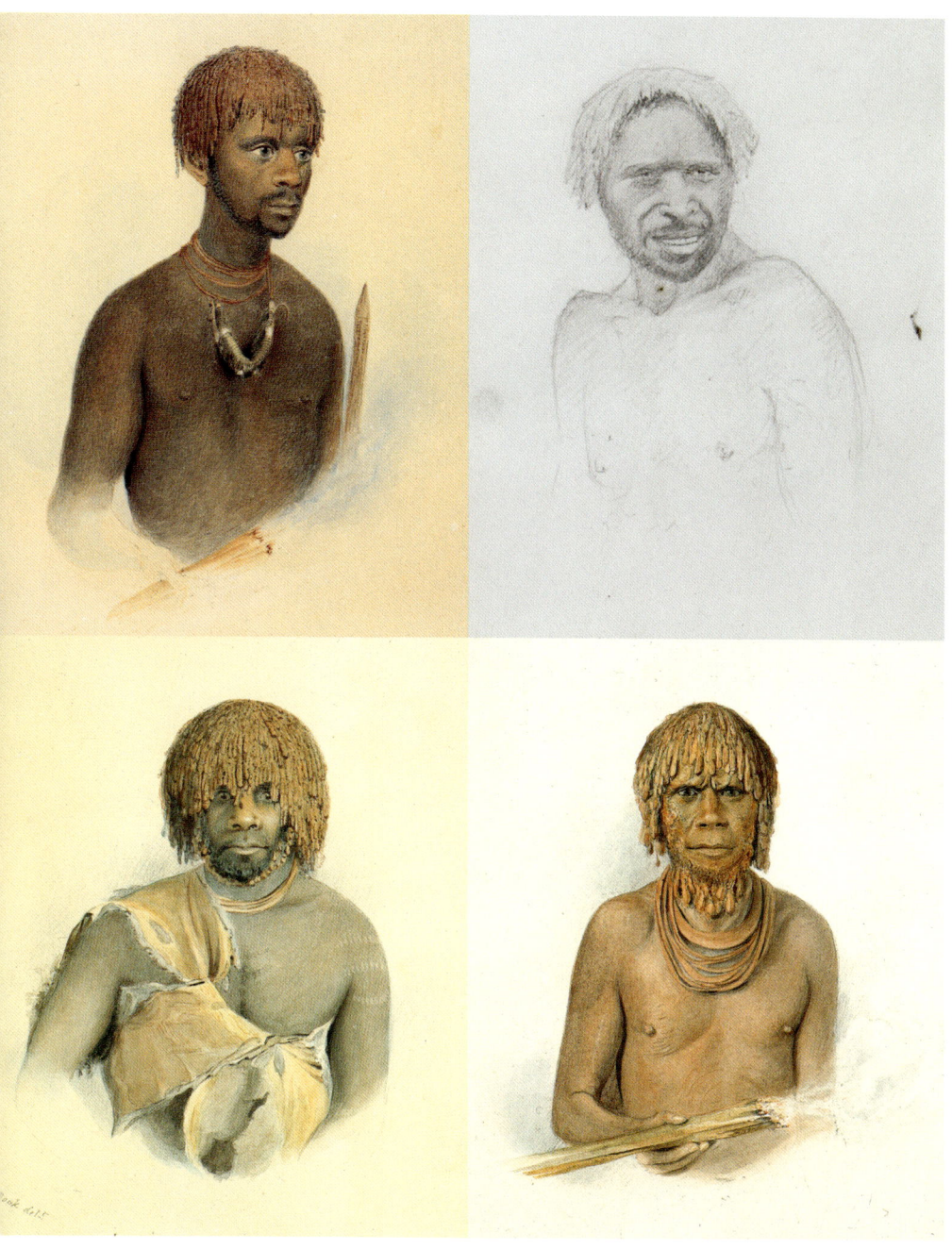

Figure 5: Tasmanian warriors (Clockwise from top). A Timmy Captured as a boy and raised by whites, he aided Robinson's conciliatory efforts in Tasmania and later in Port Phillip, where he was hung for murder in 1842. **B Tongerlongerter** Perhaps the greatest of Tasmania's resistance leaders, he was shot by whites during an ambush, forcing his kinsfolk to amputate their chief's shattered arm and cauterise the wound above the elbow. **C Mannalargenna** A warrior, shaman, chief and skilled diplomat, he waged war on the white men after being betrayed by sealers, before eventually joining Robinson's friendly mission. **D Woorrady** The last surviving man of the Bruny Island people, he was one of the longest serving and most important members of Robinson's friendly mission. (Thomas Bock 1830–34. Courtesy of the Tasmanian Museum and Art Gallery and the QVMAG.)

Figure 6: George Augustus Robinson. Although there is much debate over his character, there can be no disputing the importance of his role in ending the Black War and exiling the surviving Tasmanians. (Courtesy of the Allport Library and Museum of Fine Arts, TAHO.)

Figure 7: *Montacute, Bothwell.* In areas that were especially prone to Aboriginal attacks, settlers literally fortified their homesteads, as illustrated in the painting above. (John Glover, 1838. Courtesy of Sotheby's Australia.)

Figure 8: Conciliation Picture Board. An unknown number of these picture boards were commissioned by surveyor general George Frankland in 1829 (the mistaken title referring to Governor Davey's 1816 proclamation is a later addition). In a last-ditch attempt to convey the government's conciliatory agenda, they were distributed to people likely to encounter Aborigines. (George Frankland, 1829. Courtesy of the Allport Library and Museum of Fine Arts, TAHO.)

Figure 9: *Lieutenant John Bowen and party arriving at Risdon.* Thomas Gregson, the artist whose wartime sympathy for the Aborigines made him unpopular among his peers, was clearly influenced by the poignancy of Bowen's arrival in 1803, which sounded the beginning of Tasmania's colonisation. (Thomas Gregson, c.1860. Courtesy of the WL Crowther Library, TAHO.)

Figure 10: *The conciliation.* Although romanticised, Duterreau's painting depicts the surrender of the last Mairremmener people on 31 December 1831. With this handshake the battle for Tasmania was over, and with it 34,000 years of Aboriginal control. (Benjamin Duterreau, 1840. Courtesy of the Tasmanian Museum and Art Gallery.)

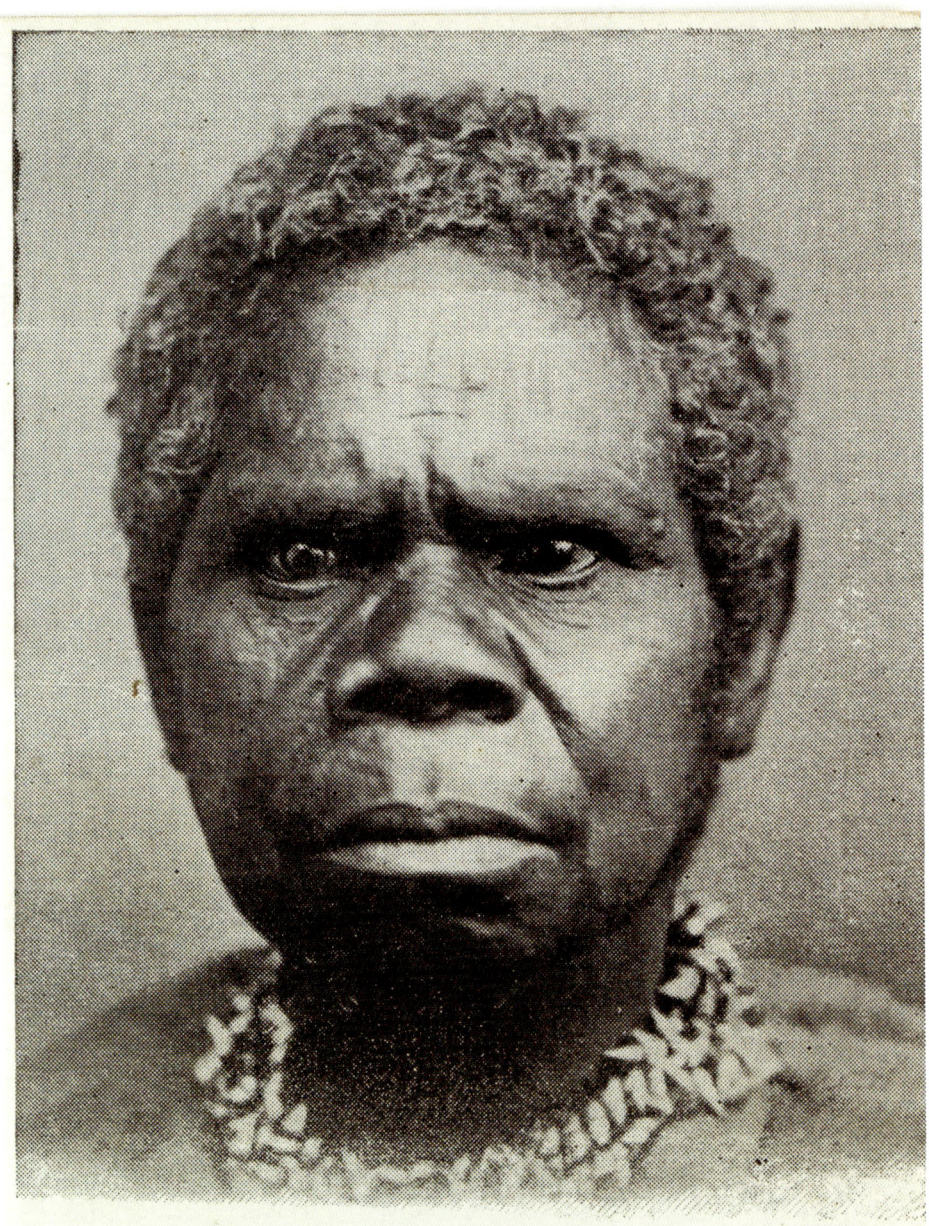

Figure 11: Trugernanna, 1866. Truganini saw many of her loved ones killed and raped by whites. After her tribe was decimated by disease in 1829, she became a key member of Robinson's friendly mission. She was thought to be the last Tasmanian when she died in 1876, and while this perception has since been revised, her passing did signal the end of an ancient way of life. (Courtesy TAHO.)

Figure 12: GP Harris' cottage Hobart Town, Van Diemen's Land c.1806 At the foot of Mt Wellington in Hobart, this hut was typical of the humble dwellings erected by early settlers. (Unknown artist. Courtesy of the National Library of Australia.)

Figure 13: *Aborigines of Tasmania*. This plausible depiction of tribal life is inaccurate only in that Tasmanians usually went about fully naked, or with just a single skin draped over their shoulders. (Robert Dowling, 1859. Courtesy of the QVMAG.)

Figure 14: *Ambush at night, Adelaide Hills c.1840s.* Although depicting South Australia in the 1840s, this image vividly illustrates a campfire ambush, the most common tactic employed by colonists' against Aborigines in Tasmania. (John Michael Skipper, 1860s. Courtesy of the Maughan family and the Art Gallery of South Australia.)

Figure 15: *Attack on settler's hut.* Tasmanians did not use shields and boomerangs, and threw firebrands, not flaming spears, but in most other details this image is representative of a typical stock hut ambush. (Unknown artist c.1870. Courtesy of the National Library of Australia.)

Figure 16: Field plan of military operations against the Aboriginal inhabitants of Van Diemen's Land. The straight lines drawn on this field plan of the Black Line indicate the colonial authorities' ignorance regarding the Tasmanian landscape. Within the first week of this epic campaign, the impossibility of maintaining a secure cordon became apparent to everyone involved. It was a disaster from the outset. (George Frankland, 1830. Courtesy of the WL Crowther Library, TAHO.)

we started cautiously towards the fire. I thought it prudent to wait till daylight, when I stationed my party in such a way, as to cover the sides of the fires, and commenced to close upon them; the fourth side was covered by the Lake. Upon closing upon them, however, we found to our great disappointment, that our labour had been thrown away upon a party of the Line.[87]

It is not clear what Lawrence's intent was, but had he executed a bloodless capture it would have been one of the first in the colony's history.

Capture, it seems, was never seriously considered a priority. On 3 November, Lawrence recorded hearing several shots down the line: 'It proved to be a Mr Glover and a constable, who had fallen in with a single native, at whom they fired several times without effect.' At 11pm on 5 November, 'the cry of look out came down the Line and two shots were heard. In the course of the day it was asserted that the natives were supposed to be in a scrubby bush; into which one of the sentries fired.' Then, on 7 November:

> About 10 o'Clock last night we were aroused by a strong fire of musketry and the cry of look out. I suppose not less than two hundred rounds were fired … one of the soldiers not being accustomed to the nocturnal ramblings of the Opossums, imagined when he saw one of them terrible vermin moving about, that it must certainly be one of the enemy.[88]

Lawrence was not the only participant to note this pattern. In total, hundreds of shots were fired at targets thought to be natives. Most of the time it was just lively marsupials or unlucky sentries, though there appears to have been several genuine sightings.[89] The only success, Edward Walpole's dawn ambush on 25 October, resulted in two natives captured (one of whom was stabbed), and two killed. Most participants were not interested in capturing blacks, except perhaps those who were wounded.

The degree to which the campaign succeeded or failed can be gauged by reference to its objectives. 'The following movements', stated Government Order no. 10, are 'directed first to surround the hostile Native Tribes, – secondly, to capture them in the county of Buckingham, progressively driving them upon Tasman's Peninsula, – and, thirdly, to prevent their escape into the remote unsettled Districts to the Westward and Eastward.'[90] Aside from the capture of two men, the operation failed in all these respects, and everybody knew it. Jorgen Jorgenson put it down 'to the want of vigilance, to sluginess [sic], and to total inattention'.[91] The men, he complained, would not patrol their posts, 'but keep close to their hut fires'.[92] This was certainly true, yet, even if the men had been more invested in the scheme, vigilance and enthusiasm were difficult to maintain in the absence of adequate food, clothing or shelter. Most focused simply on mitigating the misery of the ordeal, but nothing frustrated this project more than the landscape itself. The more lost the men became, and the more country they bypassed, the stronger their sense of futility. By 15 November, Lawrence lamented that '[a]lmost every one appears to have given up hope of success'.[93]

When the gusto had subsided, and the realities stood in stark view, no one was surprised at the result. The campaign had, after all, asked men to search thousands of hectares of mostly uncharted wilderness for a ghost-like enemy. No one denied the natives' effectiveness, both at making their incursions and eluding capture, but few imagined these 'pitiable savages' could outfox such an imposing British force. Outfoxed it was though, and the effect on the community was crushing. It had been, as Robinson put it, 'a battle with a shadow'.[94]

Black

Nowhere was the difference between the black and white experiences starker than when it came to the Black Line. On one side, the line was the all-consuming project of a united white community; on the other, it is doubtful that any of the remaining Tasmanian tribes ever grasped the full scale or meaning of the event. Knowing as we do the significance of this immense operation to the colonists, and to history, it can be easy to forget that the Tasmanians did not have a bird's-eye view. They were ignorant of anything they did not see with their own eyes, or hear from friends. They gained some understanding of the line in the weeks and months following, but what did they know at the time? Robinson's journals, together with scattered archival references, provide some record of the Aborigines' experience. Most significantly, Robinson recorded a small but telling selection of testimonies, both during and after the line, from which it is possible to paint a reasonable picture of the event from their perspective.

Lead-up to the line

Most tribes migrated away from the settlements between April and July 1830, as they had done in years past. The number of attacks over this period averaged approximately one every three days, but as in previous years, the tribes became increasingly hostile towards the end of winter and into spring. During this period, at least seven eastern tribes remained active in attacking the settlements.[95] In the north, there was a tribe on each side of the Tamar River, and one in the region of Ben Lomond. Most belligerent of all though, were the Mairremmener tribes, two of which appear to have been in the river valleys north-west of Hobart, another west of Campbell Town in the foothills of the Western Tiers, and still another in the Oyster Bay area. All these tribes were on the brink of collapse, and all were primed with grief and anger.

Collectively, Tasmanians orchestrated no less than 47 attacks in August 1830.[96] They made fewer incursions the following month, but those they did make were particularly bloody. On 10 September, for instance, a party of Mairremmener attacked the property of Thomas

Buxton at Bream Creek. They may not have known that a man named Buxton assumed ownership of the area, but they knew the country, once theirs, was now infested with malevolent beings. These beings also stored food in their huts, and this appears to have been the primary motive for the attack. An advance party speared the two stockmen who were present, while the others stormed the hut. This was a common tactic, but one of the wounded men put up a determined resistance, and the tribe was eventually forced to retreat.[97] The same day, 150 kilometres to the north-west, on the banks of the Tamar River, three sawyers were grievously speared and clubbed, one fatally.[98] The tribe responsible was probably the remnant of several tribes that had once ranged the area west of the Tamar.

These attacks, which occurred on the same day newspapers announced the Black Line, intensified the furore that was animating the whites to take such a drastic measure. But all this excitement went largely unnoticed by the people responsible for it. The war parties that made the attacks on 10 September knew nothing of each other's activities, or the effect they were having on the white community. Certainly, any hopes of terrorising the whites into submission had long since been abandoned. Their actions were now primarily orientated towards staying alive.

The line begins

Unbeknown to the Tasmanians, a storm was brewing around them in the early spring of 1830. Tribes in the north and north-east may have noticed the pressure on them reduced as the white men busied themselves with preparations for the line. It was only the tribes in the central and southeastern parts of the island – probably less than 100 individuals – that lay in the path of the intended movement. On 5 October, a tribe was surprised in a densely wooded labyrinth of valleys between the Clyde and Jordan rivers. Although one man was shot in the leg, all 'escaped in the scrub', slipping into the rear of the parties.[99]

Three other escapes were reported within the first ten days of the campaign. On 13 October, it was revealed by 'several reports' that 'some of the native tribes have been left in the rear of Lieut. Murray's Division on the Dee & the West bank of the Derwent'.[100] On the same day, an advance party stumbled upon a tribe of 'forty-two' blacks near Penstock Lagoon on the Central Plateau, but lost their trail to the westward after tracking them to the northern end of Great Lake.[101] Several days later a third tribe broke through the line at the Lower Marshes on the Jordan River.[102] On each occasion, the Tasmanians eluded their pursuers.

About the same time, another tribe comprising some 40 Mairremmener people descended on Pittwater, a now largely unprotected area well inside the line.[103] Fresh from a successful fight with an enemy tribe to the north, they ransacked eight houses, killing one man and seriously wounding three others.[104] Gauging from witnesses' reports, and the fact that the attacks took place over just two days, it is highly probable that this tribe divided itself into several war parties, operating from a central location where the women and children watched over the accumulating booty. Their plunder was substantial, but so were their losses. One man was mortally wounded with a pitchfork in a brawl with a white man, and according to the testimony of one of the Aborigines involved, four others were shot during or soon after these attacks.[105] Afterwards they retreated into the unsettled recesses of the south-east where they mistakenly thought themselves safe. These people, ignorant as they were of the operation bearing down upon them, appear to have been the only tribe not to make an early escape from the line.

The northern tribes

In the closing months of 1830, at least one tribe continued to operate along the Esk rivers in the island's north, during which time they made around a dozen attacks. Meanwhile, another very small tribe was operating in the lightly settled hinterland east of the Tamar River. They had occasionally visited George Town and, in early September, they approached that settlement one last time.[106] In the past, they probably recognised the relative safety of the township, with its opportunities for procuring introduced foods, but on this occasion the Black Line was announced soon after their arrival. They may not have known why, but the simmering animosities of many local whites were now unleashed, making it unsafe for them to remain in the area. The tribe quickly fled the town, and with the exception of two spearings along the East Tamar, they steered clear of the settlements until their surrender to Robinson on 1 November.

Their neighbours in the Ben Lomond region had, by now, coalesced into a single remnant tribe. They too had suffered heavy losses at the hands of sealers, frontiersmen and enemy tribes. By October 1830, this tribe had been reduced to just ten individuals, all men. John Batman had been hunting them for two years. As a last resort he secured the release from jail of two women, Karnebutcher and Luggenemenener, on the condition they acted as envoys to this tribe, and convinced them to turn themselves in.[107] The women were liberated on 8 August, and soon made contact, but they apparently had no intention of returning. That was, Robinson recorded, until they 'had seen the soldiers, and had been inside the Line and had run away'.[108] Luggenemenener later described to Robinson how 'the soldiers [extended] for a long way and that they kept firing off muskets. Said plenty of PAR.KUTE.TEN.NER horsemen, plenty of soldiers, plenty of big fires on the hills.'[109] Being 'afraid they [the soldiers] would shoot them', Luggenemenener convinced the others to accompany her to Batman's farm, where they arrived on 19 October. Clearly, they recognised that something big was afoot.[110]

This tribe was headed by the revered chief, Mannalargenna (see Figure 5C), who charmed Batman and his neighbours.[111] However, the initial geniality of the tribe may have been a charade. After receiving food and protection for ten days, Mannalargenna and his tribe deserted Batman's in the middle of the night, helping themselves to his dogs and provisions.[112] The following day they attacked two huts on the South Esk River, but a party of whites was in close pursuit. On 29 October a skirmish occurred at Grants Mill, west of Fingal. The following day, the tribe was surprised while plundering a hut to the town's east, and two warriors were killed.[113] Thirteen days later they arrived at Cape Portland and began making smoke signals to Robinson, who had only days before established a temporary mission on Swan Island. On 15 November, a party of envoys collected the one woman and five men, who were all that remained of this tribe, and removed them to the mission. The tribe's resumption of violence, despite their partial awareness of the line, suggests that the operation was not their primary reason for surrendering. It no doubt buttressed their sense that continued resistance was futile, but then, they already knew that.

Escaping the cordon

Early on the morning of 25 October, at the Sandspit River not far from the coast, the Mairremmener tribe that had recently been at Pittwater was awoken by white men storming their camp. Always on their guard against such attacks, they had left only one of their huts exposed. According to the lead assailant, the hut was occupied by five men, who 'appeared to have been a look out'. He reported that '[t]here were five other huts across the creek in the centre of a very thick scrub – I had fully intended to attack the main body but I found it impossible to get near enough without being heard'.[114] The attack was a clumsy one. Ronekeenarener and Weltepellemeener were wrestled into submission and captured, and two other men were shot dead as they attempted to flee, but the kinsfolk they sought to protect all managed to escape.

The survivors were now propelled into an all too familiar and distressing situation. They responded by dividing into smaller parties and heading north. One group penetrated the line several kilometres west of Prossers Bay in the early hours of 26 October, a linesman noting that '[t]he cunning of the Blacks in selecting the tempestuous night ... to escape was remarkable'.[115] The Mairremmener were loath to move at night, but Woolaytoopinneyer later told Robinson 'they saw the soldiers and the fires', and knew they had a gauntlet to run.[116] They even tethered and abandoned their dogs, which suggests they appreciated the seriousness of the situation.[117]

In the days that followed this first clandestine escape, the rest of the tribe slipped through at various points along the Prossers Plains section of the line. In places they were glimpsed and heard, and on one occasion a warrior speared a sentry in two places as he rekindled his fire. All made it through unscathed.[118] This came as no surprise to the editor of the *Launceston Advertiser*, who had been pessimistic about containing people of such 'quicksightedness and skill' within the cordon. 'Escapes have been known to be made by the Natives', he exclaimed, 'which have almost the appearance of being miraculous.'[119] Nor was Robinson surprised:

> The military operations and armed parties sent out in quest of the hostile natives has frequently been the occasion of much reflection to my mind and the futility of such endeavour has been apparent ... The natives have the advantage in every respect, in their sight, hearing, nay, in all their senses; their sense of smelling also. They can smell a smoke at a long distance, especially if the wind sets towards them. I have known instances of their scenting a kangaroo roasting by the hostile natives. They are at home in the woods; the whole country with few exceptions affords them concealment.[120]

When Robinson asked Woolaytoopinneyer, a Mairremmener woman, how she and her people managed to escape the line, she assured him 'they had no trouble in getting away'.[121]

Aboriginal guides

The Black Line was not entirely white. A number of Tasmanians participated as guides, though the details of their involvement are largely unknown. An exception was Ronekeenarener, one of the two Mairremmener men captured on 25 October. He divulged substantial information to his captors with the aid of 'a civilised Black Boy ... [who] acted as interpreter', and was then shackled and commanded to lead the white men 'to the haunts of his tribe'.[122] Ronekeenarener was praised as a shrewd guide, but since he did not lead them to his countrymen, he may have been shrewder than they realised.[123]

The only other guide we know something about is Kanneherlargenner, or as he was known to the whites, Umarrah. Apparently the leader of a tribe from the Tamar River area, Umarrah had been captured by Gilbert Robertson in November 1828, and became acquainted with the Governor when he was interviewed by the Executive Council later that year. In early 1830, he joined Robinson's expedition around the west coast, but abandoned him once they reached Macquarie Harbour. When Umarrah reappeared in Launceston in October, the Governor requested that he 'readily and cheerfully' join the line as his personal guide and advisor.[124] To this he assented, and by 22 October he had joined the white chief's entourage at Orielton.[125]

Umarrah acted as counsel to the Governor for three weeks, until one day, while 'out with two men, kangaroo hunting, all of a sudden he disappeared'.[126] It is not clear why he joined the campaign, much less why he left it, but it may have been connected to his discovery that one of his two wives was hemmed in by the forces.[127] He later pointed out to Robinson 'the way he went when he left the Line, i.e. by a circuitous route NNE through the thick forest south of the Eastern Marshes', along a traditional 'native road'.[128] Umarrah's brief career as the Governor's *aide de camp* was an undistinguished one, and there is no indication that he was in any way helpful to the operation. As

Robinson soon discovered, Tasmanian guides were only as helpful as they wanted to be.[129]

Behind the line

Some of the Aborigines who avoided the Black Line carried on plundering and killing in its rear. This was particularly true of two Mairremmener tribes: the one ambushed on 25 October, and another that evaded the operation in its early stages. The former regrouped north of the line and immediately launched attacks on four huts in the Eastern Marshes.[130] They then headed south-west, attacking a hut at Jerusalem on 7 November, where they harassed three men, speared a woman 'in several places, and then robbed the hut of every article they could carry away'.[131] Afterwards, on 9 November, they again broke up into smaller war parties that plundered five huts in Dysart Parish.[132] A tribesman was shot in one of these raids, prompting the others to retire into the hills until, for reasons unknown, three of them emerged a week later, fatally spearing the young daughter of a Bagdad settler.[133] But, with the exception of one more robbery, this was their last attack for the year. Where they went is not clear.

To the west, another tribe was taking a heavy toll on the settlements in the rear of the line. In the course of one week, they made up to a dozen attacks on properties between the Ouse and Clyde rivers. They plundered seven huts in just two days, employing the divide and attack strategy that had come to distinguish Mairremmener tactics in the later stages of the war. By 13 November, they had targeted nearly every settler in the district. Then, having accumulated a healthy store of food and blankets, they too disappeared for the remainder of the year, probably heading north onto the sparsely inhabited Central Plateau where the warmer weather would allow them to hunt in relative safety.

Knowledge of the line

What did the Tasmanians know about the Black Line? This question can be divided in two: What did they know at the time, and what did they discover later? Both questions are difficult to answer, but the first is less so. We have accounts from three of the tribes that escaped. One of these was of course Mannalargenna's people, who reported seeing soldiers firing off their guns. Another was the tribe that slipped through near Penstock Lagoon on 13 October. The following year, some of Robinson's envoys told him they had seen soldiers make 'huts and large fires' in this area, and he assumed they were referring to the Black Line.[134]

Both these tribes seem to have realised there were more parties in the field than usual, but how many did they actually see? Their escapes were in early October, well before the order was given for the impressive rows of fires that have come to be associated with the line. In fact, the parties were so widely spaced at this early stage of the campaign, that the escaping tribes probably saw two or three of them at most. The sight of multiple parties was no doubt intimidating, but armed parties were by now familiar hazards, and they were quickly evaded.

The third group that we know became partially aware of the line was the Mairremmener tribe that was ambushed on 25 October. From their perspective, the ambush itself indicated nothing out of the ordinary, but the presence of fires to the north soon alerted them to something more ominous. Depending on weather, vegetation, light and their vantage point, the tribe presumably saw evidence of multiple parties as they made their way through the line. Still, neither this tribe, nor the tribes that escaped in the early stages of the line, could have known how big the line actually was, or what the white men were up to.

What then did the Tasmanians learn of the operation in the weeks and months following their escapes? Mannalargenna's tribe probably learnt the most. At Batman's, they were joined by Mungo, a disillusioned guide who no doubt shared with them what he knew of the campaign.[135]

Later, on Swan Island, Robinson attempted to reinforce the loyalty of Mannalargenna and the other exiles by emphasising the power of the Black Line, and thus the danger of returning to the bush:

> I made known to them the military plans that were in operation against them and ... I then described to them the nature and formation of the Line by tracing it on the ground with a stick, and further informed them that the mighty enemy who were at that time engaged in capturing their countrymen to the southward would shortly appear in formidable array in front of their own territory.[136]

The governor had sent a huge force against them, and how many would he send next time? Although the whites were incapable of repeating such a costly operation, the Aborigines on Swan Island were led to believe otherwise. Robinson's explanation had the desired effect. He noted that 'the whole of them was in tears throughout the whole of the day'.[137] Then, in an almost certainly related act, 'all the aborigines tattooed themselves, the shoulder of some and back and belly of others was completely scarified'.[138]

The other tribes that escaped the line no doubt discovered further evidence of the campaign, in the form of tracks and abandoned campsites. Even though they were seeing only a fraction of the line's environmental impact, these clues probably suggested the operation was larger than they first suspected. But just how large did they think it was? From their limited exposure, they could not have appreciated its full scale, let alone its full implications. Furthermore, there was nothing in their collective memories that even bordered on a precedent for such an event. The Tasmanians would have struggled to fathom anything on that scale, and with that type of organisation. Consequently, the Black Line they experienced probably bore little resemblance to the actual Black Line.

Significance of the line

In 1831, Tasmanians made less than one-third of the attacks they had the previous year (see Figure 3, page 2), but this owed surprisingly little to the Black Line. Their hostility declined, not because the line rendered them meek and mild, but because years of warfare had drastically reduced their strength. Across the island, tribes reached the apex of their resistance at different times. Those in the Norfolk Plains region, for instance, reached theirs around 1827, while the most belligerent tribes peaked in 1830. They had taken a serious toll on the white men, but their numbers were declining, and could not be replenished. The enemy, on the other hand, somehow continued to multiply, and the balance of power swung ever more against the Aborigines. Although these shifts occurred at around the same time as the line, they bore no strong relationship to it.

The significance of the Tasmanians' experience of the Black Line is easy to overemphasise. For one, the parties comprising the line were louder and more visible than the creeping vigilantes they were used to, which made them easier to avoid, and once the tribes had evaded the line, the danger it posed was over. In fact, they may not have realised it, but in the rear of the forces they were safer than usual.

This has not prevented historians echoing Jorgen Jorgenson's claim that '[t]he marvelous facility with which the colony got eventually rid of the Blacks was entirely owing to Sir George Arthur's *levy en masse*'.[139] He insisted that Robinson's success 'was *solely* attributable to the formation of the Line; it showed the Aborigines our strength and energy'.[140] Jorgenson was referring to the historic surrender of the last of the Mairremmener people, many of whom had escaped the line at Prossers Plains. This tribe almost certainly realised the whites had executed some kind of large offensive. As disquieting as this was, however, by the time the Mairremmener surrendered, they had fought hundreds of skirmishes and dodged dozens of armed parties over the preceding decade, so the idea that the line cowered them into submission makes little sense. As we will see in Chapter 6, the Mairremmener's decision to surrender was driven by far more pressing concerns.

CHAPTER SIX

THE WAR'S END

White

The Black War has ended here after 2 months' campaign … but I fear we shall not so soon be quit of the blacks.[1]

Alexander Reid, Bothwell

The failure of the Black Line cast a dark cloud over the frontier community. It had been the biggest effort the colony was capable of mustering, and it had failed. The question now weighing on everyone's minds was expressed succinctly by William Lawrence in the line's closing days: 'If, as is most likely, the present attempt fails, I know not what more can be done, I have not as yet heard of one feasible scheme.'[2] Nowhere was this anxiety felt more acutely than 'in the breasts of lonely settlers', wrote Lawrence's fellow linesman, George Lloyd: 'the untoward result [of the operation] produced a feeling of deep despondence, and shed over their future prospects a gloom from which there seemed to be no possible relief.'[3] But, just as despair was setting in, a glimmer of hope appeared.

Colonists knew the natives did not attack as frequently in the summer months, but they seemed quieter than usual. By late January, few serious incidents had been reported, and some colonists began to suspect the line had been effective after all. 'What has become of all the Aboriginal tribes?' asked the *Colonial Times* on 28 January 1831:

> Were they all killed or taken prisoners during the late expedition? [These] are now the generally repeated questions. We are exceedingly happy to say that, to all appearances, if they were not taken or destroyed, they appear at all events to have been so much frightened as to prevent, for the present, their repeating their visits to the civilised inhabitants.[4]

But the newspaper's optimism was short lived. Even as it was going to print, couriers were bringing the news south of the spearing of a man and a child on the West Tamar.[5] Then, on 29 January, only three months after the blacks had killed her husband, Mary McCasker 'was most barbarously murdered' at Dairy Plains, and all hopes for peace seemed dashed.[6]

Experienced frontiersmen were struck by a remarkable fact: the more blacks they killed, the more there seemed to be. Europeans found it extremely hard to identify the individuals or tribes responsible for attacking them, so they were never sure how many they were facing. In hindsight, we know there could scarcely have been 100 natives operating in the settled districts in 1831, but to terrified colonists, this number would have sounded absurdly low. The frequency and geographic distribution of attacks, combined with exaggerated rumours of tribes comprising hundreds of warriors, led colonists to massively overestimate the force arrayed against them. Most assumed there remained at least 500 eastern natives, and some thought the number was in the thousands.[7] It seemed only logical that a sizeable population was necessary to generate so much commotion, but the 'vast savage hordes' that haunted the colonists' imaginations bore little resemblance to the desperate remnant they were actually facing. It was to be the final year of the war, but no one knew that then, nor did anyone suspect it.

One week in March

For reasons they did not understand, the year 1831 was particularly severe on northern colonists. In March alone, they suffered a series of brutal attacks that unleashed panic throughout the district. On the East Tamar, Mrs Cunningham:

> was at work in the garden when the natives came down. She was first speared in the back. Immediately she caught up her infant and ran towards the house, the blacks following her. As she ran she received another spear from behind; and before she could reach the house, having several times fallen, a native met her and knocked her down with a waddie. As she fell, she received another spear, which entered her body, passing nearly through her. She then drew herself over the child, when the savages came up, and stabbed her with spears about the body till she fainted … she lingered in extreme agony till the following morning, when she expired. The infant was much bruised, but is not mortally wounded.[8]

Five days later, two soldiers were wounded by another tribe at Norfolk Plains, reporting that their assailants 'exceed 100 or 150 large stout men'.[9] Everyone was put on guard and defences redoubled, but as usual, the natives made a mockery of these efforts. At 9am on 19 March, the same tribe attacked the Lawrence property at the base of the Western Tiers. This was the first of five Lake River properties attacked by this war party in as many hours. At least one man was killed and three seriously wounded.[10] One of the assigned servants on the scene hastily scribbled the following note to his master's neighbour:

> Dear Mr O'Connor, You have often been warning us against the natives. We always said they would never would come here but alas they have made their appearance … poor Crowhurst and York [are] dreadfully speared. We don't expect Crowhurst to live but one of the men that came galloped off as fast as ever he could to Dr Paton. Now what is to be done? *I am frightened out of my life.*[11]

The palpable terror exuded in this letter was representative of the feeling throughout the district. 'All is terror and dismay in this part of the Colony', wrote one local settler in the days following the attacks, 'not a man appears willing to go out to do his work.'[12] Although the level of black violence fluctuated throughout 1831, the fear, frustration and anger it produced never went away. Indeed, these emotions welled more intensely with every passing month.

Finding a solution

When he returned to Hobart after the disbanding of the Black Line, Arthur immediately convened the Executive Council to discuss the 'distressing and difficult question' of what to try next. He had finally given up on the possibility of peaceful coexistence, realising only two options remained: either the natives should be removed (by capture or conciliation) or they must be shot. Although he undoubtedly desired the former, Arthur feared the 'latter alternative ... could alone be looked to for preserving the lives of the settlers'.[13] It would appear that, having finally seen the situation for himself, Arthur came to appreciate the frustration and angst felt by those in the interior. At the very least, he was now convinced of the futility of trying to hunt down people who appeared to simply vanish into thin air, thus he disbanded the civilian roving parties.

The idea of concealing men in stock-huts, for the purpose of ambushing approaching natives, gained popularity at the same time as the roving parties were making it clear that 'travelling about at random, and scouring the country at large, can only by accident succeed'.[14] 'It would be better', wrote the *Hobart Town Courier* in February 1830, 'to remain in ambush at good commanding outposts, and wait patiently for an opportunity to arrest the blacks as they pass.'[15] In fact, even some roving parties had realised this and begun setting such traps the previous year.[16] The first vindication of the tactic occurred near Fingal on

30 October 1830, when a detachment of constables split into three parties, each of which concealed themselves in nearby huts. Major Gray reported the result to Hobart:

> the natives have been very troublesome of the past week, they have com-
> mitted robberies at almost all the huts on the road from this place to Mr
> Talbot's, when they were met by four of a party of constables from Camp-
> bell Town under Mr Sampson, on Saturday evening about four o'clock
> after nearly an hour's watching they made a rush at a man of Mr Talbot's
> who was sent out as a decoy by the constables.[17]

In the affray that followed, Talbot's man was speared in the leg, and two natives were shot dead (as noted in Chapter 5). As it happened, this success was never to be repeated, but at the time it garnered consider-able support for the tactic, and helps explain why 'ambush huts' featured strongly in post-Black Line deliberations.

The Aborigines Committee announced in its report of 4 February 1831 that it supported conciliatory aims, but 'in the meantime, for the protection of the distant settlers and stock-keepers, parties of armed men (four in number) should be stationed in the most remote stock-huts'.[18] Ostensibly, the purpose of setting these ambushes was to capture the unsuspecting assailants, but the men involved understood their remit differently. In October 1831, Robinson passed a farm at the foot of the Blue Hills in which there were 'nine men in the hut, armed with ten guns and a blunderbuss ... and these men affirm that if they had seen them [the blacks] they should certainly have shot them'.[19] To facilitate these new measures, as many as 150 stock-huts were turned into ambush huts, the number of soldiers in the interior was increased, and five strong military posts were established to intersect native migratory routes. In addition, temporary barracks were constructed at Spring Bay, Richmond and Break O'Day Plains, while the barracks at Sorell and New Norfolk were rebuilt and extended.[20]

The government's redoubled commitment to military protection for the exposed settlements was soon evident. In the north-east, Robinson found troops 'stationed at all the out-stations ... and several farms have military stationed at them', while in Hobart and Launceston, large standing forces were ready to be deployed at a moment's notice.[21] In January, for instance, no less than 50 soldiers were sent in pursuit after natives made incursions east of Launceston.[22] Not long thereafter, Lieutenant-Colonel Logan marched 93 troops from Hobart to engage a tribe that had begun 'committing depredations' in the Derwent Valley. In emulation of the Black Line, Logan deployed his men in a cordon across the Black Snake Gully and marched in this formation for three days without success.[23]

A non-military campaign of similar proportions was initiated at Norfolk Plains following the attacks of late January. The police magistrate, Malcolm Smith, ordered all the district's ticket-of-leave men, along with all the assigned convicts that local settlers could spare, to assemble at the police station on 7 February. From here the men were directed to 'such places as the natives are known to frequent' where they were to build 'sham huts' and lie in ambush.[24] Costly as this operation must have been to settlers and the government, it was undoubtedly more disagreeable to the men forced yet again from their homes into the most dangerous parts of the frontier. It is unclear how many convicts were involved, or how long they stayed in the field, but they appear to have had little success.

Despite this up-scaled military presence, the government continued to insist that 'the chief object [was] to conciliate and not to destroy these people'.[25] The major shift in its approach after the Black Line was the abandonment of 'coexistence' for a policy of exiling all captured blacks to Bass Strait. With growing fervour, the press had been calling for removal since 1826, but those on the frontier realised the problem was not what to do with the blacks once they were in custody; it was how to capture them in the first place.

Although the Governor was not sanguine about ending the war

by bloodless means, he had no choice but to try. Realising the natives' aversion to armed parties, and the latter's tendency to shoot all potential captives, Arthur sought alternative means of encouraging colonists to 'take them alive'. On 25 February 1830, Government Order no. 2 appeared in the *Hobart Town Courier*, stating that 'a reward of £5 shall be given for every adult aboriginal Native, and £2 for every child, who shall be captured, and delivered alive at any one of the police stations'. In the two years that followed this order private settlers made several captures, but their rewards greatly exceeded the promised amounts. George Anstey, for example, received 500 acres [202 ha] for taking one man, two women and a child.[26] In this case, no blood was spilled, but recognising the difficulty of the task, Arthur set no requirement for delivering captives unhurt, and no limit on the number that could be killed in the fray. This omission allowed Humphrey Howells, who led an ambush on the Shannon River in August 1831, to receive 1000 acres [405 ha] of land for capturing one native, despite killing at least two others in the process.[27] The bounties, therefore, provided no safeguard against bloodshed, just as they made no significant contribution to ending the war.

The friendly mission

The only real hope for a non-violent solution was the 'friendly mission'. In March 1829, George Augustus Robinson was appointed storekeeper at a recently established ration depot for natives on Bruny Island. Robinson never intended to be just a storekeeper though, and he immediately turned his attention to the natives' material and spiritual 'improvement'. However, his charges died quicker than he could convert them. Within six months, about two-thirds of the Bruny Islanders had died from respiratory disease.[28] Realising the enterprise was unsustainable, Robinson sought permission to draft the survivors into a 'conciliatory mission' that would journey around the island's west coast delivering a 'message of peace'. Accompanied by a troop of natives and convicts, the mission embarked on its harrowing journey on 27 January 1830.[29] In the eight months that followed, the party made contact with several tribes, laying what Robinson believed were the foundations for peaceful dialogue. But, by the time the party re-emerged in early October, the situation in the east had worsened dramatically.

When Robinson arrived on the outskirts of Launceston, preparations for the Black Line were in full swing. Coexistence, he now realised, was no longer a possibility. He resolved to continue the friendly mission, but with the new objective of securing the surrender and removal of the remaining tribes. As the line marched south, Robinson's party proceeded in the opposite direction, hoping to confer with the remnant north-east people, and success quickly followed. In November alone, Robinson and his envoys secured the surrender of 13 natives, prompting him to write to the Governor claiming he could remove 'the entire black population'.[30] Arthur may not have been entirely convinced by this, but he understood the value of the friendly mission for his reputation in London, and gave Robinson his support.

Opposition to the enterprise was widespread from the start. The public had lost all patience with the government's conciliatory rhetoric. On the frontier, Robinson regularly encountered the sneers and non-cooperation of colonists who felt the time had long since passed for diplomacy. In Launceston and Hobart, the press mocked the mission and its prospects for success.[31] The prevailing mood was epitomised by the *Launceston Advertiser*, which demanded to know: 'Can it be that we are to thus suffer these people to destroy our Fellow Colonists, and is the Government to sit down supinely and view this destruction calmly and preach conciliation? No! rather let the sentence be extermination.'[32]

Thomas and Parker

In the opening days of spring 1831, the few colonists who remained unconvinced of the necessity of exterminating the blacks, received a resounding 'I told you so' from their more pessimistic acquaintances. The brutal killing of Captain Bartholomew Thomas and his overseer James Parker at Port Sorell on 31 August shook the colony to its foundations, and triggered an unprecedented surge of fear and anger. Thomas was a highly respected veteran, whose brother Jocelyn was Colonial Treasurer and a member of the Executive Council. Thomas was sympathetic towards Aborigines. In fact, he and Parker had been attempting to conciliate the people who killed them. Outraged, the public mourned the men as martyrs of the lost cause of conciliation. Thomas and Parker were the last colonists to die in the war, but nobody knew that at the time. Indeed, in previous years native hostility had increased in the spring, so the killings were seen by many as ushering in yet another season of violence.

The public outcry was especially vitriolic in the north, where it seemed exterminationist sentiment was now pervasive. Not long after the bodies were found, the *Launceston Advertiser* denounced the killings as the 'barbarity of a race which no kindness can soften, and which nothing short of utter annihilation can subdue'. Thomas and Parker, the editor lamented, were 'victims of a mistaken faith in the sincerity of these blood-thirsty savages'.[33] For its part, Launceston's other newspaper, the recently established *Independent*, believed this latest outrage:

call[ed] aloud for retribution, deep and lasting, not only upon the perpetrators of the deeds, should they come within our power, but upon the whole race ... The whole colony cries out upon the occasion. It is useless they say, and we adopt and re-echo the opinion, to no longer attempt to hold terms with these worse than untamed beasts of prey ... What, then, is to be done? For, with the return of the season that produced the mighty armament of last year, something must be done! Otherwise what settler is there who can consider himself and his family in security from the dreadful visitations of the Aborigines![34]

But it was not just newspaper editors who felt this way. One settler wrote to the *Independent* in early October, asserting that colonists now faced a simple question: 'Are we to kill them or are they to kill us?'[35] The record suggests that most colonists agreed conciliatory measures had reached an impasse, and that the only course left was extermination.

The 'Freycinet Line'

In the tumultuous wake of the Thomas and Parker killings, a choking anxiety hung thick over the interior. The *Independent* expressed the concern on everyone's mind: 'Who can tell to what lengths they (the aborigines) may run this season, beyond all precedence?'[36] Receiving reports of 'great numbers' of native fires near Oatlands, the *Colonial Times* predicted that the tribes were 'undoubtedly approaching' the east coast and that 'the depredations of these misguided creatures, will shortly be recommenced, with more desperation than even last season.'[37] Sure enough, several weeks later they descended on the settlement at Great Swanport, robbing huts and causing panic.

On 19 October, the men at George Meredith's whaling station reported seeing between 12 and 30 natives pass onto the Freycinet Peninsula. Once the sighting was confirmed on 21 October, Meredith and the district's other settlers rallied their servants and, together with ten soldiers, formed a stationary cordon across the narrow part of the Peninsula.[38] Word was sent out and by 23 October about 100 armed men were in position.[39]

Many of the men who took up arms on the 'Freycinet Line' had served on the Black Line the previous year. Just as before, the majority of participants were convicts and soldiers who had no choice in serving. Likewise, both operations consisted of equally spaced posts between which men, under military supervision, took shifts patrolling. Compared to the Black Line though, there were some major differences in the way the Freycinet campaign was experienced. First, the men had not endured weeks of hellish marching before establishing their static cordon. And second, they were guarding an isthmus only two kilometres wide, so hopes were high that, this time, the natives would not escape.

After just four days, however, the enemy slipped through the cordon.[40] The settler John Lyne recalled his experience:

> the moon didn't rise until 10 pm and the fires were becoming low. It was my turn to patrol, I was at the time [urging] the men to keep good watch as the native dogs were seen amongst the fires in front, and after passing one of the soldiers on duty about 50 yards [45 m] I heard him call 'Halt'. He comes there firing off his gun to give the alarm and on my running quick I heard a rustle as though a mob of wild cattle were passing but could see nothing.

The news was confirmed the next morning, when Lyne and his demoralised comrades 'tracked their foot marks very plain'.[41]

This result was a huge blow to a community already exhausted from years of failed efforts to contain the native threat. George Meredith, the man who had initiated the campaign, wrote to the Governor with evident frustration:

> I must beg with deference to submit that the local government has too long delayed those energetic and efficient measures which can alone be relied upon under existing circumstances, and although the happy alternative is no longer an option, that of securing the Aborigines and removing them without the effusion of blood, their atrocities may be checked by a generally organised plan and one encouragement held out to those who from habit and experience are competent to the particular service required.[42]

One does not have to read too far between the lines here. Meredith was imploring the Governor to offer rewards to experienced black-killers, in the hope they would finish the job.

Surrender

Two months later, the job was finished, but not in the way Meredith or his fellow colonists expected. On New Year's Eve 1831, Robinson and his envoys negotiated the voluntary surrender of the once powerful Mairremmener people, of whom just 16 men, nine women and one child remained. Seven days later, Robinson and his 'conciliated blacks' walked into Hobart amidst a remarkable scene. The *Colonial Times* pointed out that it had been 'some years since the inhabitants of Hobart Town have witnessed a tribe of Aborigines in their native state'.[43] In the interest of taste, the party was issued trousers before entering the town, but this did not diminish the novelty of the spectacle. Citizens abandoned their employments and proceeded en masse to Elizabeth Street where they lined up to witness the arrival of this most infamous of 'the savage tribes'. Onlookers puzzled at how such an unimpressive remnant could have generated so much fear. The *Hobart Town Courier* remarked at how the 'very small number, which is now found to compose these tribes must strike many of our readers [as surprising], especially those who supposed them to amount to thousands'.[44]

Remembering the war

With the exception of the sporadic violence that continued in the north-west (see Chapter 7), the surrender of this last tribe signalled the end of the Black War. It took some time for incredulous colonists to accept that the removal of just 16 warriors had actually ended the violence, but it was soon apparent that 'tranquility' had indeed been restored. Everyone felt a great sense of relief, but the war had taken its toll on frontier colonists, and it would not easily be forgotten. For more than half a decade the men, women and children of the interior had lived in fear. As Louisa Meredith remarked, it was a time 'when every bush within spear throw of the house was a source of danger'; no one who had lived through the war could forget 'the horrors, and terrors, and hair-breadth escapes'.[45]

Virtually overnight, newspapers and private correspondents all but ceased discussing the blacks. Colonists would occasionally mention them publicly, but generally only when complaining about the cost of the Flinders Island mission to which the survivors had been removed. Only when it was suggested that the surviving 47 be allowed to return, did it become apparent that memories of the war were still vivid and painful. On 20 August 1847, some 200 men assembled at the Cornwall Hotel in Launceston to draft a petition against the motion. Above all, those attending insisted that the new Governor, Sir William Denison, was under a dangerous misapprehension. They maintained that neither he, nor anyone who had arrived in the colony after 1831 could appreciate the consequences 'when uncivilised creatures with all their savage and blood-thirsty propensities are admitted [*sic*] to escape into the bush to perpetrate all sorts of depredations and atrocities'.[46] Those present saw it as their duty to remind these newcomers of 'those days of terror … the dreadful state of affairs, too vivid in the memory of old colonists ever to be forgotten'.[47]

If the thought of repatriating 47 ageing and sickly natives could evoke such powerful feelings among the gentlemen of Launceston, it is fair to assume that the topic was no less emotive on the frontier. 'It is a pity', grumbled one veteran frontiersman:

> that even one of the black wretches was allowed to escape without being roasted alive which was too good for them. And now there they are the biggest villains of every tribe who were clever enough to escape summary vengeance – there they are pampered up at Flinders Island with food and clothing, and Robinson and Parson Dove to pray for them, while everything that money can do is lavished on the innocent fiends that were leaders in the warfare against the settlers … If Robinson had left us alone we soon would have demolished them, and left nothing but their bones to tell the tale.[48]

Hundreds of colonists had been killed, and many more were left physically or psychologically scarred. Not surprisingly, the horrors of the war were seared deep into their memories, and the bitterness smouldered long after the enemy had been banished.

Black

The Tasmanians knew their struggle was lost well before 1831. In the east, there remained no more than five tribes, comprising maybe 80 or 90 individuals. Isolated in small groups, they may not have been aware of just how depleted their numbers were; yet the unsustainability of their situation could not have escaped them. Most had seen the majority of their families killed, which must have had a profound effect on their attitudes and experiences. Although they no longer entertained the possibility of victory, hatred and desperation drove them to press the war. Aboriginal attacks took on an especially brutal character in 1831, even though fewer were made overall. White observers noticed that their hostilities evinced a boldness hitherto unseen; though by now, the line between bold and desperate was irrevocably blurred.

Collaborators

Not all Tasmanians were at war with the invaders. While most were being swept up in the burgeoning conflict, a few chose instead to collaborate with the invaders, and become trackers and guides for the roving parties. Notable guides included 'Black Bill', 'Mungo', Cowerterminna, Lackerla, 'Umarrah', 'Boomer Jack' and the women Karnebutcher and Numberloetinnare. However, the best known of all the roving party guides was Kickertopoller, or 'Black Tom'. Throughout the 1820s, Kickertopoller alternated between guiding and killing the white men. He had been raised from boyhood by a Hobart settler, and was first employed as a guide by exploration parties in the early 1820s. But, like many Aboriginal 'orphans', he eventually rejected white society and returned to his kinsfolk.

In contrast, most Aboriginal guides were prisoners who had agreed to assist the white men in exchange for their release. Some later absconded (Umarrah and Kickertopoller both escaped on several occasions), but others remained with the roving parties. Why they assisted the invaders is not fully understood, but we can gain some insight by examining the motivations of Robinson's envoys.

The friendly mission was a truly remarkable achievement, made possible by the skill, exertion and diplomacy of Tasmanians from regions throughout the island. It was also a harrowing and dangerous under-taking. So why did they support it? Some probably assisted Robinson with a mind to saving their surviving kinsfolk from certain death at the hands of armed white men. More often though, they had ambiva-lent or even hostile relations with the tribes Robinson was searching for. Although there were alliances between particular tribes, there was no pan-Aboriginal solidarity in Tasmania, so the envoys must have had other reasons for supporting the mission.

A number of possibilities present themselves. The envoys appear to have held Robinson in high regard – at least in the beginning – and as an influential white man they stood to gain much from his patronage. One obvious benefit was a fairly constant supply of flour, sugar, tea and tobacco. No less important was the physical security Robinson and his entourage of white servants provided. This allowed the envoys to hunt in relative safety, but above all, to sleep easy at night in the knowledge that they would not be ambushed. They also realised that Robinson was their only hope for a peaceful solution to the war, and for gaining some concessions in the process. He was, after all, a man who bore the authority of the Governor – the chief of all white men.

The envoys were the last remnants of their tribes. Woorrady, for instance, was the last adult male of the Bruny Island people, so most of the relationships, ceremonies and traditions that had once dominated his world were no more. Remarkably, this most trusted of Robinson's envoys continued to lead songs, stories and dances during his years with the mission, despite the loss of almost all his friends and family, and of the world in which he grew up. For Woorrady and the other envoys, there were just two alternatives to joining Robinson's mission: continuing to fight an unwinnable war, or languishing helplessly on a windswept island in Bass Strait.

Until recently, most historians have seen the envoys as naive dupes. In 1875, for instance, James Calder claimed Robinson 'had acquired an ascendancy so complete over those of these simple minded savages whom he had subdued to his service, as to have left them almost literally without the faculty of volition'.[49] However, the evidence tells a different story. Robinson was totally dependent on his envoys, not just for locating and negotiating with the hostile tribes, but for staying alive.[50] They understood this, and were able to exercise considerable power in their roles as guides, providers and diplomats. Indeed, to Robinson's constant frustration, they often did as they pleased.[51]

Nothing exemplifies the agency displayed by the envoys better than their subtle sabotage of Robinson's mission. From October to December 1831, Robinson and 14 envoys zigzagged across the centre of the island in quest of the much-feared Mairremmener people. The surrender of this last tribe is remembered as Robinson's finest hour, but closer inspection reveals how powerless he was without his envoys' cooperation. Despite their façade of loyalty, most were far keener to hunt and enjoy the constant supply of the white man's food than to locate the people they were sure would kill them.[52] For three months Robinson was frustrated by their manoeuvres to stall and misdirect the mission with deception and theatrics, until on 28 December, for some unknown reason:

the natives broke all their spears and threw away their waddies, except MANNALARGENNA, a proof of their desire to conform; and MAN-NALARGENNA sent away his big dog that barked … the people evinced eagerness to go after the natives, which shewed (if such a circumstance was necessary) their sincerity to do their duty. I urged them on and told them the Governor only wanted me to get to the Big River tribe and then our troubles would be over, we should not have to go after any more and they could then hunt.[53]

That afternoon, the envoys located the first signs of the Mairremmener who had conveniently eluded their search for so long. Three days later, in an atmosphere of extreme anxiety, a select embassy of eight managed to negotiate an interview with them. Robinson related his version of events in an official report:

[As the embassy returned] I heard their war whoop by which I knew they were advancing towards me. I also heard them rattle their spears as they drew nearer. At this moment MANNALARGENNA the principal chief leaped on his feet in great alarm saying that the natives were coming to spear us. He urged me to run away. Finding I would not do so he immediately took up his spears and kangaroo rug and went away. Some of the other natives were about to follow his example but I prevailed upon them to stop. From their advancing with the war whoop the aborigines as well as ourselves considered that they were coming to us with hostile intentions and that they had either killed the natives who had been sent from us, or that those natives had joined the hostile tribes.[54]

As they came closer, however, the Mairremmener lowered their spears and a surrender was negotiated (see Figure 10). How this motley assortment of collaborators managed to navigate such a strange and dangerous set of circumstances is a mystery, but clearly they were not the credulous simpletons that Calder assumed. Nor were they the traitors they are sometimes imagined to be. Indeed, by late 1830 the *opportunity* to surrender was usually all that distinguished the envoys from the war parties.

Final resistance

Over the course of the Black War, a combination of growing desperation and resentment propelled the Tasmanians to gradually abandon their traditional modes of subsistence, and devote more and more time to killing and plundering the white men. This meant that, despite their relentlessly declining population, Aboriginal belligerence intensified up until 1830. Although the capacity of the tribes to make war had been decreasing more or less since the invasion began, the extent to which they used that capacity had risen exponentially from the mid-1820s. In other words, by the time Tasmanians began investing all their resources in attacking the whites, there were scarcely any of them left. Eastern Tasmanians made more attacks than ever in 1830, but these were in fact just the death throes of their society (see Figure 3, page 2).

The pressure from armed parties increased in 1831, forcing survivors into more marginal and less familiar areas. This was especially evident in the presence of Mairremmener people in the northern foothills of the Great Western Tiers. Since 1827, this area had seen almost no violence, presumably because the local tribes had been killed off. But now it was assailed by a Mairremmener tribe that had travelled north over the Central Plateau. These people retreated south in March, but remarkably, they undertook the journey again that August. Their decision to brave the frigid plateau in the depths of winter is indicative of the danger they were facing in the south. When they reached the northern plains in late August, hungry and exhausted from their trek, they immediately began robbing stock-huts. Between 17 and 23 August, they attacked four huts, spearing a stock-keeper and a little girl, before crossing the plains, and following the Rubicon River north to Port Sorell. Here they slew their last two victims.

The circumstances surrounding the killing of Thomas and Parker speak volumes about the desperate state of the surviving Tasmanians in 1831. Robinson heard 'there was three tribes – Big River, Oyster

Bay and Port Sorell – present', but the group probably comprised the remnants of at least four different tribes.[55] And this was not the only sign of distress. There appears to have been a complete absence of children and elderly among this tribe, neither of whom were adapted to rapid, stealthy movements, let alone to crossing the plateau in winter. Among this young and motley group were several locals who had received mixed treatment from Thomas' men in the past.[56] Nevertheless, hunger seems to have prompted two men, Mackamee and Wowaree, to approach one of Thomas' huts. The Captain, whom Wowaree called 'Kandownee' (chief), gave the emissaries some bread and requested they lead him and Parker to their camp.[57] Thomas hoped to conciliate the tribe, but soon after arriving at the camp, and without warning, one of the men snatched Parker's shotgun, while another clubbed him to death with a waddie.[58] Thomas ran for his life, but did not get far before succumbing to almost a dozen spear wounds.[59]

Perhaps because of their diverse composition, those present had disagreed over whether to kill the two white men, and some of the women tried ardently to stop the slaughter.[60] Three of these women stormed off, but along with Calama-Rowenge, Mackamee and Wowaree, who were attempting to entice them back, they were captured by Thomas' men after being lured with food to the homestead. The six captives were taken to the George Town jail, where they were denied blankets, fire and food until one of the women, Nongoneepitta, agreed to direct authorities to the bodies.

Thomas' and Parker's killers were, it seems, possessed by an emphatic hatred of all white men. Mackamee told Robinson the men were slain 'in retaliation for injuries they [his people] had received from the whites'.[61] Tasmanians had long harboured such resentment, but the callous ferocity of this killing was especially characteristic of the attacks made in 1831, which suggests a peculiar bitterness was driving certain survivors to take greater risks in pursuit of indiscriminate revenge. The proportion of Aboriginal attacks that resulted in death or wounding had decreased steadily every year since 1826, but it spiked again in 1831, as did the percentage of such attacks on women and children.[62] This resurgence of brutality was not a last-ditch attempt to win the war, but a reflection of the pain and acrimony that had taken hold of the last free Tasmanians.

Seventy attacks were recorded in the east in 1831, compared to 250 the previous year (see Figure 3, page 2). This is indicative of how swiftly the fighting capacity of the remaining tribes declined. None of this was lost on the Tasmanians, who had by now accepted their fate.[63] 'They were the worn out relics of their nation', wrote John West; '[s]ome, who later gave themselves up, stated that they had been very unhappy: they had gone over the country, searching for their lost friends, of whom they could gain no tidings.'[64] Robinson also wrote of the Tasmanians' growing sense of isolation: 'My sable companions frequently asked me what had become of the natives, as they had not discovered any traces of them.'[65]

Those who continued the fight were tired and despondent, and might well have considered surrendering long before encountering the friendly mission had they reason to think a viable solution existed. Arthur was probably right when he observed in 1830:

> These miserable beings, I make no doubt, are wearied with the harassing
> life they have endured for a considerable time past, and would gladly be
> reconciled if they knew our real intentions towards them were those of
> kindness; but, unfortunately, the most conciliatory measures of the Gov-
> ernment have been already frequently rendered nugatory by the barbarity
> of runaway convicts, or of detached stock-keepers.[66]

It must have been difficult for the Tasmanians to imagine what such a solution would look like. There is no reason to think the idea of removing to an island had even occurred to them until Robinson and his envoys proposed it. At the same time, the thought of living amicably along-side the white men was clearly absurd. Why would all those thousands of independently acting white men suddenly cease trying to kill them? To the last of the free Tasmanians, hiding was the only alternative to fighting. It is telling that Robinson's offer of a bloodless escape from their nightmarish ordeal was swiftly accepted in just about every instance. For those who wanted to live, surrender was their only option.

Surrender

Robinson and his envoys secured a trickle of surrenders between November 1830 and August 1831, which was followed on 31 December 1831 by the surrender of the Mairremmener people described above. Wearied, but resolute, this last tribe agreed to accompany the mission to Hobart. Robinson wrote ahead:

> I have promised them a conference with the Lieut. Govr and that the Governor will be sure to redress all their grievances. I earnestly hope that every possible kindness and attention may be shewn to these people for they cannot and ought not to be looked upon as captives. They have placed themselves under my protection and are desirous for peace.[67]

On 7 January, this war-torn remnant arrived in the capital, and as they strode towards Government House, parting crowds of curious onlookers, they saw for the first time the true scale of what they had been fighting. The imposing buildings, the alien sounds and smells, and the sheer number of whites bombarded their senses in ways now difficult to imagine. It was an overwhelming experience, and one that confirmed the invaders' insurmountable power. According to the *Colonial Times*:

> the view with which they were induced to accompany Mr Robinson was that they should seek redress from the Governor, whom, next to Mr Robinson, they had been [led] to consider the greatest man in the Island. These men, it is said, were bent upon spearing His Excellency, provided he did not grant them the redress they were seeking. The whole mob immediately proceeded to Government House, when His Excellency came out to meet

them, and after consulting some time with those of the tame mob that could speak English, he gave to each of these savage looking warriors a loaf of bread, after which they retired to the green sward, at another part of the premises, when the tribe was sent for; On the first sound of the musical instruments the astonishment with which they listened was truly wonderful; there was a degree of fear portrayed on their countenances, but as the music continued they became more calm.[68]

Unfortunately, the condescending nature of the press coverage tells us little about how the Tasmanians experienced this extraordinary event. Adding to the mystery, no record exists of their interview with the Governor. We know only that they were soon aboard the *Tamar*, bound for Bass Strait. According to the captain, 'during the whole passage they sat on the vessel's bulwark, shaking little bags of human bones, apparently as a charm against the danger to which they felt exposed'.[69]

So what convinced the Tasmanians to surrender? Henry Reynolds argued convincingly that they chose to surrender and relocate to Bass Strait on three conditions. First, 'their customs were to be respected, and not broken into by any rash or misguided interference'.[70] It is not clear whether the Aborigines demanded Robinson promise this, but it probably carried some weight with them. Second, Robinson 'told them that they should have everything they wanted … plenty of tea, Sugar and flour, and have fine houses, Blankets, Rugs and Bedding when they came to Flinders Island'.[71] Given their fondness for such goods, and the difficulties they now had subsisting, this would have been a highly appealing offer.

The third and most contentious condition was Robinson's assurance that all Tasmanians who agreed to 'cease their depredations' could return to their country once the violence had subsided. In his journal for 27 August 1831, Robinson wrote:

I omit no opportunity of impressing upon the mind of the chief and the other natives that they are to remain in their own country; and that I am anxious to get to them for the purpose of going to others, and that I will leave a man to take care of them and that some of the [sealers'] women shall stay with them. At this arrangement they are much pleased and say it is very good indeed.[72]

There is considerable evidence that Robinson made the same promises in all his negotiations, though it is not clear whether these conditions were demanded or merely accepted by the surviving tribes.[73] They may have been willing to fight to the last if unsatisfied with Robinson's terms, but given their dire situation, they were probably drawn to any resolution that ended the torment, and preserved their lives. They could not have imagined that, within just a few years, most of them would sicken and die in a strange land. The Russian Lieutenant Vilgelm Linden, who visited Hobart in 1870, reasoned that:

It wasn't persuasion that made the indigenous Tasmanians leave their native forests – it was their hopeless situation. If they had known what awaited them, they would doubtless have chosen to die of hunger like hunted beasts in their dens.[74]

As it happens, we know nothing of the regrets the exiled Tasmanians took to their graves, though there were surely moments when they paused to envy their fallen comrades, who were spared the horror of witnessing their society gasp its last breath.

CHAPTER SEVEN

THE NORTH-WEST FRONTIER

The north-west theatre of the Black War (see Figure 1B, page xvii) was in many ways remarkably similar to the eastern theatre, but in important ways it was also very different. The first thing to note is the timing. Violence in the east began at Risdon in 1804, and had ceased by 1832. In the north-west, however, the first violence did not erupt until 1827, and it continued until 1842. The people involved in the north-west conflict were also distinctive. The colonists were exclusively servants of the Van Diemen's Land Company, a chartered enterprise that had been granted a monopoly on the region. Tasmanians in the north-west were culturally, technologically and linguistically distinct from those to the east, and they appear to have had very little contact with them.[1] Thus, there are a number of geographical and temporal, but also cultural and circumstantial features of the north-west conflict that recommend it for independent analysis.

White

The Van Diemen's Land Company was overseen by a board of directors in England, and managed in the north-west by its chief agent, Edward Curr.

In late 1826, the company's headquarters were established at Circular Head, while a survey team began searching the unexplored north-west region for suitable sheep grazing pastures. Not much was found beyond the Hampshire and Surrey hills and the areas around Circular Head and Cape Grim. These tracts, initially manned by 24 convicts and several free overseers, became the focal points of the company's grazing operations.[2] As chief agent and magistrate, Curr held total authority in the north-west. Branded the 'Potentate of the North' by the *Hobart Town Courier*, 'he was an icy man' who soon gained a reputation for ruthlessness.[3]

Sex was again the primary catalyst for conflict. There were very few white women in the colony generally, but initially there seem to have been only two in the north-west, Curr's wife and Superintendent Adey's wife. Jorgen Jorgenson, who worked for the company in 1827, warned the Governor that Curr's shepherds 'had designs of violating the [native] women'.[4] He would be repeatedly vindicated. At Circular Head in 1830, for instance, Mr Reeves told Robinson that 'a female aborigine was kept by a stock-keeper for about a month, after which she was taken out and shot'.[5] An even more graphic account was given to John Stokes of the *Beagle*, who spoke with a convict at Stony Head in 1836: 'He had spent the early part of his servitude at Circular Head, where he was for some time in charge of the native woman caught stealing flour at a shepherd's hut, belonging to the Van Diemen's Land Agricultural Company.' In the course of conversation, the man confessed 'he kept the poor creature chained up like a wild beast; and whenever he wanted her to do anything, applied a burning stick, a fire-brand snatched from the hearth, to her skin!'[6]

When the conflict began in earnest in November 1827, it was over women. Robinson's envoys told him that at Cape Grim 'the Company's shepherds had got the native women into their hut and wanted to take liberties with them, that the men resented it and speared one man in the thigh; that they [the stockmen] then shot one man dead'.[7] In response to this killing, the tribe destroyed 118 of the company's ewes, spearing and clubbing some, and herding the rest over a cliff.[8] An escalating cycle of retribution had begun, and the company's men were determined to strike a decisive blow.

Curr informed the company's directors on 14 January 1828 that the cutter *Fanny* had been sent to Cape Grim a few days after the spearing of the ewes. There, Captain Richard Frederick:

> took the opportunity of going in quest of them, with three other men. They came about nightfall on a tribe of about seventy men, but it was judged better to take day light for the intended attack, and the party drew off until morning. It rained heavily during the night and when they approached in the morning close to the Natives with the intent of attacking them, not a musket would go off and they were obliged to retreat without firing a shot.[9]

This version of events might have gone unquestioned were it not for an account given by Rosalie Hare, who was then lodging with her husband at the Curr homestead. In her journal, Hare wrote that '[w]hile we remained at Circular Head there were several accounts of considerable amounts of Natives having been shot by them (the Company's men), they wishing to extirpate them entirely, if possible. The master of the Company's Cutter, *Fanny*, assisted by four shepherds and his crew, surprised a party and killed 12'.[10] It had apparently been a close shave, as the surviving natives 'escaped but afterwards followed them. They reached the vessel just in time to save their lives.'[11] Although we cannot be certain whose version of events is more accurate, Hare, unlike Curr, had no reason to lie.

Whatever the truth, the local shepherds were determined not to rest until the entire tribe was exterminated. The end result of this resolution was the so-called Cape Grim Massacre, which has since become a by-word for the cruelty of colonisation in Tasmania. Rather than attacking at night, the men used the cape's topography to gain the element of surprise. Having some idea of the tribe's movements, company servants Weavis, Gunshannon, Nicholson and Chamberlain came upon them while they were collecting shellfish at the foot of a cliff accessible only by a steep and narrow track. From their position atop the cliff the men – one, an ex-soldier – picked off their victims below. Trapped on the beach, the natives suffered a high mortality, though Chamberlain was probably exaggerating when he claimed 30 were killed.[12]

The men's motives are somewhat obscure. They may have sought to remove the native threat, or to avenge their friend Thomas John, who had been speared two months earlier, but in Gunshannon's confession one detects something more sinister: 'He seemed to glory in the act', Robinson observed, 'and said he would shoot them whenever he met them.'[13] For his part, Curr ignored his magisterial duty, and declined to investigate the matter.

Later that year, Curr announced that 'a war of extermination' was underway: 'The recent proclamation of Martial Law ... does not speak this out in very clear terms, but it is to be the practical effect of it.'[14] The chief agent was nonchalant at the prospect of annihilating the north-west tribes. He once even confessed to offering his men spirits if they bought him back three native heads. In a letter to the company's directors, Curr admitted:

> My whole and sole object was to kill them, and this because my full con
> viction was and is that the laws of nature and of God and of this country
> all conspired to render this my duty ... As to my expression of a wish to
> have three of their heads to put on the ridge of the hut, I shall only say that
> I think it certainly would have the effect of deterring some of their com
> rades, of making the death of their companions live in their recollections.[15]

This grisly bounty reassured Curr's men that killing blacks was acceptable, yet he also gave them reason to be reticent.

On 21 August 1829, just west of Emu Bay, four company servants under the supervision of Alexander Goldie spotted two women and a girl about six years old. They shot one of the women in the back and captured the other two. One of the men approached the wounded woman and executed her with an axe.[16] Several weeks later, Goldie mentioned the killing in a letter to Curr. He had no reason to expect rebuke given Curr's well-known attitude towards blacks, but the calculating manager reported the matter to the Governor, hoping to present himself as humane, while shrewdly incriminating Goldie, with whom he had recently fallen out.[17] The case was brought to the attention of Attorney General Alfred Stephen. Goldie ought to have been convicted, since the proclamation of martial law stated clearly 'that defenceless women and children be invariably spared', but according to Stephen, the natives were 'open enemies to the King, in a state of actual warfare against him', and thus 'the Pursuit of the Natives by Mr Goldie and his party, was lawful'.[18]

Following Curr's unexpected reaction, Goldie went on a tour of the company's stock-huts warning the other employees to keep quiet about any killings.[19] But this did nothing to quell the actual violence. At the Hampshire and Surrey hills, where the headhunting incident had followed a series of violent encounters, Robinson discovered in 1830 that the men 'evince a hostile feeling towards the aborigines and declare they will shoot them whenever they may find them'.[20]

Shooting blacks may not have exhausted the men's tactical repertoire. In 1830, Mr Robson informed Robinson that he had once:

> proposed to the shepherds at the Surrey Hills to give them some poison to use for the destruction of the hyaena [thylacine]. The men said that they did not require it then but if Mr R would let them have some in the summer they would find a use for it. He asked them why they should find a use for it in the summer more than now. They said, 'Oh, Sir, we will poison the natives' dogs'. Mr R took it away with him, their object, he said, being to

poison the natives by putting it in the flour &c. No doubt hundreds have been destroyed in this way.[21]

Eleven years later, in 1841, Curr wrote to his overseer, Adolphus Schayer, after receiving a 'report, resting on very good foundation I believe, that it was intended to get rid of the natives by leaving poisoned damper in the huts, having reached the Government, is the cause in my opinion, of the present investigation … I beg you to communicate to me (and in a separate letter) anything you may have heard connected to this topic'.[22] Neither of these references proves that poison was used, though these men certainly had the motives and the means to employ such tactics had they chosen to.

In response to the resurgence of violence in 1841, Curr had his servants experiment with novel ways of killing blacks. In August of that year, the Chief Agent confided in a friend that he had 'tried the effect of spring guns in the huts, which they have once discharged, and must have escaped from almost by miracle. I am now trying a man-trap, also in one of the huts.'[23] The company's men did their utmost to assist Curr in putting down this latest wave of attacks, and they may well have been successful.

In December 1842, sealers at the Arthur River captured the Lanne family – an adult couple with three boys under the age of eight; purportedly the last of the free blacks. However, it is unlikely that these were the people responsible for the recent attacks.[24] Witnesses to the attacks described up to nine assailants (presumably adult males), yet William Lanne – well known for his placid nature – was the only adult male in the family. The implication is that there was probably another group responsible, and the fact that they were not heard of after February 1842 suggests Curr's efforts were not fruitless after all.

North-west Tasmania appears to have been the breeding ground for an especially sordid strain of white violence. It was a place where, according to Hare, men 'consider[ed] the massacre of these people an honour'.[25] This is not to suggest that native resistance in the region was ineffectual, or that colonists in the north-west did not live in fear. Following an attack at Emu Bay, for instance, the stockmen were discovered 'in a dreadful state of alarm'; two of them 'so reduced and altered by the constant state of dread in which they existed' that they were 'no longer the same men'.[26] Blacks in the north-west made 64 recorded attacks on colonists and property between 1827 and 1842, taking a substantial physical and psychological toll on the men they targeted.[27] Nevertheless, the company's men, with their unbridled violence, clearly dominated the conflict. North-west Tasmania was one of the most remote frontiers in the Empire, and the only force of law within 200 kilometres was a callous magistrate who cared nothing for the welfare of the natives, and everything for the company's profits. The surviving evidence provides us with a mere snippet from which we must infer the rest, and as with elsewhere in the colony, the tip of the north-west's empirical iceberg bodes ominously for that which went unrecorded.

Black

The Greater north-west of Tasmania was home to at least a dozen tribes. Our insight into their experience of the Black War comes from a slim, but surprisingly rich, catalogue of evidence, comprised largely of Van Diemen's Land Company records, on the one hand, and Robinson's journals on the other. The picture that emerges from these sources is tantalisingly incomplete, though there were some clear differences between the experiences and responses of north-west Tasmanians and those of their eastern neighbours, just as there were also many parallels. Local Aborigines are likely to have known little about the conflict in the east; their world was the north-west and their story is unique.

By the time white men first set foot in the north-west in late 1826, the tribes in the region had no doubt heard of them, but what preconceptions they held is impossible to know. There had been isolated contacts with the strangers before 1826, the first being in 1803 when a sealing vessel under Captain Chase had an apparently non-violent encounter with a tribe on the Hunter Islands. The next recorded contact between north-west people and sealers occurred about 1820, when the latter killed two men and abducted at least seven women at Cape Grim.[28] However, sealers had operated in western Bass Strait consistently from the turn of the century, so there were almost certainly other encounters.

Between 1815 and 1824, five exploratory voyages also visited the north-west and Macquarie Harbour. Brief encounters were recorded on four of these expeditions, but only the meeting with James Kelly's whaleboat crew in January 1816 ended in violence.[29] Local men initially welcomed the five strangers as they hauled their boat onto the beach at Robbins Island, but following a misunderstanding over some swans, they began showering them with stones. Kelly claimed he and his men shot several in self-defence.[30] The only other hostile contact with whites occurred in the vicinity of Macquarie Harbour, where a penal station had been established in 1822. In its 11 years of operation, a trickle of convicts escaped from this hellish prison into the surrounding wilderness, many of whom were never seen again. Two women, who were familiar with the region, told Robinson the local Aborigines 'killed plenty of prisoner white men from Macquarie Harbour'.[31]

Most north-west Tasmanians, however, did not see their first white man, sheep, oxen, horses or stock-huts until the Van Diemen's Land Company began its operations in the late 1820s, by which time the war in the east was already reaching its apex. The arrival of these strangers was initially cause for great curiosity, and many tribes gained a voyeuristic familiarity with them.[32] During the first 12 months of the company's presence, there is circumstantial evidence suggesting that at least one tribe engaged in prostitution, probably in exchange for dogs and other novelties.[33] But this state of affairs came to an abrupt end with the November 1827 dispute over the violation of women at Cape Grim. Superintendent Reeves later described another incident that occurred at Cape Grim around this time: 'Thomas, a man in the Company's employ, enticed some aborigines by holding up a large damper to them, and when one drew near he offered him a piece of bread on the end of a large knife and whilst the man was in the act of taking it off, he rushed forward and ripped him up.'[34] The violence then quickly spread and, from 1828, most tribes found themselves at war with the strangers.

A total of 16 separate acts of violence against Aborigines were recorded in the north-west, but this cannot account for the destruction of the tribes in this region. With the exception of the two devastating ambushes at Cape Grim in February 1828, most of the recorded incidents seem to have involved only one or two victims. Yet, by the time Robinson collected what he believed was the final remnant in 1834, the north-west Tasmanians had been all but wiped out. The only known outbreak of disease occurred at Macquarie Harbour in 1833, so we must assume that violence (not all of it perpetrated by white men) played a significant role in the decline of the north-west tribes.[35]

After the killings at Cape Grim, Robinson observed that 'the [north-west] natives call the white people NOW.HUM.MOE, devil, and when they hear the report of a gun they say the NOW.HUM.MOE have shot another tribe of natives'.[36] But, though they were afraid of their new nemeses, Robinson also noted that the north-west Aborigines were a vengeful people who 'never forget an injury'.[37] For instance, one of the Cape Grim killers 'was severely speared afterwards at the Surrey Hills, as was several others, when the natives came down and robbed the hut and made an attack upon the shepherds and speared them'.[38] Likewise, following the Goldie incident described above, the killer was soon after speared. According to Robinson, 'the husband of this woman took it so much to heart that he vowed to revenge her death on every white man he had the chance to meet, and which it appears he has done in numerous instances'.[39] At the Arthur River, an Aborigine named Edick swore a similar oath to one of Robinson's envoys that he and his people 'would murder every white man they met with'.[40] In this, they were occasionally successful, such as when three company men were killed at the Surrey and Hampshire hills in three separate spearings in July and October 1831. They also inflicted heavy losses on the company's sheep and oxen.[41] Compared to Tasmanians in the south-east, however, the toll that north-west tribes took on the invaders was less severe.

The north-west tribes' preoccupation with internecine conflict may help explain their lower efficiency in combating the white invaders. From the time of his first mission in 1830, to his final visit in 1834, Robinson recorded as many as ten internecine conflicts in the north-west. Most of these disputes involved competition over women, which was no doubt exacerbated by sealers and stockmen, who abducted a considerable number for themselves.[42] Nevertheless, the paucity of the record precludes any judgment on the comparative importance of internecine and white violence in bringing about the demise of the north-west tribes.

In 1834, all the violence ceased. Robinson declared: 'The work is done, the great evil is removed', and most assumed that every last Tasmanian had been killed or removed.[43] Five years later, however, they resurfaced and, between September 1839 and February 1842, made at least 18 attacks on company men and property. Presumably, this was just one tribe that had attempted to live remote from white settlement, but for some reason resumed their hostilities. Whatever their motivations, this tribe made their final attack at Table Cape on 27 February 1842, and then disappeared forever. Their fate, as suggested above, was probably not natural death. Either way, the circumstances and motivations that triggered this aftershock of the Black War are unclear. We are also ignorant of what this remnant – the last of the free Tasmanians – went through during their final campaign. Their attitudes and experiences can only be surmised; all we can be sure of is that despair was among the emotions they felt, and hope was not.

CHAPTER EIGHT

THE SEA FRONTIER

It was on the sea frontier[1] (see Figure 1C, page xvii) that the European sealers of Bass Strait encountered the Aborigines of northern and eastern Tasmania.[2] Sealers rarely crossed paths with the stockmen of the interior, and their experiences of the Black War were very different, but the Aborigines had to deal with both threats. Eventually, tribes from Mount Cameron in the north-west to Bruny Island in the south-east felt the impact of the sealers' lust, but none suffered more than the north-east tribes. Between 1810 and 1832, sealers killed or abducted several hundred natives, and instituted a brutal system of female slavery.[3] Paradoxically, they also sired the first generation of mixed-descent Tasmanians who have, in recent decades, established themselves as a powerful cultural and political presence in the state.

There are some illuminating parallels between the sea frontier and the conflict in the interior. For one, the sealers' socioeconomic backgrounds, as well as their motives and tactics, were very similar to those of the stockmen and sawyers of mainland Tasmania. Likewise, both frontiers were poorly policed borderlands, populated by sex-deprived and brutalised men. This was not a coincidence, nor was the fact that the conflict on both frontiers occurred over roughly the same period. We must also appreciate the differences between the two frontiers. There was, for instance, little geographic overlap between the scenes of violence, and the sealers felt themselves more engaged in a system of slavery than a war. But to fully understand the Black War it must be seen as a multifaceted and interconnected conflict, in which the sea frontier played a pivotal role.

White

After the discovery of huge seal colonies in Bass Strait in 1797, sealing quickly became Australia's first major export industry.[4] Over the decade that followed, scores of large sealing gangs returned seasonally from Port Jackson. But they were not concerned with conservation, and by 1810, the seal colonies were so depleted that most sealers moved on. Thereafter, only small crews were able to eke out a living from the remaining seals. Most of these crews operated seasonally from Launceston or Hobart, but some eventually took up residence in Bass Strait.

In addition to the authorised sealing crews, runaways sometimes managed to steal a vessel and establish themselves in Bass Strait. Even on authorised vessels, criminals were routinely smuggled out of the Tamar and Derwent estuaries.[5] In 1826, Captain Whyte, aided by a party of the 40th Regiment, sailed to the islands for the purpose of 'ridding Bass's Straits of [the] many bad characters, who have so long infested it'.[6] Whyte apprehended 18 prisoners, but many more avoided his purge.[7] In response, Governor Arthur commissioned an investigation into the situation, headed by Lieutenant-Colonel William Balfour. The commission found the straits:

> provide constant Shelter and secure retreat for runaways, and villains of the worst description. Almost every Rock throughout the Straits has become the habitation of some one or more accurately the most desperate and lawless of mankind ... The whole of the Straits seem to present one continued scene of Violence, Plunder, and the commission of every species of Crime.[8]

When Robinson arrived in Bass Strait to establish his mission in 1830, most of the remaining 40 or so sealers were permanent residents. They lived predominately on the Furneaux Islands, but some ventured as far as Kangaroo Island and King George's Sound. By this time, seals in Bass Strait had become too scarce to support seasonal operations, but by exploiting the skilled labour of native women, these men had diversified their economy to include cropping, hunting and mutton-birding. Thanks to Robinson and his associates, the experiences of these sealers are relatively well documented.

The allure of naked, exotic women to sex-deprived sailors should present no surprise. Initially, sex was the sealers' primary motivation for acquiring native women, but their captives' full potential soon became apparent. According to the sealer James Munro, 'when the black women was first brought over from the main, they were intended principally to gratify the sealers, but that on one occasion the sealers happening to be away for a short time, they found on their return a quantity of kangaroo which the black women had caught, at sight of which the sealers resolved to make them hunt in future'.[9] In addition to hunting, sealers compelled women to perform a multitude of tasks, from making clothes and preparing food, to crewing boats and diving for shellfish. At many of these tasks they were more competent than their masters, and there is no doubt that, as Robinson observed, the sealers became 'dependent upon these slaves for their subsistence'.[10]

Some sealers, up until at least 1816, were able to establish trading relationships with coastal tribes, and in doing so became partially acquainted with their language and way of life. In exchange for women, or for assistance in abducting women from other tribes, sealers traded seal carcasses, dogs and a variety of European goods. In making these exchanges, sealers may also – wittingly or unwittingly, sincerely or insincerely – have entered into kinship relations. If so, they failed to uphold the abiding obligations that accompanied them.

Trade opportunities evaporated as relations broke down. Still, up to

100 sealers continued to operate in the straits during the early and mid-1820s, and they all desired women. Consequently, the practice of gin raiding became widespread. According to Captain James Hobbs, who knew the straits well, 'when [the sealers] could not purchase women they shot the men and carried their wives away'.[11] Indeed, the missionary James Backhouse, who spent considerable time in the straits from 1832, asserted that '[m]ost of these women were originally kidnapped' – a claim consistent with all the evidence.[12]

The abduction and enslavement of native women in Bass Strait went back to at least the early 1810s. In 1815, Major William Stewart reported that:

> For several years it had been the practice for whaleboats, twenty to thirty feet [6–9 m] long, to clear out of Hobart and Port Dalrymple apparently with only two or three men on board, but in fact with several convicts hidden … These buccaneers raided the Tasmanian mainland for aboriginal women and they traded in them … keep[ing] them as Slaves or Negroes, hunting and foraging for them, who they transfer and dispose of from one to another as their own property; very few of whom ever see their Native Home [again.][13]

If the practice was common in 1815, it was entrenched by the early 1820s. A number of women told Robinson of how they were abducted by sealers who 'rushed upon them at their fires and shot the men'.[14] The sealers' method of abducting women was the same as the stock-keepers'. They would scour the horizon for signs of smoke, then creep up and ambush their victims as they slept. The key difference was that the sealers could retreat to the islands, and thereby avoid the stockmen's dilemmas of how to contain captured women, and evade tribal retribution. This geographical fact made all the difference.

The sealers were especially fond of little girls. Writing about the prevalence of child abduction, Robinson observed that '[m]any such instances have occurred: James Munroe [*sic*] had Jumbo ever since she was a child, and several others the same'.[15] Elsewhere he recorded that 'Ruth' was abducted at age nine, 'Poll' at age eight, 'Little Kit' 'when a girl', 'Sally' 'when a little girl', 'Fanny' at age nine, 'Tekartee' 'when a little girl', 'Margaret' when an 'infant', and the list could go on.[16] There were obvious reasons why the sealers preferred children to adults, and sexual gratification was only one of them. For one, their inexperience and lack of strength made them more vulnerable in ambushes. Taken young, they were also more likely to grow submissive, and if prepubescent, they would not burden their masters with unwanted children. What is more, they would hold their value as labourers and concubines longer.

What evolved in Bass Strait was a genuine slave trade – what Robinson called 'the African slave trade in miniature'.[17] In 1830, the onetime sealing captain, James Kelly, testified that 'every man [had] from two to five of these women for his own use'.[18] Confirming Kelly's observation, Robinson recorded the names of 50 sealers who collectively possessed at least 124 women.[19] Two women may have been the average, but some sealers were more extravagant. 'Harrington', for instance, 'procured 10 or 15 women, placed them on different islands, and left them to procure Kangaroo skins for him.'[20]

Women were commonly traded from sealer to sealer in exchange for cash or commodities.[21] 'Tekartee' and 'Isaac', for example, were sold at different times for 'some seal skins', 'Sarah' was sold for four skins, 'Pung' cost John Thomas a mere guinea, Munro paid £7 for 'Emma', and these are just some of the recorded transactions.[22] Slave owners also prostituted their women. The slave Wottecowidyer told Robinson that the sealers used to 'make them cohabit with the other men for a kangaroo skin'.[23] Likewise, Sall told him 'that Brown sent her to sleep with the [other] sealers for one night and they gave him a kangaroo skin'.[24] This was chattel slavery in the most literal sense.

In addition to treating native women as disposable property, some sealers appear to have taken sadistic pleasure in torturing them. As early as 1815, Stewart observed that the sealers, 'by way of punishment, half hang them [their women], cut their heads with Clubs in a Shocking Manner, or flog them most unmercifully with Cats [whips] made from Kangaroo Sinews'.[25] One of these women told Robinson that 'the sealers beat the black women plenty; they cut a piece of flesh off a woman's buttock ... They cut them with broad sealers' knives. Said they tied them up and beat them with ropes.'[26] Such punishments could be incurred for trying to escape, but also for more trivial offences. According to Munro, 'if they should happen to return with a small quantity [of game] they would tie them up to a tree and flog them'.[27] If any of John Harrington's harem of slaves failed to procure a satisfactory amount of game, he 'used to punish them', according to Kelly, 'by tying them up to trees for 24 or 36 hours together, flogging them at intervals'.[28]

Mortality was high among enslaved women.[29] Kelly testified that sealers 'not infrequently killed the women in cold blood if they were stubborn'.[30] Robinson learnt of several specific cases. Robert Gamble, for instance, shot two women, and Jem Everitt killed a woman on Woody Island 'because she would not get mutton birds'.[31] Robinson heard that some sealers went so far as to 'burn their women alive'.[32] Such evidence leaves no doubt that Bass Strait was home to a culture of unrestrained violence – but why?

The story of how the sealers came to think and behave the way they did began in childhood. Most were raised in poverty and transported or apprenticed at a young age. Even those who experienced kindness in early life were brutalised by the oppressive systems of convictism and maritime indenture. Moving to the Bass Strait islands did nothing to soften these men, and it took away the legal and social restraints that may otherwise have moderated their behaviour. If they could evade the wrath of their victims, and the occasional government vessel, the sealers were basically free to live lawlessly and indulge their carnal desires.

The sealers fancied themselves as rebels, hard drinking buccaneers who shunned the hierarchical and authoritarian strictures of colonial society. They took pride in being their own masters.[33] However, there is little indication that their renegade lives brought them happiness. There was an inevitable trade-off between the freedom they sought in Bass Strait and the torments this entailed. Most sealers appear to have eked out a rather wretched existence on the windswept and mostly barren islands of Bass Strait.[34] Their work was hard, dangerous and uncomfortable, and it supported only the most meagre subsistence. Perhaps worst of all though, sealers' lives appear to have been almost devoid of love, and an atmosphere of distrust corroded their friendships as well.

Among the sealers it was every man for himself, 'the weak being obliged to give way to the stronger'.[35] Robinson observed that '[t]hese men consider it a fortunate circumstance when anyone is drowned, as they say they was in their debt and seize upon their property'.[36] The scramble for a dead man's slaves was pitiless, but not everyone could wait.[37] In John Taylor's case, his sealing associates stole his concubine and child while he was out sealing.[38] In other instances, sealers expedited the process by murdering their fellow sealers in order to gain possession of their slave women.[39]

Violence was so much a part of sealers' lives that they became largely inured to it. 'It is not improbable that they were sensible of kindness', wrote John West, 'but it is very certain that this was not their ordinary lot. Unanimous testimony permits no doubt that they [the sealers' slaves] experienced the severity, which men of low intellect, and of fierce and capricious passions, inflict on women of an inferior race.'[40] Such women, it seems, gave sealers an opportunity to be masters instead of slaves themselves. They were certainly hard, and often ruthless men, but the unforgiving world in which they lived did not favour the weak, or reward the humane. The sealers were the products of their environment, and to that extent they were both inhuman, and all too human.

Black

The Aborigines of northern Tasmania would have heard rumours about the mysterious white men long before they first encountered them. Those they eventually did meet were sealers, who introduced them to dogs and other exotic goods. In 1816, a tribe from Cape Portland encountered James Kelly and his whaleboat crew, who were circumnavigating Tasmania. The tribe's chief, Mannalargenna,[41] was familiar with one of Kelly's men, the sealer George Briggs, and tried to enlist his help in a raid against his brother Tolo. When Briggs refused, Kelly observed that Mannalargenna 'seemed greatly dissatisfied, and told Briggs in a very hostile tone that he had often before gone with him to fight other tribes when he (Briggs) wanted women'. Mannalargenna threatened to press the white men into his service, but Kelly, Briggs and the others managed to steal away that evening.

Tolo, who was also acquainted with Briggs, headed a large tribe that was congregated at Eddystone Point. He encountered the men five days after they had evaded his brother, and ordered six women to help them hunt seals on nearby George Rocks. During this time, Tolo busied his people hunting and skinning kangaroos to trade for the seal carcasses. After the exchange was completed, Tolo's people danced on the beach as the boatmen pulled away.[42]

It is clear from Kelly's account that some Tasmanians were also complicit in the slave trade. This was confirmed by a woman from Mannalargenna's tribe, who told Robinson 'her people took the black women from the natives at Port Dalrymple and sold them to the sealers for dogs, mutton birds, flour &c'.[43] The firsthand experience of being sold into slavery was affectingly captured by Lowhenunhe, who reported:

> that the sealers at the straits carry on a complete system of slavery; that they barter in exchange for women flour and potatoes; that she herself was bought off the black men for a bag of flour and potatoes; that they took

her away by force, tied her hands and feet, and put her in the boat; that white man beat black woman with a rope.[44]

Lowhenunhe seems to have been taken from her people by an enemy tribe that then sold her on to the sealers, and this appears to be how the majority of 'exchanged' women ended up in Bass Strait.

The only known exception occurred when Mannalargenna bestowed his daughter on George Briggs in the early 1810s.[45] However, this was not a commercial transaction; the chief was attempting to build an alliance with the powerful newcomers. 'Trading' their own women in perpetuity was never in a tribe's best interest – they held too much social and economic value. Regardless, by 1820, violence and betrayal had destroyed all exchange relationships – both commercial and diplomatic – and the coastal tribes increasingly found themselves under attack.[46]

'Tyereelore', a word of unknown origin, was the name north-east Tasmanians gave to women enslaved on the islands. Practically all accounts describe the Tyereelore's lives as full of violence and despair. Some of these women confided in Robinson following their emancipation, telling him:

> that the sealers flog the women, that all the women have been flogged and that they tie them up to trees and flog them on the buttock. BULL.RUB said Black Jack flogged her because she had not caught some kangaroo, gave her two dozen [lashes], and at another time Jack Brown flogged her; and TAN.LE.BONE.YER had been flogged several times … The white men flog the black women for nothing and flog the women belonging to other white men. Thomson beat the women on the head with a stick or tomahawk, plenty of blood.

With Robinson probing further, Bullrub revealed that the sealers also starved the women, who were forced to live on whatever food they could procure themselves.[47] Likewise, the east coast woman, Looerryminer, explained to Backhouse how the sealers:

flogged the women who did not pluck Mutton-birds, or do other work to their satisfaction. She spread her hands to the wall, to shew the manner in which they were tied up, said a rope was used to flog them with, and cried out with a failing voice till she sank upon the ground, as if exhausted. This woman's statements were confirmed by others, several of whom have escaped to the settlement.[48]

These examples form part of a substantial body of testimonial evidence that confirms the prevalence of gratuitous violence, and explains why the Tyereelore were so often terrified of their white masters.

Like most protracted ordeals, there were moments of respite, if not laughter and enjoyment. There may even have been unrecorded exchanges of kindness between master and slave. Indeed, several Tyereelore remained with the sealers after the rest relocated to Flinders Island, and within a generation they and their ageing masters had established a functioning community that still exists today. However, although we can speculate on the possible consolations of their condition, the evidence for the period 1810–32 invariably portrays the Tyereelore's life as one of suffering and misery, or what the *Hobart Town Gazette* called 'a cruel chain of unspeakable torment!'[49]

In late December 1830, Robinson concluded '[t]here was not a woman kept in captivity but what earnestly desired and longed for their liberty, and many attempts have been made by them to get away'.[50] Escape from the islands was very difficult, but this did not prevent women from trying. Backhouse recalled that when he visited Green Island, 'two women, called Isaac and Judy, took the opportunity of escaping by it, while the sealers were asleep – Two other women waded and swam from Green Island to the Settlement – a distance of three miles [5 km].'[51] Some Tyereelore were willing to take great risks to free themselves from their appalling circumstances. At least eight drowned while attempting escape, and many others suffered severe punishments after they were intercepted by their masters.[52]

When Robinson came to liberate the Tyereelore, the sealers did all they could to subvert him.[53] This often involved physical threats. A north-east woman named Wobberty, for instance, recalled how her master ordered her and her fellow slaves 'to run away in the bush; [and] that he scolded them for coming [back] and said that he would shoot them'.[54] Other times, sealers tried to brainwash their slaves into thinking Robinson and his agents were coming to murder them. In one case, a sealer at Penguin Island 'had given one of the women a gun and had told her to shoot the first man that should attempt to take her'.[55]

When they were finally emancipated, the Tyereelore were overjoyed. Robinson observed this on a number of occasions, as did the missionaries Backhouse and Walker.[56] Above all though, emancipation from the sealers enabled the Tyereelore to be reunited with their loved ones. These were always highly emotional occasions, sometimes moving Robinson to tears.[57] His assistant, Anthony Cottrell, recorded a reunion between two sisters: 'Neither spoke for some time, but throwing their arms round each other's necks, they remained in that attitude, the tears trickling down their cheeks, until at length … they began to talk and laugh, and exhibit all the demonstrations of extravagant joy.'[58] These reunions were often bittersweet, however, as women learnt from exiled relatives that their country had been entirely usurped, and their people decimated.

Women were not the only victims of the Bass Strait slave trade. It was widely acknowledged that sealers frequently killed men when raiding for women. Adolphus Schayer, for instance, reported that the sealers 'often killed their parents or friends who tried to prevent this violence'.[59] The physical evidence also attested to this. Robinson found that 'at every boat harbour along the whole line of the [north-east] coast the bones of the murdered aborigines are strewed over the face of the earth and bleaching in the sun … Several skulls have been found perforated by musket balls.'[60] Even more revealing are the eyewitness testimonies. In one instance, described by two recently liberated Tyereelore:

the sealers rushed them and took several [women], and then anchored their boat off the surf and enticed the natives to the beach and discharged several guns at them and killed several. One man, when he saw the sealers about to fire, dived under water and came up and laid hold of the stern post of the boat. They towed him out to sea and when the man let go and was swimming to shore, they fired at him. He dived and they pulled after him and shot him.[61]

North-east tribes suffered terribly from the loss of their wives and providers. Some attempted to replenish their dwindling female populations by raiding enemy tribes, but they too were short of women.[62] Not surprisingly, when Robinson first encountered tribesmen in the north-east, they 'complained in the strongest terms … of the hardships incumbent upon [them from] the deprivation of their women'.[63] Survival became a desperate struggle for tribes with insufficient women, a situation compounded by the constant fear of when the next attack might occur. Robinson found '[t]heir fear of the sealers is such the natives would approach the coast very cautiously, if at all'.[64]

Aggrieved tribesmen could take their time in exacting revenge on stockmen or sawyers, but once in their boats, the sealers were beyond their reach. In fact, there are only three cases on record in which Tasmanians managed to assail a party of sealers.[65] Seven sealers were killed and three wounded in these reprisals, yet the sea frontier was still a very one-sided conflict. Tasmanian men were warriors, with strong conceptions of justice and honour, so their inability to avenge these wrongs, or to rescue their women, was both frustrating and emasculating.

Survivors nonetheless strove to maintain communication with their enslaved womenfolk. At Peak Hill on the north coast, Robinson witnessed male survivors:

kindle a fire the smoke of which is a signal to the female aborigines which had been torn from them by the merciless sealers, the wife from the fond embrace of her husband, the daughter from her parent, the sister from her brother, the female from her lover, and had been transported by these lawless and cruel men to the islands ... The females of the Island make smoke in answer to the men, and they also dance on these hills and sing an aboriginal song which is a relation to love complaints.

'What a wretched existence' the north-east men now led, Robinson observed, 'all their females gone, torn from them.'[66] It is, therefore, no surprise that these men were elated when Robinson promised he would restore their women to them.[67]

Between November 1830 and May 1831, Robinson secured the release of some two dozen women, and the scenes of reunion described in his journals convey vividly the emotions felt by both the enslaved and their families. But their rejoicing was short lived. Soon after the emancipations began, Governor Arthur was persuaded by the cynical, but charismatic, figures of Munro and Tucker that the sealers were decent men who should be allowed to keep one woman each.[68] They returned to the straits waving the Governor's decree victoriously in Robinson's face.

When the chief Mannalargenna discovered the sealers artifice he 'was in a rage, and said, "No, no, no, they be bad men and by and by me tell the Governor"'.[69] That same week, he unexpectedly met his daughter on Preservation Island. Robinson observed that 'daughter and parent was alternately in tears and on MANNALARGENNA being necessarily obliged to take his leave of his offspring, a strong emotion of kindred affection was manifest and they were both suffused in tears'. The chief 'importuned me to get his daughter', Robinson lamented, 'but in this there is more difficulty than he can suppose'.[70] Mannalargenna had endured a great deal at the hands of the sealers, who had shot him, and enslaved his sister and three of his daughters.[71] Worse still, this revered warrior had been all but powerless to stop them destroying everything he cared about.

By November 1830, the Tasmanian population in the greater north-east had been reduced to just 74, of whom only three were women.[72] At the same time, no less than 70 women, mostly from the north-east, were living with the sealers.[73] Some tribes were initially complicit in trading women, but without the benefit of hindsight, they could never have imagined the sealers would become so rapacious. Once they became aware of their lethal potential they had nowhere to turn, because the white men were now advancing overland as well. From the Tasmanians' perspectives, the coast and the interior were two fronts of the same War, the sealers and the stockmen two faces of the same enemy.

CONCLUSION

Given the importance of the Black War to Australian and world history, the preceding exploration of how it was experienced is long overdue. Posterity remembers it for its tragic outcome; what many consider an indelible stain on a callous empire. But for the thousands of Aborigines and colonists who endured it, the war looked radically different. For them, it was a cycle of violence, misery and fear, compounded on both sides by the incomprehensibility of the enemy. Indeed, there has never been a war fought between such fundamentally different people. The ethical and legal questions that animate historians were far from the minds of those involved. Thus, in exploring these peoples' attitudes and experiences, I have sought to illuminate the war from important and neglected angles. Above all, this unique approach has contributed a fresh layer to our understanding, and what follows is a synthesis of its more salient insights.

White perspectives

The Black War has almost invariably been approached from the point of view of the colonial administration, and the near annihilation of the

Tasmanians has frequently been blamed on the government's failure to punish those who harmed them. However, despite his neglect in failing to follow up several egregious cases, Governor Arthur's actual control over the frontier was minimal. He admonished settlers to keep their servants in check, but maintaining constant surveillance was impossible. In isolated regions, the threat of Aboriginal revenge was often all that checked the behaviour of brutalised and sex-deprived convicts.

The colony's gender imbalance led predictably to frontiersmen abducting and raping Aboriginal women. As the violence spiralled further out of control in the late 1820s, sex became less important than defeating the enemy, whom many considered sub-human. But, just as frontiersmen encountered few legal or moral obstacles to killing Aborigines, they had very little protection against being killed themselves. For this reason, many colonists killed Aborigines as much from a sense of self-preservation as from feelings of hatred or lust. The blacks made everyone on the frontier feel intensely vulnerable, to the point where killing them came to be considered a public service.

Aboriginal attacks generated immense hatred, grief and frustration, but the emotion colonists expressed above all others was fear. Everyone on the frontier felt some fear, but for those in exposed areas, it could be paralysing. Most pressing among settlers was their fear of economic loss, and for the safety of family and friends. Convicts, however, were understandably more concerned for their own safety. The blacks were so effective and so elusive that they took on a terrifying mystique in the minds of frontiersmen. Many turned their dwellings into makeshift fortresses, and refused to venture beyond them without guns, dogs or companions. In extreme cases, fear drove people from their farms. Indeed, whether it was their intention or not, Tasmania's Aborigines succeeded in producing a kind of hysteria among many of their invaders.

The Black Line was the ultimate expression of this hysteria. For a brief period, it offered colonists hope, but it also gave them a way to channel years of pent-up frustration and fear. The operation remains the largest domestic offensive in Australia's military history: a *levée en masse* involving one-fifth of all adult males in the colony. It has traditionally been called a 'volunteer' operation, yet about 80 per cent of participants served under duress. This is one of the many reasons the line failed. Indeed, it was a tactical and logistical disaster that demoralised the frontier community, while having no serious impact on the Aborigines.

The Black War cost colonists in a number of significant ways. The extent to which violence retarded the colony's economic and population growth is difficult to measure, though its cost to settlers in labour and property was a constant source of complaint. Even greater was the cost in human life. Depending on how one measures the population of frontier colonists, between three and six per cent were killed or wounded by Aborigines, and many more survived pursuits and sieges. But the most costly toll of all was psychological.

Black perspectives

If examining the Black War through the colonists' eyes has its difficulties, glimpsing it from the perspectives of the Tasmanians – a mysterious and preliterate people – poses immense challenges. Nevertheless, it has been possible to distil some of their core attitudes and experiences from the observations of Europeans. Careful analysis of these sources reveals that most Tasmanians understood little about the white men, and at least some seem to have believed they were malevolent ancestor spirits returned from the dead. However, none of this prevented them from recognising the strangers' destructive power, or from treating them as invaders.

Attacks launched by Tasmanians were sometimes overtly political, especially those involving arson and stock killing, but they were also motivated by more proximate causes. These provocations, and their responses to them, changed over the course of the war. When seeking revenge, for instance, Aborigines initially targeted specific perpetrators, but as the insults mounted, they began to treat all whites as enemies. Another major change was that, as the soaring white population overwhelmed the game-rich plains and valleys, European foods and blankets became necessities rather than luxuries. Thus, Tasmanians experienced a priority shift from killing on principle to plundering for survival.

The invasion of their homelands cost most Tasmanians their life, but it cost all of them their way of life. Over the course of the 1820s, their population plummeted, their social and ceremonial networks broke down, and they found moving and hunting more dangerous with every passing year. When near the settlements, tribes were forced to sleep around tiny campfires in inconspicuous places, with sentinels constantly on guard. From sundown to sunrise they wrestled against cold and fear, questioning every sound, and watching for the slightest stirring among their dogs. Tasmanians had always dreaded the malevolent spirits that lurked in the night, but during the war their slumbers were haunted by more tangible spectres.

When they could, the surviving tribes sought refuge in the remote and inhospitable recesses of the island, but often the dangers of cold and starvation outweighed those of bayonets and bullets. Incessantly harried by dozens of armed parties, the wounded had no time to recuperate, and the strong were sometimes obliged to abandon them, along with infants and the elderly. These crushing expedients, together with the constant loss of kinsfolk in campfire ambushes, caused a great cloud of sadness, anger and despair to descend on the survivors. From the perspectives of the Tasmanians, the Black War was a war of attrition, of trying to run, fight and survive as their society collapsed around them. Not surprisingly, the Conciliator's offer to relieve them of this hellish existence was readily accepted.

General themes and comparisons

The Black War exhibited many features common to guerrilla wars throughout history: stealthy raiding parties, hit-and-run ambushes, sabotage and a high casualty rate among noncombatants. But the most distinctive feature of the conflict was its solar rhythm. Every attack on colonists or their property was conducted during daylight hours, and with few exceptions, colonists attacked Aborigines at night. This day/night pendulum of violence could well distinguish the Black War as unique in the history of warfare.

The guerrilla tactics employed on the Tasmanian frontier were remarkably uniform. Robinson observed that 'the practice of [convicts] is to come upon [the blacks] and to fire at them – a similar practice to the blacks in their attacks upon the whites'.[1] Colonists found that the only reliable way to kill or capture Aborigines was to spot their camp-fires, then ambush them as they slept. On the other hand, most colonists were killed or wounded when Aboriginal war parties ambushed them in or about their huts. Although the numerically superior colonists were ultimately victorious, the tactics used by both sides were comparably effective.

Between 1824 and 1831, Aborigines made at least 833 attacks on colonists in the east, killing or wounding 437 of them (see Figure 3, page 2). Although in hindsight they did not fully exploit tactics such as arson, the Tasmanians nonetheless proved themselves to be skilful and dangerous foes, mounting a resistance that dwarfs anything encountered elsewhere in the Australian colonies. For their part, colonists killed something like 600 eastern Aborigines during the war years, mostly in clandestine ambushes. The majority of these attacks were conducted not by troops or roving parties, but by vigilante groups comprised largely of convicts and ex-convicts.

Aborigines and colonists both demonstrated skill and resolve in their attacks, each taking a heavy toll on the other. Given its profoundly unequal result, the suggestion that the Black War was a fight between equally competent adversaries can seem ludicrous. Keith Windschuttle has asserted: 'Either the Aborigines were not the great guerrilla warriors they have been portrayed or their death toll was much lower than has been claimed.'[2] However, this non sequitur ignores the historical fact that martial prowess never guarantees victory. In the American Civil War, for instance, the confederates were often more effective strategists and fighters than their union antagonists, but out-numbered and out-resourced, they ultimately lost the struggle. Likewise, the Tasmanians' guerrilla tactics were highly effective; but for every colonist they killed, another 50 poured into their country, and they could do little to alter the result of the war.

The near extermination of the Tasmanians cannot help but evoke emotions such as guilt, sadness and contempt in any feeling person. Yet it is misleading to think of the Black War as a battle between good and evil. The traditional dichotomies of strong and weak, cowardly and courageous, victim and victimiser simply do not stand up to scrutiny. Practically everyone saw themselves as the victims. White and black alike, most were just trying to survive the nightmare in which they found themselves. There were of course many cruel individuals, but they too were victims of their circumstances, assumptions, hatreds, frustrations, fears and sadnesses. They were human beings, with all the fallibility and vulnerability that comes with being a member of that species. This is not justification, but nor is it condemnation. Judgment contributes nothing to our understanding. The war was at once the effect and the cause of untold suffering, fear and malice. It was an extraordinary event that drove ordinary people to do the unthinkable. The real story of the Black War can only be told by those who lived and died in its clutches, and it is to them we must turn if we are to truly understand this appalling tragedy.

SELECT BIBLIOGRAPHY

Online resources

New Zealand History Online, 'End of the New Zealand Wars', nzhistory.net.nz/
war/new-zealand-wars/end

R v Farrell, Supreme Court of Van Diemen's Land, 11 August 1824, law.mq.edu.
au/research/colonial_case_law/tas/cases/case_index/1824/r_v_farrell

Robinson GA, 'Speech of G. A. Robinson to the Australian Aborigines Protection
Society', 19 October 1838, law.mq.edu.au/research/colonial_case_law/nsw/
other_features/correspondence/robinson_speech_1838

Story to Bonwick, n.d., University of Tasmania library special and rare materials
collection, eprints.utas.edu.au/2228

xyris.com.au

Newspapers

Colonial Advocate
Colonial Times
Derwent Star
Hobart Town Courier
Hobart Town Gazette
Independent
Launceston Advertiser
Launceston Examiner
Tasmanian
Tasmanian and Port Dalrymple Advertiser

Archive files
NLA, MS3251, miscellaneous correspondence mostly pertaining to bushrangers and Aborigines.
TAHO, CD9/1, CD11/1–2, CD20/1, daily registers of articles issued from the colonial store, 1830–35.
TAHO, CSO1/316–31 (pagination is sometimes confused, CSO1/324 is unpaginated).
TAHO, GO52/1/6, letterbooks of general outward correspondence 1833–36.
TAHO, LC347, miscellaneous legal correspondence, Launceston 1825–27.

Unpublished papers and accounts
Allen J, 'Notebook of John Allen, 1837–76, and other assorted papers', GSPHS.
Amos A, 'Diary of Adam Amos 1822–25', TAHO, NS323/1/1.
Arthur G, 'George Arthur's Papers', SLNSW, ML, A1771.
Australian Bureau of Statistics, 'Tasmanian Statistics 1804–1902', Canberra, 1989, SLT, 319.46 TAS.
Balfour W, 'Balfour report, 5 May 1826', TAHO, CSO1/36, pp. 180–96.
Batman J, 'Diary of John Batman', unpublished, NLA, N994.6, B333.
Beams JR, unpublished family account, 1947, Beams family papers, Flowery Gully, private collection.
Bradstreet R, 'Richard Bradstreet letter, 16 January 1824', TAHO, NS690/1/9.
Dumaresq, 'Dumaresq family papers, 1821–84', TAHO, NS953.
Dumaresq E, 'Diary of Edward Dumaresq', 1829–30, TAHO, NS953/1/376.
Emmett HJ, 'Reminiscences of the Black War', 1873, TAHO, NG1216.
Hudspeth WH, 'The British Army in Tasmania', c.1940, Royal Society of Tasmania archive, RS3/4(3).
Laing A, 'The Alexander Laing story', 1867, TAHO, NS1332/1/12.
Lawrence RW, 'Journal of Robert William Lawrence, 1829–30', QVMAG, CHS53–33/2.
Lennox G, 'The Van Diemen's Land Company and the Tasmanian Aborigines: a re-appraisal', unpublished draft, SLT, TL.Q 994.60049915 LEN, 1991.
O'Connor R, 'Roderic O'Connor's papers', Connorville, private collection.

Theses
Clements N, '"Wriggle, and Shuffle, and Twist"': attitudes towards Aborigines in the Tasmanian press 1825–1831', Hons thesis, University of Tasmania, History & Classics and Riawunna, 2007.
—— 'Frontier conflict in Van Diemen's Land', PhD thesis, University of Tasmania, Humanities, 2013.

McMahon JF, 'The British Army and the counter insurgency campaign in Van Diemen's Land, with particular reference to the Black Line', MA thesis, University of Tasmania, History & Classics, Hobart, 1995.

Taylor J, 'A study of the Palawa (Tasmanian Aboriginal) place names', MA thesis, University of Tasmania, Riawunna, 2006.

Articles and papers

Aksar Y, 'The specific intent (*dolus specialis*) requirement of the crime of genocide: confluence or conflict between the practice of Ad Hoc Tribunals and the ICJ', *Uluslararası İlişkiler*, vol. 6, no. 23, 2009, pp. 113–26.

Anderson S, 'French anthropology in Australia, the first fieldwork report: François Péron's "Maria Island anthropological observations"', *Aboriginal History*, vol. 25, 2001, pp. 228–42.

Bowdler S, 'The empty coast: conditions for human occupation in southeast Australia during the late Pleistocene', *Terra Nullius*, vol. 32, 2010, pp. 177–85.

Boyce J, 'A dog's breakfast … lunch and dinner: canine dependency in early Van Diemen's Land', *Tasmanian Historical Research Association (THRA) Papers & Proceedings*, vol. 51, no. 4, 2004, pp. 194–213.

Broome R, 'The statistics of frontier conflict', in BA & SG Foster (ed.), *Frontier conflict: the Australian experience*, National Museum of Australia, Canberra, 2003.

Clark I & Cahir DA, 'Understanding "Ngamadjidj": Aboriginal perceptions of Europeans in nineteenth century western Victoria', *Journal of Australian Colonial History*, vol. 13, 2011, pp. 105–24.

Clements N, '"Army of sufferers": The experience of Tasmania's Black Line', *Journal of Australian Studies*, vol. 37, no. 1, 2013, pp. 19–33.

Connor J, 'British frontier warfare logistics and the "Black Line", Van Diemen's Land (Tasmania), 1830', *War in History*, vol. 9, no. 2, 2002, pp. 143–58.

Davies RH, 'On the Aborigines of Van Diemen's Land', *Tasmanian Journal of Natural Science*, vol. 2, 1846, pp. 409–20.

Diamond J, 'In black and white: how have ordinary people, so often throughout history, brought themselves to commit genocide?', *Natural History*, vol. 97, no. 10, 1988, pp. 8–14.

Fels M, 'Culture contact in the county of Buckinghamshire, Van Diemen's Land, 1803–11', *THRA Papers & Proceedings*, vol. 29, no. 2, 1982, pp. 47–69.

Finnane M, 'Just like a "nun's picnic"? violence and colonisation in Australia', *Current Issues in Criminal Justice*, vol. 14, no. 3, 2003, pp. 299–306.

Gover E, 'Tasmania through Russian eyes (nineteenth and early twentieth centuries)', *THRA Papers & Proceedings*, vol. 37, no. 4, 1990, pp. 150–64.

Gregg I, 'A young Englishman's observations of the Aboriginals during five years in Van Diemen's Land: who was Dr John Barnes?', *Tasmanian Ancestry*, vol. 21, no. 1, 2000, pp. 19–24.

Horton D, 'Tasmanian adaptation', *Mankind*, vol. 12, no. 1, 1979, pp. 28–34.

Leigh, 'Of the Aboriginal Inhabitants of Van Diemen's Land', *Missionary Notices to the Methodist Conference*, vol. 3, 1820, pp. 241–43.

Lennox G, 'The Van Diemen's Land Company and the Tasmanian Aborigines: a re-appraisal', *THRA Papers & Proceedings*, vol. 37, no. 4, 1990, pp. 165–208.

Maxwell-Stewart H, '"I could not blame the rangers": Tasmanian bushranging, convicts and convict management', *THRA Papers & Proceedings*, vol. 42, no. 3, 1995, pp. 109–26.

McFarlane I, 'Adolphus Schayer: Van Diemen's Land and the Berlin papers', *THRA Papers & Proceedings*, vol. 57, no. 2, 2010, pp. 105–18.

Meredith C, 'Verbal remarks on the Aborigines of Tasmania', *Royal Society of Tasmania Papers & Proceedings*, 1873, p. 28.

Merry K, 'The cross-cultural relationships between the sealers and the Tasmanian Aboriginal women at Bass Strait and Kangaroo Island in the early nineteenth century', *The Flinders University Online Journal of Interdisciplinary Conference Papers*, vol. 3, no. 1, 2003, pp. 80–88.

Taylor JA, 'Windschuttle's *The fabrication of Aboriginal history*: linguistic matters', *Tasmanian Historical Studies*, vol. 9, 2004, pp. 100–6.

Vanderwal R, 'Adaptive technology in south west Tasmania', *Australian Archaeology*, vol. 8, 1978, pp. 107–27.

Books and book chapters

Alexander A, *Tasmania's convicts: how felons built a free society*, Allen & Unwin, Crows Nest, 2010.

Backhouse J, *A narrative of a visit to the Australian colonies*, Hamilton, Adams & Co., London, 1843.

Bayly CA, *Imperial meridian: the British Empire and the World, 1780–1830*, Longman, Harlow, 1989.

Begg AC & Begg NC, *The world of John Boultbee*, Whitecoulls, Christchurch, 1979.

Bellingshausen, FGT, *The voyage of Captain Bellingshausen to the Antarctic Seas, 1819–1821*, Kraus Reprints, Nendeln, 1967.

Billot C, *John Batman: the story of John Batman and the founding of Melbourne*, Hyland House, Melbourne, 1979.

Bonwick J, *The last of the Tasmanians, or the Black War of Van Diemen's Land*, S. Low, Son & Marston, London, 1870.

—— *The daily life and origins of the Tasmanians*, Sampson Low, London, 1870.

—— *The lost Tasmanian race*, Johnson Reprint Corporation, New York, 1970.

Bowden KM, *Captain James Kelly of Hobart Town*, Melbourne University Press, Carlton, 1964.

Boyce J, *Van Diemen's Land*, Black Inc., Melbourne, 2008.

Brown PL (ed.), *Clyde Company Papers*, vol. 1, Oxford University Press, London, 1949.

Calder G, *Levée, line and martial law: a history of the dispossession of the Mairremmener people of Van Diemen's Land 1803–1832*, Fullers, Launceston, 2010.

Calder JE, *Some accounts of the wars, extirpation, habits, etc. of the native tribes of Tasmania*, Henn & Co., Hobart, 1875.

Cameron P, *Grease and ochre: the blending of two cultures at the colonial sea frontier*, Studies in the History of Aboriginal Tasmania, Fullers, Launceston, 2011.

Campbell AH, *John Batman and the Aborigines*, Kibble, Malmsbury, 1987.

Chapman P. (ed.), *The Diaries and Letters of GTWB Boyes, Volume One, 1820–1832*, Oxford University Press, Melbourne, 1985.

Clark J, 'Devils and horses: religious and creative life in Tasmanian Aboriginal society', in M Roe (ed.), *The flow of culture: Tasmanian studies*, Australian Academy of the Humanities, Canberra, 1987, pp. 50–72.

Cohn-Sherbok D & Sudqi El Alami D, *The Palestine-Israeli conflict: a beginner's guide*, 2nd edn, Oneworld, London, 2002.

Cowan J, *The New Zealand Wars: a history of the Māori campaigns and the pioneering period*, vol. 2, RE Owen, Wellington, 1956.

Curthoys A, 'Genocide in Tasmania: the history of an idea', in AD Moses (ed.), *Empire, colony, genocide: conquest, occupation and subaltern resistance in world history*, Berghahn Books, New York, 2008, pp. 228–51.

Damousi J, *Depraved and disorderly: female convicts, sexuality and gender in colonial Australia*, Cambridge University Press, Melbourne, 1997.

Darwin C, *The voyage of the Beagle*, Bantam, New York, 1972.

Dyer C, *The French explorers and the Aboriginal Australians 1772–1839*, University of Queensland Press, St. Lucia, 2005.

Fenton P, *James Fenton of Forth: a Tasmanian pioneer 1820–1901: a collection of essays by and about James Fenton (1820–1901), his family and friends*, Educare, Melbourne, 2001.

FitzSymonds E, *A looking glass for Tasmania: letters, petitions and other manuscripts relating to Van Diemen's Land 1808–1845*, Sullivan's Cove, Adelaide, 1980.

Gammage B, *The biggest estate on earth: how Aborigines made Australia*, Allen & Unwin, Crows Nest, 2011.

Gover E, *Australia in the Russian mirror: changing perceptions, 1770–1919*, Melbourne University Press, Carlton, 1997.

Graeme-Evans A, *Tasmanian rogues and absconders 1803–1875*, vols 1 & 2, Regal Publications, Launceston, 1994.

Grey J, *Military history of Australia*, 3rd edn, Cambridge University Press, Melbourne, 2008.

Hare R, *The voyage of the* Caroline *from England to Van Diemen's Land and Batavia in 1827–28*, I Marriott (ed.), Longmans, Green & Co., London, 1927.

Hartwell RM, *The economic development of Van Diemen's Land 1820–1850*, Melbourne University Press, Carlton, 1954.

Hobler G, *The diaries of pioneer George Hobler, October 6, 1800–December 13, 1882*, vol. 1, C & H Reproductions Inc., 1992.

Hodgen MT, *Early anthropology in the sixteenth and seventeenth centuries*, Oxford University Press, London, 1964.

Hughes R, *The fatal shore*, Pan, London, 1988.

Jones R, 'Tasmanian tribes', in NB Tindale (ed.), *Aboriginal tribes of Australia: their terrain, environmental controls, distribution, limits and proper names*, Australian National University Press, Canberra, 1974, pp. 319–54.

Leavitt TWH & Fenton J, *The jubilee history of Tasmania illustrated*, vols 1 & 2, Wells & Leavitt, Melbourne, 1881.

Lennox J & Wadsley J, *Barrack Hill: a history of Anglesea Barracks 1811–2011*, Defence Publishing Service, Canberra, 2011.

Lloyd GT, *Thirty-three years in Tasmania and Victoria: being the actual experience of the author interspersed with historic jottings, narratives, and counsel to emigrants*, Houlston & Wright, London, 1862.

Locke J, *Two treatises of government*, P Laslett (ed.), Cambridge University Press, Cambridge, 1960.

McFarlane I, 'Cape Grim', in R Manne (ed.), *Whitewash: on Keith Windschuttle's fabrication of Aboriginal history*, Black Inc., Melbourne, 2003, pp. 277–98.

—— *Beyond awakening: the Aboriginal tribes of north west Tasmania: a history*, Fullers, Launceston, 2008.

McKay A (ed.), *Journals of the land commissioners for Van Diemen's Land, 1826–28*, THRA, Hobart, 1962.

Marshal PJ & Williams TG, *The great map of mankind: perceptions of new worlds in the age of enlightenment*, Harvard University Press, Harvard, 1982.

Marslen TJ, *The friend of Australia: or, a plan for exploring the interior and for carrying on a survey of the whole continent of Australia*, Hurst, Chance & Co., London, 1830.

Melville HS, *The history of Van Diemen's Land from the year 1824 to 1835*, G Mackaness (ed.), Horwitz-Grahame, Sydney, 1965.

Meredith L, *My home in Tasmania*, Bunce, New York, 1853.

Montagu J (ed.), *Statistical returns from Van Diemen's Land 1824–1835*, government printer, Hobart, 1836.

Morgan S, *Land settlement in early Van Diemen's Land: creating an antipodean England*, Cambridge University Press, Oakleigh, 1992.

Mulvaney DJ & Kamminga J, *Prehistory of Australia*, Allen & Unwin, Crows Nest, 1999.

Nicholas S (ed.), *Convict workers: reinterpreting Australia's past*, Cambridge University Press, Melbourne, 1988.

Nicholls M (ed.), *The diary of the Reverend Robert Knopwood 1803–1838: first chaplain of Van Diemen's Land*, THRA, Hobart, 1977.

Oxley D, *Convict maids: the forced migration of women to Australia*, Cambridge University Press, Melbourne, 1996.

Parramore W, *The Parramore letters: letters from William Thomas Parramore, sometime private secretary to Lieutenant Governor Arthur of Van Diemen's Land, to Thirza Cropper, his fiancée in Europe and England, the majority from 1823 to 1825*, DC Shelton (ed.), self-published, Epping, 1993.

Pinker S, *The better angels of our nature: why violence has declined*, Penguin, New York, 2011.

Plomley NJB (ed.), *Weep in silence: a history of the Flinders Island Aboriginal settlement*, Blubber Head Press, Hobart, 1987.

—— 'Robinson's adventures in Bass Strait', in S Murray-Smith (ed.), *Bass Strait: Australia's last frontier*, Australian Broadcasting Commission, Sydney, 1987, pp. 42–51.

—— (ed.), *Jorgen Jorgenson and the Aborigines of Van Diemen's Land: being a reconstruction of his 'lost' book on their customs and habits*, Blubber Head Press, Hobart, 1991.

—— *The Aboriginal/settler clash in Van Diemen's Land, 1803–1831*, QVMAG, Launceston, 1992.

—— *The Tasmanian tribes and cicatrices as tribal indicators among the Tasmanian Aborigines*, QVMAG, Launceston, 1992.

—— *The Tasmanian Aborigines*, Plomley Foundation, Launceston, 1993.

—— (ed.), *Friendly mission: the Tasmanian journals and papers of George Augustus Robinson, 1829–1834*, 2nd edn, Quintus, Hobart, 2008.

Plomley NJB & Henley KA, *The sealers of Bass Strait and the Cape Barren Island community*, Blubber Head Press, Hobart, 1990.

Plomley NJB & Piard-Bernier J, *The General: the visits of the expedition led by Bruny d'Entrecasteaux to Tasmanian waters in 1792 and 1793*, QVMAG, Launceston, 1993.

Prinsep, *The journal of a voyage from Calcutta to Van Diemen's Land: comprising a description of that colony during a six months' residence: from original letters*, Smith & Elder, London, 1833.

Reynolds H, *An indelible stain? the question of genocide in Australia's history*, Penguin, Ringwood, 2001.

—— *The law of the land*, Penguin, Camberwell, 2003.

—— 'Terra Nullius reborn', in R. Manne (ed.), *Whitewash: on Keith Windschuttle's fabrication of Aboriginal history*, Black Inc., Melbourne, 2003, pp. 109–38.

—— *Fate of a free people*, 2nd edn., Penguin Books, Camberwell, 2004.

—— *A history of Tasmania*, Cambridge University Press, Melbourne, 2011.

—— *Forgotten war*, NewSouth Publishing, Sydney, 2013.

Robson LL, *A history of Tasmania: volume one, Van Diemen's Land from the earliest times to 1855*, Oxford University Press, Melbourne, 1983.

Roth HL, *The Aborigines of Tasmania*, F King & Sons, Halifax, 1899.

Rousseau JJ, *Discourse on the origin and the foundations of inequality among men*, NK Singh (ed.), Global Vision Publishing House, Delhi, 1754.

Rudé G, *Protest and punishment: the story of the social and political protesters transported to Australia 1788–1868*, Oxford University Press, London, 1978.

Ryan L, *The Aboriginal Tasmanians*, 2nd edn, Allen & Unwin, Crows Nest, 1996.

—— *Tasmanian Aborigines: a history since 1803*, Allen & Unwin, Crows Nest, 2012.

Shakespeare N, *In Tasmania*, Random House, Milsons Point, 2004.

Sharland, M, *Stones of a century*, Oldham, Bedome & Meredith, Hobart, 1952.

Shaw AGL (ed.), *Van Diemen's Land: copies of all correspondence between Lieutenant-Governor Arthur and his Majesty's Secretary of State for the Colonies, on the subject of the military operations lately carried on against the Aboriginal inhabitants of Van Diemen's Land*, THRA, Hobart, 1971.

Smith B, *European vision and the South Pacific*, 2nd edn, Harper & Row, Sydney, 1985.

Stoddart E, *The Freycinet Line, 1831: Tasmanian history and the Freycinet Peninsula*, Freycinet Experience, Coles Bay, 2003.

Stokes JL, *Discoveries in Australia*, vol. 2, T & W Boone, London, 1846.

Stoney HC, *A residence in Tasmania*, Smith & Elder & Co., London, 1856.

Taylor JA, 'Aboriginal language of health and well-being in Tasmania', in P Richards, B Valentine & T Dunning (eds), *Effecting a cure: aspects of health and medicine in Launceston*, Myola House of Publishing, Launceston, 2006, pp. 3–18.

Thomas B, *Henry Hellyer's observations: journals of life in the Tasmanian bush 1826–1827*, North Down Press, Latrobe, 2011.

Turnbull C, *Black War: The extermination of the Tasmanian Aborigines*, 3rd edn, Sun Books, Melbourne, 1974.

Walker GW, *The life and labours of George Washington Walker*, J Backhouse & C Tylor (eds), Bennett & Brady, London, 1862.

Watson C, Chapman P & Jetson T (eds), *Historical Records of Australia*, ser. 1, 3, 4, Library Committee of the Commonwealth Parliament; Australian Government Publishing Service, Sydney & Canberra, 1914–23; 1997–2008.

West J, *The history of Tasmania with copious information respecting the colonies of New South Wales, Victoria, South Australia, &c., &c., &c.*, vol. 2, H Dowling, London, 1852.

Windschuttle K, *The fabrication of Aboriginal history: volume one, Van Diemen's Land 1803–1847*, Macleay Press, Sydney, 2002.

NOTES

INTRODUCTION

1   Broome, 'Statistics of frontier conflict', pp. 89–90.

2   Clements, 'Frontier conflict', pp. 279–339, pp. 339–41.

3   Clements, 'Frontier conflict', pp. 323–31.

4   H Reynolds, *Forgotten war*, NewSouth Publishing, Sydney, 2013.

5   New Zealand History Online, 'End of the New Zealand Wars', nzhistory.net.nz/war/new-zealand-wars/end; J Cowan, *The New Zealand Wars: a history of the Māori campaigns and the pioneering period*, vol. 2, RE Owen, Wellington, 1956, pp. 552–53.

6   Cowan, *The New Zealand Wars*, pp. 235–43.

7   See M Finnane, 'Just like a "nun's picnic"? violence and colonisation in Australia', *Current Issues in Criminal Justice*, vol. 14, no. 3, 2003, pp. 299–306.

8   As Fig. 1 illustrates, the colonial and Aboriginal populations changed dramatically over the course of the war. The crude averages used here assume the increases and decreases were linear, which is basically accurate for the colonists, but we cannot know in the Aboriginal case.

9   J Grey, *Military history of Australia*, 3rd edn, Cambridge University Press, Melbourne, 2008, pp. 119–20. Australia had the highest casualty rate of any Commonwealth country during World War I.

10 Clements, 'Frontier conflict', pp. 323–31.

11 S Pinker, *The better angels of our nature: why violence has declined*, Viking, New York, 2011, p. 53. Pinker sampled 27 conflicts between non-state societies and nine conflicts between states.

12 R Hughes, *The fatal shore*, Pan, London, 1988, p. 120.

13   LL Robson, *A history of Tasmania: volume one, Van Diemen's Land from the earliest times to 1855*, Oxford University Press, Melbourne, 1983; NJB Plomley, *The Aboriginal/settler clash in Van Diemen's Land, 1803–1831*, Queen Victoria Museum and Art Gallery (QVMAG), Launceston, 1992; H Reynolds, *Fate of a free people*, 2nd edn, Penguin Books, Camberwell, 2004 (first published in 1995); J Boyce, *Van Diemen's Land*, Black Inc., Melbourne, 2008; G Calder, *Levée, line and martial law: a history of the dispossession of the Mairremmener people of Van Diemen's Land 1803–1832*, Fullers, Launceston, 2010.

14   Windschuttle, *Fabrication*, p. 129.

15   Windschuttle, *Fabrication*, p. 386. Unless we accept that luck indulged the Tasmanians continuously for 34,000 years, this conclusion need not be taken seriously.

16   Windschuttle, *Fabrication*, p. 98.

17   *Friendly mission*, p. 427.

18   The term 'envoys' will be used throughout this book to refer to those Aborigines who aided Robinson's mission.

CHAPTER ONE: *Background*

1   A McKay (ed.), *Journals of the land commissioners for Van Diemen's Land, 1826–28*, Tasmanian Historical Research Association (THRA), Hobart, 1962, p. 67.

2   Prinsep, *The journal of a voyage from Calcutta to Van Diemen's Land: comprising a description of that colony during a six months' residence: from original letters*, Smith & Elder, London, 1833, p. 79.

3   Leigh, 'Of the Aboriginal inhabitants of Van Diemen's Land', *Missionary Notices to the Methodist Conference*, vol. 3, 1820, p. 242.

4   JJ Rousseau, *Discourse on the origin and the foundations of inequality among men*, NK Singh (ed.), Global Vision Publishing House, Delhi, 1754, p. 68.

5   J West, *The history of Tasmania with copious information respecting the colonies of New South Wales, Victoria, South Australia, &c., &c., &c.*, vol. 2, H Dowling, London, 1852, p. 3.

6   e.g. PJ Marshal & TG Williams, *The great map of mankind: perceptions of new worlds in the age of enlightenment*, Harvard University Press, Harvard, 1982, p. 293.

7   B Smith, *European vision and the South Pacific*, 2nd edn, Harper & Row, Sydney, 1985, p. 87.

8   M Hodgen, *Early anthropology in the sixteenth and seventeenth centuries*, Oxford University Press, London, 1964, p. 362.

9   Hodgen, *Early anthropology*, pp. 361–66.

10   CA Bayly, *Imperial meridian: the British Empire and the world, 1780–1830*, Longman, Harlow, 1989, p. 256.

11   Bayly, *Imperial meridian*, p. 133.

12   Verdict on the validity of Statute 20, 1822, *Historical Records of Australia* (*HRA*), ser. 4, vol. 1, p. 414.

13   J Locke, *Two treatises of government*, P Laslett (ed.), Cambridge University Press, Cambridge, 1960, p. 329.

14   H Reynolds, *The law of the land*, Penguin, Camberwell, 2003, pp. 19–23.

15   e.g. *Colonial Times*, 11 May 1827, 23, 30 April 1830; *Independent*, 15 October 1831; *Launceston Advertiser*, 15 February 1830, 26 September 1831; *Tasmanian*, 21 December 1827, 28 November 1828, 25 June 1831; N Clements, "Wriggle, and Shuffle, and Twist': attitudes towards Aborigines in the Tasmanian press 1825–1831', Hons thesis, University of Tasmania, 2007.

16   Secondary sources informing this section include: S Nicholas (ed.), *Convict workers: reinterpreting Australia's past*, Cambridge University Press, Melbourne, 1988; Robson, *A history of Tasmania*, section 2; A Alexander, *Tasmania's convicts: how felons built a free society*, Allen & Unwin, Crows Nest, 2010; S Morgan, *Land settlement in early Van Diemen's Land: creating an antipodean England*, Cambridge University Press, Oakleigh, 1992.

17   J Montagu (ed.), *Statistical returns from Van Diemen's Land 1824 to 1835*, government printer, Hobart, 1836, fig. 17; Australian Bureau of Statistics, 'Tasmanian statistics 1804–1902', Canberra, 1989, State Library of Tasmania (SLT), 319.46 TAS.

18   J Montagu (ed.), *Statistical returns of Van Diemen's Land from 1824–35*, government printer, Hobart, 1836, table 36.

19   Alexander, *Tasmania's convicts*, pp. 22–27.

20   A Graeme-Evans, *Tasmanian rogues and absconders 1803–1875*, vol. 2, Regal Publications, Launceston, 1994, p. 2.

21   Reynolds, *Fate of a free people*, p. 100; WH Hudspeth, 'The British Army in Tasmania', c.1940, Royal Society of Tasmania archive, RS3/4(3); JF McMahon, 'The British Army and the counter insurgency campaign in Van Diemen's Land, with particular reference to the Black Line', MA thesis, University of Tasmania, History & Classics, Hobart, 1995, p. 56.

22   J Diamond, 'In black and white: how have ordinary people, so often throughout history, brought themselves to commit genocide?', *Natural History*, vol. 97, no. 10, 1988, p. 8.

23   Clements, 'Frontier conflict', pp. 282–83.

24 M Fels, 'Culture contact in the county of Buckinghamshire, Van Diemen's Land, 1803–11', *THRA Papers & Proceedings*, vol. 29, no. 2, 1982, pp. 59–63.

25 Government Order, 17 May 1817, in *Hobart Town Gazette*, 24 May 1817.

26 West, *History of Tasmania*, p. 11.

27 Clements, 'Frontier conflict', pp. 283–84.

28 Blue Book for 1822, in Australian Bureau of Statistics, 'Tasmanian statistics 1804–1902'.

29 J Lennox and J Wadsley, *Barrack Hill: a history of Anglesea Barracks 1811–2011*, Defence Publishing Service, Canberra, 2011, p. 34.

30 e.g. D Oxley, *Convict maids: the forced migration of women to Australia*, Cambridge University Press, Melbourne, 1996.

31 N Shakespeare, *In Tasmania*, Random House, Milsons Point, 2004, pp. 98–99; Boyce, *Van Diemen's Land*, pp. 237–40; Alexander, *Tasmania's convicts*, pp. 122–29; J Damousi, *Depraved and disorderly: female convicts, sexuality and gender in colonial Australia*, Cambridge University Press, Melbourne, 1997.

32 *Tasmanian*, 10 December 1830.

33 West, *History of Tasmania*, p. 94.

34 Government Order, 25 June 1813, in NJB Plomley (ed.), *Friendly mission: the Tasmanian journals and papers of George Augustus Robinson, 1829–1834*, 2nd edn., Quintus, Hobart, 2008, p. 27.

35 NJB Plomley & KA Henley, *The sealers of Bass Strait and the Cape Barren Island community*, Blubber Head Press, Hobart, 1990, pp. 25–26.

36 *Hobart Town Gazette*, 27 March 1819.

37 M Nicholls (ed.), *The diary of the Reverend Robert Knopwood 1803–1838: first chaplain of Van Diemen's Land*, THRA, Hobart, 1977, p. 99.

38 West, *History of Tasmania*, p. 9.

39 *Colonial Times*, 16 June 1826.

40 Boyce, *Van Diemen's Land*, pp. 84–87.

41 See Chapter 8.

42 *R v. Farrell*, Supreme Court of Van Diemen's Land, 11 August 1824, law.mq.edu.au/research/colonial_case_law/tas/cases/case_index/1824/r_v_farrell; various testimonies, January 1825, Tasmanian Archive and Heritage Office (TAHO), LC347; *Colonial Times*, 2 February, 6 July 1827; *Colonial Advocate*, 1 August 1828; JC Sutherland's diary, 4 May 1830, TAHO, NS61/1/3.

43 *Colonial Advocate*, 1 August 1828.

44 e.g. Nicholls, *Diary of the Reverend Robert Knopwood*, pp. 232, 277, 293–94; *Hobart Town Gazette*, 26 September 1818; *HRA*, ser. 3 vol. 2, pp. 741, 750; Bonwick, *Last of the Tasmanians*, p. 59.

45 *Hobart Town Gazette*, 12 November 1825.

46 *Hobart Town Gazette*, 26 December 1818.

47 e.g. Bigge report, in C Turnbull, *Black War: The extermination of the Tasmanian Aborigines*, 3rd edn, Sun Books, Melbourne, 1974, p. 61.

48 West, *History of Tasmania*, pp. 127–28.

49 Government Proclamation, 13 March 1819, in *Hobart Town Gazette*, 27 March 1819.

50 Sorell to Arthur, 22 May 1824, *HRA*, ser. 3, vol. 4, pp. 134–55.

51 *Hobart Town Gazette*, 16 July 1824.

52 JA Taylor, 'A study of the Palawa (Tasmanian Aboriginal) place names', MA thesis, University of Tasmania, Riawunna, 2006.

53 S Bowdler, 'The empty coast: conditions for human occupation in southeast Australia during the late Pleistocene', *Terra Nullius*, vol. 32, 2010, pp. 177–79.

54 NJB Plomley, *The Tasmanian Aborigines*, Plomley Foundation, Launceston, 1993, pp. 45–55.

55 e.g. Plomley, *The Tasmanian Aborigines*, p. 42; R. Vanderwal, 'Adaptive Technology in South West Tasmania', *Australian Archaeology*, vol. 8, 1978, pp. 107–27; D Horton, 'Tasmanian adaptation', *Mankind*, vol. 12, no. 1, 1979, pp. 28–34.

56 e.g. R Jones, 'Tasmanian tribes', in NB Tindale (ed.), *Aboriginal tribes of Australia: their terrain, environmental controls, Distribution, limits and proper names*, Australian National University Press, Canberra, 1974, p. 325.

57 Jones, 'Tasmanian tribes', p. 324.

58 NJB Plomley, *Tasmanian tribes and cicatrices as tribal indicators among the Tasmanian Aborigines*, QVMAG, Launceston, 1992. p. 3.

59 Plomley, *Tasmanian tribes and cicatrices*, p. 5.

60 Calder, *Levée, line and martial law*. Calder, with John Taylor, derived 'Mairremmener' from a suffix form common to names of certain constituent tribes. It was not contemporaneous.

61 J Backhouse, *A narrative of a visit to the Australian colonies*, Hamilton, Adams & Co., London, 1843, pp. 105–6.

62 Clements, 'Frontier conflict', p. 21.

63 J Taylor, 'Windschuttle's *The fabrication of Aboriginal history*: linguistic matters', *Tasmanian Historical Studies*, vol. 9, 2004, p. 102.

64 Robinson's speech to Australian Aborigines Protection Society, 19 October 1838, law.mq.edu.au/research/colonial_case_law/nsw/other_features/correspondence/robinson_speech_1838.

65 Jones, 'Tasmanian tribes', p. 328.

66   B Gammage, *The biggest estate on earth: how Aborigines made Australia*, Allen & Unwin, Crows Nest, 2011.

67   Plomley, *The Tasmanian Aborigines*, pp. 32–39.

68   e.g. Plomley, *Friendly mission*, pp. 62, 69–70, 143, 172–73.

69   Plomley, *Friendly mission*, p. 319; J Bonwick, *The daily life and origins of the Tasmanians*, Sampson Low, London, 1870, p. 89.

70   Plomley, *Friendly mission*, pp. 400, 670–71.

71   *Hobart Town Courier*, 4 April 1829.

72   JA Taylor, 'Aboriginal language of health and well-being in Tasmania', in P Richards, B Valentine & T Dunning (eds), *Effecting a cure: aspects of health and medicine in Launceston*, Myola House of Publishing, Launceston, 2006, pp. 3–18.

73   G Lloyd, *Thirty-three years in Tasmania and Victoria: being the actual experience of the author interspersed with historic jottings, narratives, and counsel to emigrants*, Houlston & Wright, London, 1862, p. 44.

74   NJB Plomley & J Piard-Bernier, *The General: the visits of the expedition led by Bruny d'Entrecasteaux to Tasmanian waters in 1792 and 1793*, QVMAG, Launceston, 1993, p. 295.

75   e.g. Jeffreys, *Van Diemen's Land*, pp. 118–24; Plomley, *Friendly mission*, p. 562; NJB Plomley (ed.), *Weep in silence: a history of the Flinders Island Aboriginal settlement*, Blubber Head Press, Hobart, 1987, p. 420.

76   Pinker, *The better angels of our nature*, pp. 2–3, 36–55.

77   e.g. Plomley, *Friendly mission*, pp. 425, 652; Plomley, *Weep in silence*, p. 512; Clark to Colonial Secretary (CS), 29 October 1830, TAHO, Colonial Secretary's Office (CSO) 1/316, pp. 706–11.

78   e.g. Shaw, *Van Diemen's Land*, p. 55; West, *History of Tasmania*, p. 20; Plomley, *Friendly mission*, pp. 291–92.

79   e.g. Plomley, *Friendly mission*, pp. 291–92, 410–11, 592–93, 586–87.

80   e.g. Plomley, *Friendly mission*, pp. 431–32, 448–49, 586–87; West, *History of Tasmania*, pp. 81–82; Fels, 'Culture contact', p. 59.

81   Plomley, *Friendly mission*, pp. 408–9.

82   Plomley, *Friendly mission*, p. 405.

83   Plomley, *Friendly mission*, p. 405.

84   Plomley, *Friendly mission*, pp. 406, 409.

85   Plomley, *Friendly mission*, pp. 894–95.

86   Plomley, *Friendly mission*, p. 399.

87   Plomley, *Friendly mission*, p. 433.

88   Plomley, *Friendly mission*, pp. 405–6.

89   e.g. the pademelon's creation, in Plomley, *Friendly mission*, p. 406.

90   e.g. Gilbert Robertson's journal, 13 January 1829, TAHO, CSO1/331, p. 115; *Hobart Town Courier*, 21 March 1829; Plomley, *Friendly mission*, pp. 523–24, 596.

91   GW Walker, *The life and labours of George Washington Walker*, J Backhouse & C Tylor (ed.), Bennett & Brady, London, 1862, pp. 100–1, 110.

92   e.g. Plomley, *Friendly mission*, pp. 166–67, 426, 634–35, 756–57.

93   Plomley, *Friendly mission*, pp. 429–30, 445–47, 521–24, 572–76.

94   e.g. Backhouse, *A narrative*, pp. 104–20.

95   e.g. NJB Plomley (ed.), *Jorgen Jorgenson and the Aborigines of Van Diemen's Land: being a reconstruction of his 'lost' book on their customs and habits*, Blubber Head Press, Hobart, 1991, pp. 67–68; J Bonwick, *The daily life and origins of the Tasmanians*, Sampson Low, London, 1870, p. 48.

96   Walker, *Life and labours*, p. 108.

97   e.g. Curr to CS, 5 February 1830, TAHO, CSO1/330, p. 85.

98   Plomley, *Jorgen Jorgenson*, p. 67.

99   e.g. Plomley, *Friendly mission*, pp. 670–71, 907–9.

100   e.g. Plomley, *Friendly mission*, pp. 69–70, 184–85, 300–1.

101   Plomley, *Friendly mission*, p. 572.

102   Plomley, *Friendly mission*, p. 532.

103   Plomley, *Friendly mission*, p. 334.

104   Davies, 'On the Aborigines of Van Diemen's Land', p. 418.

105   e.g. Davies, 'On the Aborigines of Van Diemen's Land', p. 416; Horton, 'Tasmanian adaptation', p. 33.

106   I McFarlane, 'Adolphus Schayer: Van Diemen's Land and the Berlin papers', *THRA Papers & Proceedings*, vol. 57, no. 2, 2010, pp. 105–118.

107   e.g. Lloyd, *Thirty-three years*, pp. 43–49; Plomley, *Jorgen Jorgenson*, p. 68.

108   Plomley & Piard-Bernier, *The General*, p. 369.

109   S Anderson, 'French anthropology in Australia, the first fieldwork report: François Péron's "Maria Island anthropological observations" ', *Aboriginal History*, vol. 25, 2001, pp. 236–37.

110   This belief was common in mainland Australia (I Clark & DA Cahir, 'Understanding "Ngamadjidj": Aboriginal perceptions of Europeans in nineteenth century Western Victoria', *Journal of Australian Colonial History*, vol. 13, 2011, pp. 105–24).

111   West, *History of Tasmania*, p. 90.

112   e.g. Plomley, *Friendly mission*, p. 64; Plomley, *Weep in silence*, p. 507.

113   Plomley, *Weep in silence*, p. 1015.

114   Plomley, *Friendly mission*, p. 557.

115   Plomley, *Friendly mission*, p. 408.

116   See Chapter 8.

117   Plomley, *Friendly mission*, p. 408.

118   e.g. Plomley, *Friendly mission*, pp. 143, 260; Backhouse, *A narrative*, p. 103; Bonwick, *Daily life and origins*, pp. 85, 87.

119   Clements, 'Frontier conflict', pp. 326–30. There was a report of two probably detribalised women with catarrh at Jerusalem in 1827, but another source contradicts the report.

120   Plomley, *Friendly mission*, p. 63.

121   Plomley, *Friendly mission*, pp. 78–79, 175–76, 212–15, 404–6; Hurling & Smith depositions, 26 June 1827, TAHO, CSO1/316, pp. 15–27; Backhouse, *A narrative*, p. 181.

122   Risdon was held by Lieutenant William Moore, who ordered his men to open fire with muskets. A cannon (reportedly loaded with grapeshot) was also fired. For the main accounts of this affray, see Calder, *Levée, line and martial law*, pp. 232–43.

123   Fels, 'Culture contact', pp. 55–58.

124   Clements, 'Frontier conflict', p. 283.

125   Oxley's report on Port Dalrymple, 1810, *HRA*, ser. 3, vol. 1, p. 769.

126   Lloyd, *Thirty-Three Years*, p. 55.

127   Plomley, *The Tasmanian Aborigines*, p. 46.

128   e.g. Plomley, *Friendly mission*, pp. 171–72, 287–88, 685–89; J Boyce, 'A dog's breakfast … lunch and dinner: canine dependency in early Tasmania', *THRA Papers & Proceedings*, vol. 51, no. 4, 2004, pp. 194–213.

129   e.g. Plomley, *Friendly mission*, p. 118.

130   *Tasmanian and Port Dalrymple Advertiser*, 12 January 1825.

131   e.g. West, *History of Tasmania*, pp. 9, 15–16; National Library of Australia (NLA), MS3251/2/4, pp. 31–33; *Tasmanian and Port Dalrymple Advertiser*, 12, 19 January 1825.

132   C Meredith, 'Verbal remarks on the Aborigines of Tasmania', *Royal Society of Tasmania Papers & Proceedings*, 1873, p. 28.

133   McMinn deposition, 16 March 1830, TAHO, CSO1/323, pp. 197–98.

134   e.g. Plomley, *Friendly mission*, p. 78; Plomley, *Jorgen Jorgenson*, p. 59.

135   See Chapters 3 and 4.

136   Brodribb to Aborigines Committee (AC), 11 March 1830, in Shaw, *Van Diemen's Land*, p. 52.

137   *Hobart Town Gazette*, 17, 24 April 1819.

138   West, *History of Tasmania*, p. 10.

139   West, *History of Tasmania*, pp. 9–10; *Derwent Star*, 29 January 1810.

140 Calder, *Some accounts of the wars, extirpation, habits, etc. of the native tribes of Tasmania*, Henn & Co., Hobart, 1875, pp. 94–95.

141 Reynolds, *Fate of a free people*, p. 41.

142 Plomley, *Friendly mission*, p. 165.

143 *Colonial Times*, 29 September 1826, p. 3.

144 e.g. Clark to Vicary, 8 September 1830, TAHO, CSO1/316, p. 618; *Colonial Times*, 10 November 1826; Plomley, *Friendly mission*, p. 541.

145 McKay deposition, 24 September 1831, TAHO, CSO1/316, pp. 981–83.

146 West, *History of Tasmania*, p. 272.

147 Parramore to family, 19 November 1823, in W Parramore, *The Parramore letters: letters from William Thomas Parramore, sometime Private Secretary to Lieutenant Governor Arthur of Van Diemen's Land, to Thirza Cropper, his fiancée in Europe and England, the majority from 1823–1825*, DC Shelton (ed.), self-published, Epping, New South Wales, 1993, pp. 30–31.

148 FGT Bellingshausen, *The voyage of Captain Bellingshausen to the Antarctic Seas, 1819–1821*, Kraus Reprints, Nendeln, Liechtenstein, 1967, p. 355. Bellingshausen conducted his investigations from Sydney.

149 Clements, 'Frontier conflict', pp. 334–35.

CHAPTER TWO: *Attitudes*

1   *Hobart Town Gazette*, 8 April 1825.

2   *Colonial Times*, 1 December 1826. Original capitalisation.

3   See Clements, ' "Wriggle, and Shuffle, and Twist" ', pp. 39–41.

4   These boards, attributed to surveyor-general George Frankland, were to be nailed to trees or otherwise distributed among the natives in an effort to convey the government's intentions. Nothing is known of their efficacy, though they were widely ridiculed.

5   West, *History of Tasmania*, p. 37.

6   G Hobler, *The diaries of pioneer George Hobler, October 6, 1800–December 13, 1882*, vol. 1, C & H Reproductions, 1992, p. 94.

7   *Tasmanian*, 19 February 1830.

8   *Launceston Advertiser*, 6 July 1829.

9   *Colonial Advocate*, 1 May 1828. Original italics.

10   Brown to AC, 5 February 1830, TAHO, CSO1/323, pp. 125–26.

11   *Colonial Times*, 27 August 1830.

12   *Tasmanian*, 26 February 1830.

13   Hudspeth to AC, 16 March 1830, TAHO, CSO1/323, p. 331.

14   West, *History of Tasmania*, p. 37.

15   Steel to Arthur, 15 June 1829, TAHO, CSO1/316, pp. 281–83.

16   e.g. *Colonial Times*, 19 March 1830; *Hobart Town Courier*, 20 December 1828, 7 March 1829.

17   TAHO, CSO1/322.

18   Curtain to CS, 5 March 1828, TAHO, CSO1/316, p. 113.

19   *Hobart Town Courier*, 13 March 1830.

20   Hobbs to AC, 9 March 1830, in Shaw, *Van Diemen's Land*, p. 51.

21   AC report, 19 March 1830, in Shaw, *Van Diemen's Land*, p. 45.

22   Anstey to CS, 16 November 1829, State Library of New South Wales (SLNSW), Mitchell Library (ML), A1771, vol. 28, p. 101.

23   Robertson to Anstey, 12 November 1829, SLNSW, ML, A1771, vol. 28, pp. 94–99.

24   Gray to Arthur, 24 October 1830, TAHO, CSO1/316, p. 696.

25   Robertson to AC, 4 March 1830, in Shaw, *Van Diemen's Land*, p. 48.

26   *Tasmanian*, 5 March 1830.

27   Garrison Order, 12 December 1828, in Shaw, *Van Diemen's Land*, p. 31.

28   Executive Council minutes, 14 June 1826, in Reynolds, *Fate of a free people*, p. 102.

29   e.g. Reynolds, *Fate of a free people*, p. 102; Brown to AC, 5 February 1830, TAHO, CSO1/323, pp. 140–49.

30   Brown to AC, 5 February 1830, TAHO, CSO1/323, pp. 144.

31   Brown to AC, 5 February 1830, TAHO, CSO1/323, p. 146.

32   e.g. Westwood deposition, 17 January 1829, TAHO, CSO1/316, pp. 220–22.

33   Armstrong deposition, 1 April 1829, *HRA*, ser. 1, vol. 15, p. 317.

34   e.g. Simpson to CS, 2 December 1828, TAHO, CSO1/316, p. 207; Brown to AC, 5 February 1830, TAHO, CSO1/323, pp. 149–50.

35   See Clements, ' "Wriggle, and Shuffle, and Twist" '.

36   Clements, 'Frontier conflict', p. 347.

37   H Melville, *The history of Van Diemen's Land from the year 1824 to 1835*, G Mackaness (ed.), Horwitz-Grahame, Sydney, 1965, pp. 31–32.

38   *Colonial Times*, 8 December 1826.

39   O'Connor to Parramore, 11 December 1827, TAHO, CSO1/323, p. 75.

40   Clark to Arthur, 8 November 1826, SLNSW, ML, A1771, vol. 28, p. 20.

41   West, *History of Tasmania*, p. 18.

42   Amos diary, 14, 15 December 1823, 10 January, 25, 28, 29 March, 23 May, 12 July 1824, TAHO, NS323/1/1.

43   e.g. Plomley, *Friendly mission*, p. 460; Hobler, *Pioneer George Hobler*, p. 176.

44   *Colonial Times*, 2 July 1830.

45   Bonwick, *Last of the Tasmanians*, pp. 57–58.

46   HL Roth, *The Aborigines of Tasmania*, F King & Sons, Halifax, 1899, p. 172. Some of these stories were undoubtedly coloured by bravado, but they are too numerous to be dismissed.

47   e.g. *Hobart Town Gazette*, 26 December 1818; *Tasmanian*, 25 June 1831; *Colonial Advocate*, 1 April, 1 May 1828; *Colonial Times*, 8 October 1830; Plomley, *Friendly mission*, p. 95; Clements, ' "Wriggle, and Shuffle, and Twist" ', pp. 16–21.

48   Draft of Robinson's unfinished book, in NJB Plomley, 'Robinson's Adventures in Bass Strait', in S Murray-Smith, *Bass Strait: Australia's Last Frontier*, Australian Broadcasting Commission, Sydney, 1987, p. 43.

49   West, *History of Tasmania*, p. 269.

50   JL Stokes, *Discoveries in Australia*, T & W Boone, London, 1846, vol. 2, pp. 459–60.

51   AC report, 19 March 1830, in Shaw, *Van Diemen's Land*, p. 41.

52   *Hobart Town Courier*, 13 November 1830.

53   Bradstreet to family, 16 January 1824, TAHO, NS690/1/9.

54   Barnes to AC, 10 March 1830, TAHO, CSO1/323, p. 300.

55   Plomley, *Friendly mission*, p. 207.

56   *Colonial Times*, 2 July 1830.

57   P Fenton, *James Fenton of Forth: a Tasmanian pioneer 1820–1901: a collection of essays by and about James Fenton (1820–1901) his family and friends*, Educare, Melbourne, 2001, pp. 201–2.

58   *Launceston Advertiser*, 28 March 1831.

59   e.g. Plomley, *Friendly mission*, p. 100; West, *History of Tasmania*, p. 9; *Colonial Times*, 17 September, 8 October 1830.

60   Roth, *Aborigines of Tasmania*, p. 172.

61   Hobbs to AC, 9 March 1830, in Shaw, *Van Diemen's Land*, pp. 49–51.

62   Plomley, *Friendly mission*, p. 629.

63   Plomley, *Friendly mission*, p. 100.

64   Leavitt and Fenton, *Jubilee history*, pp. 53–54.

65   Plomley, *Friendly mission*, p. 379.

66   Clements, 'Frontier conflict', pp. 330–31.

67   *Hobart Town Gazette*, 29 November 1826.

68   e.g. *Hobart Town Courier*, 19 April 1828.

69   Melville, *History of Van Diemen's Land*, p. 73.

70   Government Proclamation, 15 April 1828, in *Hobart Town Courier*, 19 April 1828.

71   Government Proclamation, 1 November 1828, in *Hobart Town Courier*, 8 November 1828. Original capitalisation.

72   *Launceston Advertiser*, 5 October 1831.

73   e.g. Arthur to CS, 13 March 1830, TAHO, CSO1/316, p. 455.

74   Fenton, *James Fenton of Forth*, p. 201.

75   Alexander, *Tasmania's convicts*, p. 24.

76   e.g. L Ryan, *The Aboriginal Tasmanians*, Allen & Unwin, Crows Nest, 1996, p. 255; Boyce, *Van Diemen's Land*, pp. 258–322; A Curthoys, 'Genocide in Tasmania: the history of an idea', in AD Moses (ed.), *Empire, colony, genocide: conquest, occupation and subaltern resistance in world history*, Berghahn Books, New York, 2008, pp. 244–46.

77   H Reynolds, 'Genocide in Tasmania', in AD Moses (ed.), *Genocide and settler society: frontier violence and stolen indigenous children in Australian history*, Berghahn Books, New York, 2004, pp. 127–29; Curthoys, 'Genocide in Tasmania', p. 229. Reynolds and Curthoys present examples of this claim, but do not make it themselves.

78   Murray to Arthur, 5 November 1830, in Shaw, *Van Diemen's Land*, p. 56.

79   H Reynolds, *An indelible stain? the question of genocide in Australia's history*, Penguin, Ringwood, 2001, pp. 13–33, 49–86; H Reynolds, *Forgotten war*, NewSouth Publishing, Sydney, 2013, pp. 138–41, 148–57.

80   Reynolds, *An indelible stain?*, pp. 15–32; Reynolds, *Forgotten war*, pp. 148–50.

81   Y Aksar, 'The specific intent (*dolus specialis*) requirement of the crime of genocide: confluence or conflict between the practice of Ad Hoc Tribunals and the ICJ', *Uluslararası İlişkiler*, vol. 6, no. 23, 2009, pp. 113–126.

82   e.g. Wood to AC, 7 March 1830, TAHO, CSO1/323, pp. 295–98; Barnes to AC, 10 March 1830, TAHO, CSO1/323, p. 299; Clark to AC, 15 March 1830, TAHO, CSO1/323, pp. 319–325; Anstey to AC, 18 March 1830, TAHO, CSO1/323, p. 340.

83   Henry Reynolds first made this argument in *Fate of a free people*.

84   Plomley, *Friendly mission*, p. 585.

85   Plomley, *Friendly mission*, p. 101.

86   Plomley, *Friendly mission*, pp. 335, 762–63, 891.

87   Robertson to Lascelles, 17 November 1828, TAHO, CSO1/331, p. 175.

88   *Colonial Times*, 10 November 1826.

89   Sherwin deposition, 23 January 1830, TAHO, CSO1/316, pp. 430–33.

90   Bellingshausen, *The voyage of Captain Bellingshausen*, p. 355.

91   Plomley, *Friendly mission*, p. 585.

92   Robinson to CS, 5 January 1832, in Plomley, *Friendly mission*, pp. 602–3.

93   Robinson to Executive Council, 23 February 1831, in Shaw, *Van Diemen's Land*, p. 81.

94   Plomley, *Friendly mission*, p. 318.

95   Simpson to CS, 4 September 1828, TAHO, CSO1/316, p. 160.

96   Moriarty to CS, 25 August 1831, TAHO, CSO1/316, p. 941; Smith to CS, 7 September 1831, TAHO, CSO1/316, pp. 954–57.

97   Robinson to CS, 24 February 1831, in Plomley, *Friendly mission*, p. 470.

98   GF Story to J Bonwick, n.d., University of Tasmania library special and rare materials collection, eprints.utas.edu.au/2228.

99   e.g. O'Connor to AC, 17 March 1830, in Shaw, *Van Diemen's Land*, pp. 54–55; Plomley, *Friendly mission*, pp. 298–300, 309–12, 412, 451–52.

100   Plomley, *Friendly mission*, p. 585.

101   e.g. *Hobart Town Courier*, 20 December 1828, 26 March 1831; *Colonial Times*, 1 October 1830; Williams to CS, 16 December 1828, TAHO, CSO1/316, pp. 210–12; Robinson to Arthur, 20 November 1830, TAHO, CSO1/317, pp. 216–33.

102   Plomley, *Jorgen Jorgenson*, p. 70.

103   Meredith, 'Verbal Remarks on the Aborigines of Tasmania', p. 28.

104   Lloyd, *Thirty-three years*, p. 57.

105   Robinson to CS, 27 October 1836, SLNSW, ML, A2188, vol. 28, p. 310.

106   Plomley, *Friendly mission*, p. 87.

107   Plomley, *Friendly mission*, pp. 253–54.

108   Simpson to CS, 8 March 1831, TAHO, CSO1/316, pp. 890–93.

109   AC report, 19 March 1830, in Shaw, *Van Diemen's Land*, pp. 39–40.

110   Bonwick, *Last of the Tasmanians*, p. 60.

111   Dry to AC, 7 March 1830, TAHO, CSO1/323, p. 289.

112   Roberts deposition, 16 July 1825, NLA, MS3251/1/4, p. 10.

113   *Hobart Town Courier*, 13 February 1830.

114   Chadwick deposition, 31 August 1829, TAHO, CSO1/316, pp. 296–300.

115   Plomley, *Friendly mission*, pp. 70–72.

116   e.g. Vicary to CS, 9 February 1830, TAHO, CSO1/316, pp. 402–3; Jorgenson to Anstey, 24 February 1830, TAHO, CSO1/320, section D; Anstey to CS, 31 December 1830, TAHO, CSO1/316, p. 771; *Colonial Times*, 12, 19 November 1830.

117   Plomley, *Friendly mission*, p. 562.

118   Executive Council minutes, 23 February 1831, in Shaw, *Van Diemen's Land*, pp. 80–82.

119   *Colonial Times*, 26 January 1827.

120   e.g. Barnes to AC, 10 March 1830, TAHO, CSO1/323, pp. 299–305; O'Connor to AC, 17 March 1830, in Shaw, *Van Diemen's Land*, pp. 54–55.

121   O'Connor to AC, 17 March 1830, in Shaw, *Van Diemen's Land*, pp. 54–55.

122   *Colonial Times*, 3 September 1830.

123   *Hobart Town Courier*, 31 January 1829.

124   Plomley, *Jorgen Jorgenson*, p. 63.

125   TJ Marslen, *The friend of Australia: or, a plan for exploring the interior and for carrying on a survey of the whole continent of Australia*, Hurst, Chance & Co., London, 1830, p. 241.

126   *Hobart Town Courier*, 11 December 1830.

127   *Launceston Advertiser*, 25 October 1830.

128   *Tasmanian*, 28 November 1828.

129   Plomley, *Jorgenson and the Aborigines*, p. 114. Jorgenson paraphrasing.

CHAPTER THREE: *Warfare*

1   For more on population, see Clements, 'Frontier conflict', pp. 323–31.

2   Leavitt & Fenton, *Jubilee history*, p. 53.

3   *Hobart Town Gazette*, 11 November 1826.

4   AC report, 19 March 1830, in Shaw, *Van Diemen's Land*, p. 36.

5   Clark to AC, 15 March 1830, TAHO, CSO1/323, pp. 319–25.

6   Plomley, *Friendly mission*, p. 105.

7   Goldie to Curr, 16 September 1829, in McFarlane, *Beyond awakening*, p. 110.

8   *Launceston Advertiser*, 26 October 1829; Plomley, *Friendly mission*, p. 278.

9   *Colonial Times*, 5 April 1836.

10   Plomley, *Friendly mission*, p. 377.

11   Plomley, *Friendly mission*, p. 379. Robinson believed this was a different incident from the one above.

12   Fenton, *James Fenton of Forth*, p. 201.

13   Perry deposition, 14 March 1826, NLA, MS3251/2/2, pp. 215–17.

14   Simpson to CS, 18 March 1828, TAHO, CSO1/316, pp. 122–24.

15   JR Beams (great-grandson of Thomas), 1947, Beams family papers, Flowery Gully, private collection.

16   Quotation: John Batman referring to roving party objectives, in AH Campbell, *John Batman and the Aborigines*, Kibble, Malmsbury, 1987, p. 54.

17   Anstey to Arthur, 14 November 1828, in Plomley, *Jorgen Jorgenson*, pp. 81–82. Original italics.

18   *Hobart Town Courier*, 12 September 1829; Jorgenson to Arthur, 5 January 1828, in Plomley, *Jorgen Jorgenson*, pp. 33–37.

19   E Gover, *Australia in the Russian mirror: changing perceptions, 1770–1919*, Melbourne University Press, Carlton, 1997, p. 45.

20   Armstrong deposition, 1 April 1829, *HRA*, ser. 1, vol. 15, p. 317.

21   Government notice, in *Hobart Town Gazette*, 29 November 1826.
22   Danvers to Anstey, 9 December 1828, TAHO, CSO1/320, section E.
23   Anstey to CS, 9 December 1828, TAHO, CSO1/329, p. 269; *Hobart Town Courier*, 13 December 1828.
24   Ayton deposition, 15 March 1830, TAHO, CSO1/330, p. 109.
25   Batman to Anstey, 7 August 1829, TAHO, CSO1/320, section B.
26   C Billot, *John Batman: The story of John Batman and the founding of Melbourne*, Hyland House, Melbourne, 1979, p. 48.
27   CS to Simpson, 4 August 1830, in Reynolds, *Fate of a free people*, p. 114.
28   West, *History of Tasmania*, pp. 31–32.
29   Lloyd, *Thirty-three years*, pp. 107, 157; Plomley, *Jorgen Jorgenson*, p. 56.
30   *Ambush at Night* depicts a campfire ambush in South Australia a decade after the Black War, but I am aware of no other artist representations of the tactic.
31   Plomley, *Friendly mission*, p. 527.
32   Reynolds, *Fate of a free people*, p. 72.
33   e.g. *Launceston Advertiser*, 2 August 1830; Curr to Directors, 14 January 1828, in McFarlane, *Beyond awakening*, p. 91.
34   Reynolds, *Fate of a free people*, p. 72.
35   e.g. Melville, *History of Van Diemen's Land*, pp. 78–79; *Colonial Times*, 19 March 1830; Williams deposition, 30 June 1827, TAHO, CSO1/316, pp. 28–33.
36   e.g. *Hobart Town Courier*, 9 October 1830; *Tasmanian*, 11 June 1830; Robertson to Lascelles, 17 November 1828, TAHO, CSO1/331, pp. 170–71.
37   Leavitt & Fenton, *Jubilee history*, pp. 53–54.
38   Hobler, *Pioneer George Hobler*, p. 40.
39   Hobler, *Pioneer George Hobler*, p. 60. Hobler's neighbour was Richard Dry.
40   *Tasmanian*, 16 May 1828.
41   *Colonial Times*, 30 January 1829.
42   *Hobart Town Courier*, 13 November 1830; *Colonial Times*, 1 June 1831.
43   Plomley, *Friendly mission*, p. 292.
44   Plomley, *Friendly mission*, p. 425.
45   Plomley, *Friendly mission*, p. 431.
46   Plomley, *Friendly mission*, pp. 448–49.
47   Plomley, *Friendly mission*, p. 425.
48   Plomley, *Friendly mission*, pp. 452, 518, 692; KM Bowden, *Captain James Kelly of Hobart Town*, Melbourne University Press, Carlton, 1964, pp. 42–43; Calder, *Some accounts*, p. 33.
49   Plomley, *Friendly mission*, p. 531.

50   Plomley, *Friendly mission*, p. 531.

51   Plomley, *Friendly mission*, p. 395.

52   Plomley, *Friendly mission*, p. 523; Calder, *Some accounts*, pp. 31–32.

53   Plomley, *Friendly mission*, p. 297.

54   Plomley, *Friendly mission*, p. 395.

55   e.g. Nicholls, *The Diary of the Reverend Robert Knopwood*, pp. 128, 171; Plomley, *Friendly mission*, p. 405; Simpson to Arthur, 3 October 1830, TAHO, CSO1/316, pp. 656–59; Roth, *Aborigines of Tasmania*, pp. 67–68; 73–74.

56   Plomley, *The Tasmanian Aborigines*, pp. 47–48; Plomley, *Friendly mission*, p. 255.

57   Walker, *Life and labours*, pp. 46–47.

58   Plomley, *The Tasmanian Aborigines*, p. 48; Plomley, *Friendly mission*, pp. 59–60.

59   Plomley, *Friendly mission*, pp. 59–60.

60   *Hobart Town Courier*, 13 December 1828.

61   Lascelles to Arthur, 16 June 1829, TAHO, CSO1/316, p. 275.

62   Story to Arthur, 25 October 1831, TAHO, CSO1/316, pp. 1015–19; Plomley, *Friendly mission*, pp. 295–96, 309–12, 454, 526–27, 604.

63   e.g. Gray to Arthur, 23 October 1830, TAHO, CSO1/316, pp. 691–95; *Friendly mission*, pp. 302, 819, 889.

64   Anstey to AC, 18 March 1830, TAHO, CSO1/323, p. 343.

65   *Tasmanian*, 18 April 1828.

66   *Hobart Town Courier*, 18 October 1828.

67   *Colonial Times*, 16 July 1830.

68   Calder, *Some accounts*, p. 51.

69   Péron's Maria Island report, in Plomley, *The Baudin expedition*, pp. 89–90.

70   Vicary to CS, 12 February 1830, TAHO, CSO1/316, pp. 404–5.

71   L Meredith, *My home in Tasmania*, Bunce, New York, 1853, p. 86.

72   Clark to CS, 29 October 1830, TAHO, CSO1/316, p. 710.

73   Hooper to Anstey, 19 August 1830, TAHO, CSO1/316, pp. 571–74.

74   *Colonial Times*, 16 July 1830.

75   Smith to Parramore, 22 March 1830, TAHO, CSO1/316, pp. 480–82.

76   Executive Council minutes, 27 July 1830, in Shaw, *Van Diemen's Land*, p. 63.

77   Hobbs to AC, 9 March 1830, in Shaw, *Van Diemen's Land*, p. 50.

78   *Hobart Town Courier*, 8 December 1827.

79   Harte to CS, 20 March 1830, TAHO, CSO1/316, pp. 126–28.

80   *Hobart Town Courier*, 6 June 1829.

81   E FitzSymonds, *A looking glass for Tasmania: letters, petitions and other manuscripts relating to Van Diemen's Land 1808–1845*, Sullivan's Cove, Adelaide, 1980, pp. 35–36.

82   Roth, *Aborigines of Tasmania*, p. 136; Darling to Arthur, 4 May 1832, SLNSW, ML, A1771, p. 108.

83   Plomley, *Friendly mission*, p. 541.

84   *Hobart Town Courier*, 8 March 1828.

85   John Allen file, Glamorgan Spring Bay Historical Society archive.

86   e.g. Simpson to CS, 23 August 1830, TAHO, CSO1/316, pp. 581–82; Anstey to CS, 21 December 1830, TAHO, CSO1/316, pp. 768; Plomley, *Friendly mission*, p. 568; Story to Bonwick, n.d., Utas ePrints no. 2228.

87   Scott to Douglas, 30 September 1830, TAHO, CSO1/316, pp. 652–55.

88   *Colonial Times*, 22 October 1830.

89   Calder, *Some accounts*, p. 100.

90   *Hobart Town Courier*, 8 March 1828.

91   Simpson to CS, 4 September 1828, TAHO, CSO1/316, p. 160.

92   Hobler, *Pioneer George Hobler*, pp. 128–29.

93   Vicary to CS, 9 August 1830, TAHO, CSO1/316, pp. 550–58.

94   Anstey to CS, 23 August 1830, TAHO, CSO1/316, pp. 591–94.

95   Brown to AC, 5 February 1830, TAHO, CSO1/323, p. 135.

96   e.g. Anstey to CS, 31 December 1830, TAHO, CSO1/316, pp. 772–74; *Hobart Town Gazette*, 19 October 1816; *Hobart Town Courier*, 25 October 1828, 11 September 1830.

97   e.g. *Hobart Town Courier*, 12 April 1828; Clark to CS, 24 March 1828, TAHO, CSO1/316, p. 134; Anstey to CS, 24 August, 31 December 1830, TAHO, CSO1/316, pp. 593, 770, 774.

98   Hobler, *Pioneer George Hobler*, pp. 94–95.

99   *Colonial Advocate*, 1 April 1828.

100   *Ibid*. Original italics.

101   Clements, 'Frontier conflict', p. 347.

102   Oxen: Plomley, *Friendly mission*, pp. 220, 586; *Hobart Town Gazette*, 6 August 1824; Clark to CS, 29 October 1830, TAHO, CSO1/316, p. 710. Horses: *Hobart Town Courier*, 13 December 1828, 28 August 1830; *Tasmanian*, 12 December 1828; Lyttleton to CS, 31 January 1831, TAHO, CSO1/316, p. 856; *Hobart Town Courier*, 8 March 1828; Meredith, *My home in Tasmania*, p. 81.

103   Sheep: Jones deposition, 15 March 1830, TAHO, CSO1/323, pp. 191–96; *Hobart Town Gazette* of 29 April 1825; *Hobart Town Courier*, 21 June, 13 December 1828; Clark to CS, 29 October 1830, CSO1/316, p. 707;

Colonial Times, 29 September 1826, 26 March 1830. Cattle: *Colonial Advocate*, 1 May 1828; Plomley, *Friendly mission*, pp. 636–68; *Hobart Town Gazette*, 6 August 1824; Clark to CS, 29 October 1830, TAHO, CSO1/316, p. 710.

104   Abbot to CS, 12 November 1827, TAHO, CSO1/316, pp. 64–65; *Tasmanian*, 16 November 1827; *Tasmanian*, 25 April 1828; Anstey to Arthur, 21 December 1830, TAHO, CSO1/316, p. 776. Cattle herds were much smaller, though losses were comparable.

105   Clements, 'Frontier conflict', p. 346.

106   e.g. Bonwick, *The lost Tasmanian race*, p. 65; McKay, *Journals of the land commissioners*, p. 94.

107   Clark to AC, 15 March 1830, TAHO, CSO1/323, p. 321.

108   Robertson to AC, 4 March 1830, in Shaw, *Van Diemen's Land*, p. 48.

109   Clark to CS, 29 October 1830, TAHO, CSO1/316, pp. 706–11.

110   See Chapter 5.

111   Gray to Arthur, 19 October 1830, TAHO, CSO1/316, pp. 684–87.

112   *Tasmanian*, 22 October 1830.

113   Walpole to Arthur, 29 October 1830, TAHO, CSO1/324.

114   Plomley, *Friendly mission*, p. 297.

115   e.g. West, *History of Tasmania*, p. 85; Plomley, *Friendly mission*, pp. 292, 345, 411, 586.

116   Roth, *Aborigines of Tasmania*, p. 73.

117   Robertson to Lascelles, 17 November 1828, TAHO, CSO1/331, pp. 170–73.

118   Gilbert Robertson's journal, 2 November 1829, TAHO, CSO1/331, pp. 85–86.

119   Hobler, *Pioneer George Hobler*, pp. 186–87.

120   Plomley, *Weep in silence*, p. 512.

CHAPTER FOUR: *Experience*

1   Vicary to CS, 15 June 1830, TAHO, CSO1/316, pp. 525–28.

2   *Hobart Town Courier*, 25 October, 1 November 1828.

3   Clements, 'Frontier conflict', p. 343.

4   *Tasmanian*, 26 February 1830.

5   West, *History of Tasmania*, p. 34.

6   See H Maxwell-Stewart, '"I could not blame the rangers": Tasmanian bush-ranging, convicts and convict management', *THRA Papers & Proceedings*, vol. 42, no. 3, 1995, pp. 109–26.

7   *Colonial Times*, 5 January 1827.

8   *Hobart Town Gazette*, 6 August 1824; *Colonial Times*, 1 June 1831.

9   Bryan to Smith, 10 November 1827, TAHO, CSO1/316, pp. 58–59.
10   O'Connor to Parramore, 11 December 1827, TAHO, CSO1/323, pp. 63–75.
11   John Allen file, Glamorgan Spring Bay Historical Society archive; Allen to Arthur, 15 March 1828, TAHO, CSO1/170, p. 38.
12   *Colonial Times*, 19 February 1830.
13   RM Hartwell, *The economic development of Van Diemen's Land 1820–1850*, Melbourne University Press, Carlton, 1954, pp. 179–82.
14   Hobbs to Anstey, 20 May 1830, TAHO, CSO1/316, pp. 509–10.
15   *Colonial Advocate*, 1 May 1828.
16   e.g. Hartwell, *Economic Development*, p. 118.
17   Arthur to Buxton, 31 January 1835, TAHO, GO52/1/6, p. 250.
18   Clements, 'Frontier conflict', pp. 281–321.
19   e.g. *Hobart Town Courier*, 18 April 1829.
20   Clements, 'Frontier conflict', pp. 281–321.
21   H Reynolds, *A history of Tasmania*, Cambridge University Press, Melbourne, 2011, p. 61.
22   Vicary to CS, 16 February 1830, TAHO, CSO1/316, p. 416.
23   *Hobart Town Courier*, 13 November 1830, p. 3.
24   P Chapman (ed.) *The Diaries and Letters of GTWB Boyes, Volume One, 1820–1832*, Oxford University Press, Melbourne, 1985, p. 378.
25   e.g. *Colonial Times*, 19 November 1830, p. 2.
26   G Rudé, *Protest and punishment: The story of the social and political protesters transported to Australia 1788–1868*, Oxford University Press, London, 1978. Hamstringing involved the slicing of an animal's hamstring muscle, laming it. I am grateful to Andrew Gregg for inspiring this paragraph.
27   *Hobart Town Courier*, 18 October 1828.
28   Coronial inquest, 11 October 1828, TAHO, CSO1/316, p. 166.
29   *Hobart Town Courier*, 26 September 1829.
30   This is a remarkable fact, especially given the sexual violence and deprivation natives themselves suffered. They probably had cultural reasons for restraining themselves.
31   Clements, 'Frontier conflict', p. 343.
32   Clements, 'Frontier conflict', p. 342.
33   Dalrymple to CS, 28 October 1828, TAHO, CSO1/316, pp. 189–90.
34   *Colonial Times*, 26 November 1830.
35   Hayes to Arthur, 1 December 1830, TAHO, CSO1/316, p. 751.
36   Plomley, *Friendly mission*, p. 594.
37   West, *History of Tasmania*, p. 35.

38   A Laing, 'The Alexander Laing story', unpublished reminiscences of Pittwater's District Constable, 1819–38, TAHO, NS116/1, p. 56.

39   Torlesse to Vicary, 15 February 1830, TAHO, CSO1/316, pp. 422–23.

40   Minnitt to Arthur, 22 August 1831, TAHO, CSO1/316, p. 939.

41   Plomley, *Friendly mission*, p. 580.

42   James to CS, 23 May 1830, TAHO, CSO1/320, section F.

43   Plomley, *Friendly mission*, p. 561.

44   *Hobart Town Courier*, 25 October 1828.

45   e.g. Macguinnis to CS, 8 March 1830, TAHO, CSO1/316, pp. 446–48.

46   *Colonial Times*, 29 December 1826.

47   *Hobart Town Courier*, 22 March 1828.

48   Young to Williams, 1 November 1829, TAHO, CSO1/316, pp. 335–36.

49   e.g. Hobler, *Pioneer George Hobler*, p. 40; Plomley, *Friendly mission*, p. 865.

50   Plomley, *Friendly mission*, p. 885.

51   Thomas, *Henry Hellyer's observations*, pp. 41–42.

52   Prinsep, *Journal of a voyage*, pp. 88–89.

53   Prinsep, *Journal of a voyage*, p. 78.

54   Lascelles to CS, 10 June 1829, TAHO, CSO1/316, p. 273.

55   *Launceston Advertiser*, 7 February 1831.

56   *Colonial Times*, 1 June 1831; Laplace, in Roth, *Aborigines of Tasmania*, p. 40.

57   Anstey to CS, 13 October 1828, TAHO, CSO1/316, p. 177.

58   Meredith, *My home in Tasmania*, p. 84. This statement was made by Louisa Meredith, who did not arrive in the colony until 1840, though her husband Charles had been one of the earliest Oyster Bay settlers.

59   e.g. Curtain to CS, 7 February 1828, TAHO, CSO1/316, pp. 94–97.

60   e.g. Plomley, *Friendly mission*, pp. 574, 865.

61   *Launceston Advertiser*, 20 December 1830.

62   This is a relatively elaborate example of the types of fortification used by colonists.

63   WH Hudspeth to Sharland, no date, in M Sharland, *Stones of a century*, Oldham, Bedome & Meredith, Hobart, 1952, p. 56.

64   e.g. Plomley, *Friendly mission*, pp. 319, 541.

65   e.g. *Colonial Times*, 25 May 1831; Vicary to CS, 15 June 1830, TAHO, CSO1/316, pp. 525–28.

66   e.g. *Hobart Town Courier*, 5 June 1830; Beams' Ford account, Beams family papers, private collection.

67   e.g. Wood to Arthur, 14 June 1830, TAHO, CSO1/316, pp. 521–24.

68   *Hobart Town Courier*, 20 March 1830.

69   *Hobart Town Courier*, 13 March 1830.

70   Inhabitants of the Clyde to Arthur, 27 February 1830, TAHO, CSO1/316, pp. 438–43.
71   e.g. Meredith Senior to Arthur, 26 July 1824, in FitzSymonds, *A looking glass for Tasmania*, pp. 35–36.
72   Vicary to CS, 16 February 1830, TAHO, CSO1/316, p. 416.
73   Phillips to Smith, 21 April 1830, TAHO, CSO1/316, pp. 489–92.
74   Hobler, *Pioneer George Hobler*, p. 169.
75   Clark to CS, 2 November 1829, TAHO, CSO1/316, pp. 346–48.
76   Plomley, *Friendly mission*, pp. 174–75.
77   *Hobart Town Gazette*, 6 August 1824.
78   *Hobart Town Courier*, 5 April 1828.
79   Simpson to CS, 1 April 1828, TAHO, CSO1/316, pp. 137–38.
80   For robbery, see Plomley, *Friendly mission*, p. 745. For arson, see Plomley, *Friendly mission*, p. 253; PL Brown (ed.), *Clyde Company papers*, vol. 1, Oxford University Press, London, 1949, p. 99. For stock killing, see Plomley, *Friendly mission*, pp. 600, 881. For killing, see Western deposition, 11 February 1826, NLA, MS3251/2/2, pp. 131–35; Brown to AC, 5 February 1830, TAHO, CSO1/323, pp. 120–21.
81   Clements, 'Frontier conflict', pp. 279–81.
82   Plomley, *Friendly mission*, p. 865.
83   HC Stoney, *A residence in Tasmania*, Smith & Elder & Co., London, 1856, p. 33.
84   *Colonial Times*, 30 June 1835.
85   e.g. Walker, *Life and labours*, p. 97.
86   Fear of the dark, rather than the night, may explain why Aborigines were occasionally known to move by torch or moon light.
87   Plomley, *Friendly mission*, p. 406.
88   e.g. Roth, *Aborigines of Tasmania*, pp. 53–57; Hare, *Voyage of the Caroline*, p. 41; Hobbs to AC, 9 March 1830 & Robertson to AC, 4 March 1830, in Shaw, *Van Diemen's Land*, p. 48.
89   Brown to AC, 5 February 1830, TAHO, CSO1/323, pp. 139–40.
90   Plomley, *Jorgen Jorgenson*, p. 67.
91   Plomley, *Friendly mission*, pp. 555.
92   Plomley, *Weep in silence*, pp. 324–25.
93   *Ibid.*
94   Plomley, *Friendly mission*, p. 237.
95   *Tasmanian*, 25 June 1830. This ambush is described in Chapter 3.
96   e.g. Plomley, *Friendly mission*, p. 599.
97   Plomley, *Friendly mission*, p. 585.

98   Brown to AC, 5 February 1830, TAHO, CSO1/323, pp. 136–37.

99   *Launceston Advertiser*, 2 August 1830.

100   Robertson to Lascelles, 17 November 1828, TAHO, CSO1/331, pp. 170–71.

101   Walpole to Arthur, 29 October 1830, TAHO, CSO1/324; *Hobart Town Courier*, 6 November 1830.

102   Robertson to AC, 4 March 1830, in Shaw, *Van Diemen's Land*, p. 48.

103   *Colonial Times*, 19 March 1830.

104   Plomley, *Friendly mission*, p. 587.

105   e.g. Melville, *History of Van Diemen's Land*, pp. 71–72; Plomley, *Friendly mission*, p. 295; *Colonial Times*, 18 September 1829, 19 March 1830.

106   Plomley, *Friendly mission*, pp. 555.

107   Robinson to CS, 11 May 1838, in Reynolds, *Fate of a free people*, p. 37.

108   Plomley, *Friendly mission*, p. 568.

109   Batman to Anstey, 1 February 1830, TAHO, CSO1/320, section B.

110   e.g. Gilbert Robertson's journal, 14 November 1829, TAHO, CSO1/331, pp. 88–89.

111   Gilbert Robertson's journal, 27 September 1829, TAHO, CSO1/331, p. 84.

112   Hellyer to Robinson, c. 25 August 1830, in Plomley, *Friendly mission*, p. 272.

113   Plomley, *Friendly mission*, p. 529.

114   Vicary to CS, 25 May 1830, TAHO, CSO1/316, pp. 515–16.

115   Brown to AC, 5 February 1830, TAHO, CSO1/323, p. 137.

116   Brodribb to AC, 11 March 1830, in Shaw, *Van Diemen's Land*, p. 52.

117   e.g. *Colonial Times*, 22 May 1829; Curr to CS, 5 September 1831, TAHO, CSO1/316, pp. 950–53; Jorgenson to Anstey, 14 July 1829, TAHO, CSO1/320, section D.

118   Brown to AC, 5 February 1830 TAHO, CSO1/323, pp. 136–37.

119   Plomley, *Friendly mission*, p. 577.

120   *Hobart Town Courier*, 1 November 1828.

121   Plomley, *Friendly mission*, p. 924.

122   HJ Emmett, 'Reminiscences of the Black War', 1873, TAHO, NG1216, p. 1.

123   West, *History of Tasmania*, p. 30.

124   Plomley, *Friendly mission*, p. 549.

125   Robinson's speech to the Australian Aborigines Protection Society, 19 October 1838.

126   Plomley, *Weep in silence*, p. 464.

127 *Hobart Town Courier*, 23 October 1830; William Grant's journal, 13 February 1829, TAHO, CSO1/331, pp. 126–27; Plomley, *Friendly mission*, pp. 59, 776.

128 e.g. Roth, *Aborigines of Tasmania*, pp. 22, 162–63; Meredith, *My home in Tasmania*, p. 143.

129 Thomas, *Henry Hellyer's observations*, pp. 23–24; Roth, *Aborigines of Tasmania*, p. 163; I Gregg, 'A young Englishman's observations of the Aboriginals during five years in Van Diemen's Land: who was Dr John Barnes?', *Tasmanian Ancestry*, vol. 21, no. 1, 2000, p. 21.

130 Emmett, 'Reminiscences', p. 1.

131 West, *History of Tasmania*, p. 79.

132 Plomley, *Weep in silence*, p. 300.

133 *Hobart Town Courier*, 3 October 1829.

134 Plomley, *Friendly mission*, p. 550.

135 Plomley, *Friendly mission*, p. 546.

136 e.g. Plomley, *Friendly mission*, pp. 592–93.

137 e.g. C Dyer, *The French explorers and the Aboriginal Australians 1772–1839*, University of Queensland Press, St. Lucia, Queensland, 2005, pp. 151–52; Plomley, *Friendly mission*, pp. 88, 109–10, 777, 809, 868, 869.

138 Robinson to Arthur, 15 January 1830, TAHO, CSO1/317, pp. 128–29.

139 Gray to Arthur, 19 October 1830, TAHO, CSO1/316, pp. 684–87.

140 Plomley, *Friendly mission*, p. 665.

141 Plomley, *Friendly mission*, p. 88.

142 Plomley, *Friendly mission*, p. 809.

143 Plomley, *Friendly mission*, p. 816.

144 Walker, *Life and labours*, pp. 103–4.

145 Reminiscence dictated to Alexander McKay, in Calder, *Some accounts*, pp. 104–5.

146 Plomley, *Friendly mission*, p. 83.

147 Walsh to Robinson, 28 July 1838, in Plomley, *Weep in silence*, p. 569.

148 Backhouse, *A narrative*, p. 105.

149 e.g. Brown to AC, 5 February 1830, TAHO, CSO1/323, p. 139; Thomas, *Hellyer's observations*, p. 12; *Colonial Advocate*, 1 May 1828; *Colonial Times*, 10 November 1826; Roth, *Aborigines of Tasmania*, pp. 119–20; Plomley, *Friendly mission*, pp. 282, 335.

150 West, *History of Tasmania*, p. 66.

151 Plomley, *Friendly mission*, p. 536.

152 Plomley, *Friendly mission*, pp. 172–73.

153 Plomley, *Jorgen Jorgenson*, p. 68.

CHAPTER FIVE: *The Black Line*

1   Shaw, *Van Diemen's Land*, pp. 4–5. Many of this Chapter's themes are elaborated on in my article '"Army of sufferers": The experience of Tasmania's Black Line', *Journal of Australian Studies*, vol. 37, no. 1, 2013, pp. 49–63.

2   Clements, 'Frontier conflict', pp. 282–321.

3   Government Order no. 9, 9 September 1830, in *Hobart Town Courier*, 11 September 1830.

4   *Ibid.*

5   Clements, '"Army of sufferers"', pp. 21–22.

6   Anstey to CS, 14 October 1830. TAHO, CSO1/324.

7   *Hobart Town Courier*, 11 September 1830.

8   John Batman's diary, 25 September 1830, NLA, N994.6; TAHO, CSO1/316, pp. 646–59.

9   *Colonial Times*, 1 October 1830.

10 Emmett to CS, 17 September 1830, TAHO, CSO1/328, p. 182; Emmett, 'Reminiscences', p. 2.

11 Emmett, 'Reminiscences', p. 2; government memorandum, 1 October 1830, in 'Dumaresq family papers', TAHO, NS953/1/476.

12 Lloyd, *Thirty-three years*, p. 227.

13 Government Order no. 9, 9 September 1830, in *Hobart Town Courier*, 11 September 1830.

14 Party roll calls, 18–20 November 1830, TAHO, CSO1/324.

15 Plomley, *Friendly mission*, p. 258.

16 Robinson to wife, 6 October 1830, in Plomley, *Friendly mission*, p. 467.

17 *Launceston Advertiser*, 11 October 1830.

18 RW Lawrence's journal, 5 October 1830, QVMAG, CHS53–33/2.

19 Lawrence journal, 6–8 October 1830.

20 Lawrence journal, 8 October 1830.

21 Emmett, 'Reminiscences', p. 2.

22 *Ibid.*

23 Lawrence journal, 8–13 October 1830.

24 Lawrence journal, 15, 16 October 1830.

25 Lawrence journal, 15 October 1830.

26 *Ibid.*

27 Lawrence journal, 22 October 1830.

28 Government Order no. 10, 22 September 1830, in *Hobart Town Courier*, 25 September 1830; Commissariat memorandum, 9 September 1830, TAHO, CSO1/329, p. 229.

29 Foodworks 7, Xyris Software (Australia) Pty Ltd, Kenmore Hills, QLD.

30   Lawrence journal, 13 November 1830.

31   Lloyd, *Thirty-three years*, p. 223.

32   Gray to CS, 1 November 1830, TAHO, CSO1/316, pp. 714–17.

33   Douglas to Arthur, 30 October 1830, TAHO, CSO1/324; *Hobart Town Courier*, 30 October 1830.

34   Douglas to Arthur, 25 October 1830, TAHO, CSO1/324.

35   Emmett, 'Reminiscences', p. 5.

36   Douglas to Arthur, 3 November 1830, TAHO, CSO1/324.

37   *Colonial Times*, 22 October 1830.

38   Lloyd, *Thirty-three years*, p. 219.

39   Bonwick, *Last of the Tasmanians*, p. 156.

40   Plomley, *Friendly mission*, pp. 348–49.

41   Lawrence journal, 15 October 1830.

42   Arthur to CS, 20 November 1830, TAHO, CSO1/329, p. 168.

43   e.g. Plomley, *Friendly mission*, p. 349.

44   McDowell to Moodie, 25 October 1830, TAHO, CSO1/329, p. 126.

45   Mahon to Douglas, 12 November 1830, TAHO, CSO1/324.

46   Commissariat distribution log, October–November 1830, TAHO, CD11/1–2, pp. 394–95.

47   Arthur to Douglas & Wentworth, 24 October 1830, TAHO, CSO1/324.

48   Emmett, 'Reminiscences', p. 4.

49   This was the Walpole incident (discussed below).

50   *Colonial Times*, 19 November 1830.

51   Emmett, 'Reminiscences', p. 5.

52   Plomley, *Friendly mission*, p. 349.

53   Lawrence journal, 7 November 1830.

54   Lawrence journal, 18 October 1830.

55   *Hobart Town Courier*, 13 November 1830.

56   *Ibid.*

57   Lawrence journal, 18 October 1830.

58   Eighty-four volunteers served in Hobart, and 56 in Launceston. George Town (and possibly other smaller towns) also raised guards.

59   *Launceston Advertiser*, 11 October 1830.

60   Burnett to Arthur, 15 October 1830, in Reynolds, *An indelible stain?*, p. 69.

61   Melville, *History of Van Diemen's Land*, p. 99.

62   Burnett to Arthur, 23 October 1830, in Reynolds, *An indelible stain?*, p. 69.

63   Anstey to CS, 21 December 1830, TAHO, CSO1/316, p. 768.

64   Emmett, 'Reminiscences', p. 6.

65   Lawrence journal, 15 November 1830.

66 e.g. *Launceston Advertiser*, 25 October 1830.

67 Circular, 31 October 1830, TAHO, CSO1/324.

68 Douglas to Arthur, 11 November 1830, TAHO, CSO1/324.

69 Emmett, 'Reminiscences', p. 6.

70 e.g. *Colonial Times*, 3 December 1830; *Hobart Town Courier*, 27 November 1830.

71 e.g. Lawrence journal, 15 November 1830; Plomley, *Jorgen Jorgenson*, p. 108.

72 Lloyd, *Thirty-three years*, p. 219.

73 *Launceston Advertiser*, 15 November 1830.

74 Douglas to Arthur, 30 October 1830, TAHO, CSO1/324.

75 TAHO, CSO1/324; *Hobart Town Courier*, 13 November 1830.

76 Lawrence journal, 17 November 1830.

77 e.g. Jorgenson to Anstey, 30 November 1830, TAHO, CSO1/320, section D.

78 *Colonial Times*, 24 September 1830.

79 *Launceston Advertiser*, 27 September 1830.

80 *Ibid.*

81 *Launceston Advertiser*, 4 October 1830.

82 Plomley, *Friendly mission*, p. 258.

83 *Colonial Times*, 8 October 1830.

84 *Colonial Times*, 17 September 1830. Substantial sums could be made selling native skulls.

85 *Tasmanian*, 24 September 1830.

86 *Ibid.*

87 Lawrence journal, 8–9 October 1830.

88 Lawrence journal, 7 October 1830.

89 e.g. Douglas to Arthur, 25 October 1830, TAHO, CSO1/324.

90 Government Order no. 10, 22 September 1830, in *Hobart Town Courier*, 25 September 1830.

91 Jorgenson to C Arthur, 30 November 1830, TAHO, CSO1/320, section D.

92 Jorgenson to Arthur, 9 November 1830, TAHO, CSO1/324.

93 Lawrence journal, 15 November 1830.

94 Plomley, *Friendly mission*, p. 585.

95 This figure has been deduced by plotting all confirmed reports on a map.

96 Clements, 'Frontier conflict', pp. 312–14.

97 Aubin to CS, 18 September 1830, TAHO, CSO1/316, pp. 629–30; *Colonial Times*, 1 October 1830.

98 *Colonial Times*, 17 September 1830; Lyttleton to CS, 13, September 1830, TAHO, CSO1/316, p. 621.

99   Edward Dumaresq's diary, 5 October 1830, TAHO, NS953/1/376.

100 Arthur to Captain Donaldson, 13 October 1830, TAHO, CSO1/324.

101 *Hobart Town Courier*, 30 October 1830.

102 Arthur to Captain Donaldson, 17 October 1830, TAHO, CSO1/324.

103 Plomley, *Friendly mission*, pp. 522–23; Walpole to Arthur, 29 October 1830, TAHO, CSO1/324.

104 Clements, 'Frontier conflict', p. 315.

105 *Hobart Town Courier*, 20 November 1830; Walpole to Arthur 29, October 1830, TAHO, CSO1/324.

106 Lyttleton to CS, 13 September 1830, TAHO, CSO1/316, p. 621.

107 Robinson to Arthur, 20 November 1830, TAHO, CSO1/317, pp. 216–33; Batman diary, August–September 1830.

108 Plomley, *Friendly mission*, pp. 309–12.

109 *Ibid.*

110 *Ibid.*

111 e.g. W Gray to Arthur, 23 October 1830 & J Gray to Arthur, 19 October 1830, TAHO, CSO1/316, pp. 684–95. This man, identified here as 'Limogana', was almost certainly Mannalargenna. The timing and details all confirm this assertion, as do the writings of Jorgenson (Plomley, *Jorgen Jorgenson*, p. 113) and West (*History of Tasmania*, p. 59).

112 Mannalargenna left his young son at Batman's.

113 W Gray to CS, 1, 11 November 1830, TAHO, CSO1/316, pp. 714–17; *Hobart Town Courier*, 13 November 1830.

114 Walpole to Arthur, 29 October 1830, TAHO, CSO1/324.

115 *Hobart Town Courier*, 30 November 1830; Plomley, *Weep in silence*, pp. 324–25.

116 Plomley, *Friendly mission*, p. 209.

117 C Darwin, *The voyage of the Beagle*, Bantam, New York, 1972, p. 38; *Hobart Town Courier*, 13 November 1830.

118 Douglas to Arthur 27 October 1830, TAHO, CSO1/316, pp. 703–4; *Hobart Town Courier*, 6, 30 November 1830; *Colonial Times*, 5 November 1830.

119 *Launceston Advertiser*, 11 October 1830.

120 Plomley, *Friendly mission*, pp. 584–86.

121 Plomley, *Friendly mission*, p. 209.

122 Walpole to Arthur, 29 October 1830, TAHO, CSO1/324; Arthur to Murray, 20 November 1830, SLNSW, ML, A1771, p. 53.

123 Lawrence journal, 11 November 1830.

124 Plomley, *Friendly mission*, p. 124.

125   *Hobart Town Courier*, 23 October 1830; Arthur to Gordon, 19 October 1830, CSO1/324.

126   *Colonial Times*, 19 November 1830.

127   Plomley, *Friendly mission*, pp. 522–23.

128   Plomley, *Friendly mission*, p. 525.

129   See Chapter 6.

130   *Hobart Town Courier*, 13 November 1830.

131   *Colonial Times*, 12 November 1830.

132   *Ibid.*; *Hobart Town Courier*, 13, 20 November 1830.

133   *Hobart Town Courier*, 20 November 1830; *Launceston Advertiser*, 6 December 1830.

134   Plomley, *Friendly mission*, p. 575.

135   Batman to Frankland, 18 November 1830, TAHO, CSO1/316, pp. 742–44. After fleeing Batman's with Mannalargenna, Mungo does not appear in the record again.

136   Robinson's report, February 1831, in Plomley, *Friendly mission*, pp. 470–71.

137   Plomley, *Friendly mission*, p. 317.

138   *Ibid.*

139   Plomley, *Jorgen Jorgenson*, p. 99. Such scholars include Calder, *Levée, line and martial law*, pp. 187–89; J Connor, 'British frontier warfare logistics and the 'Black Line', Van Diemen's Land (Tasmania), 1830', *War in History*, vol. 9, no. 2, 2002, p. 143; McMahon, 'The British Army and the counter-insurgency campaign', pp. 90–94; Ryan, *Tasmanian Aborigines*, p. 112; Reynolds, *Fate of a free people*, p. 51.

140   Plomley, *Jorgen Jorgenson*, p. 99. Original italics.

CHAPTER SIX: *The war's end*

1   Reid to Williams, December 1830, in Brown, *Clyde Company papers*, p. 110.

2   Lawrence journal, 15 November 1830.

3   Lloyd, *Thirty-three years*, p. 234.

4   *Colonial Times*, 28 January 1831.

5   Lyttleton to CS, 31 January 1831, TAHO, CSO1/316, p. 854.

6   Smith to CS, 7 February 1831, TAHO, CSO1/316, pp. 65–76.

7   *Tasmanian*, 18 June 1831; Robinson to AC, 23 February 1831, in Shaw, *Van Diemen's Land*, p. 80; O'Connor to AC, 16 March 1830, in Shaw, *Van Diemen's Land*, pp. 54–55; Kelly to AC, 10 March 1830, in Shaw, *Van Diemen's Land*, p. 51.

8   *Hobart Town Courier*, 26 March 1831.

9   *Ibid.*

10   Smith to CS, 21 March 1831, TAHO, CSO1/316, p. 905; *Hobart Town Courier*, 26 March 1831; *Independent*, 11 April 1831; *Tasmanian*, 8 April 1831.

11   Unsigned letter, O'Connor's papers, Connorville, item 7, miscellaneous letters folder. My italics. I am indebted to Andrew Gregg for this letter.

12   *Tasmanian*, 8 April 1831, p. 112.

13   Executive Council minutes, 30 November 1830, in Reynolds, *Fate of a free people*, pp. 118–19.

14   *Hobart Town Courier*, 13 February 1830.

15   *Ibid.*

16   e.g. Batman diary, July–August 1830.

17   Major Gray to CS, 1, 11 November 1830, TAHO, CSO1/316, pp. 714–17.

18   AC report, 4 February 1831, in Shaw, *Van Diemen's Land*, pp. 76–78.

19   Plomley, *Friendly mission*, p. 530.

20   Executive Council minutes, 30 November 1830, in Reynolds, *Fate of a free people*, p. 119; Sharland to Parramore, 25 June 1831, TAHO, CSO1/323, pp. 279–81.

21   Plomley, *Friendly mission*, p. 375; *Colonial Times*, 8 October 1830.

22   *Launceston Advertiser*, 31 January 1831.

23   Logan to Arthur, 14 March 1831, TAHO, CSO1/316, pp. 901–4.

24   Smith to CS, 31 January 1831, TAHO, CSO1/316, pp. 857–58.

25   Lascelles to CS, 29 June 1831, TAHO, CSO1/317, pp. 449–50.

26   Arthur to CS, 30 July 1830, TAHO, CSO1/317, pp. 169–70.

27   Howells to Vicary, 5 August 1830, TAHO, CSO1/316, pp. 545–47; Vicary to CS, 16 August 1830, TAHO, CSO1/316, pp. 564–66.

28   Robinson's report of 23 September 1829 (TAHO, CSO1/317, pp. 83–91) gave the figure of 22 dead, but this included several casualties among a visiting party from the south-west.

29   Plomley, *Friendly mission*, p. 276.

30   Robinson to Arthur, 20 November 1830, TAHO, CSO1/317, pp. 216–33.

31   e.g. *Colonial Times*, 22 February, 1 March 1831; *Launceston Advertiser*, 14 March 1831.

32   *Launceston Advertiser*, 7 February 1831.

33   *Launceston Advertiser*, 19 September 1831.

34   *Independent*, 24 September 1831.

35   *Independent*, 15 October 1831.

36   *Independent*, 17 September 1831.

37   *Colonial Times*, 17 August 1831.

38   Story to Arthur, 25 October 1831, TAHO, CSO1/316, pp. 1015–22.

39   *Ibid.*; Aubin to CS, 31 October 1831, TAHO, CSO1/316, pp. 1041–44; *Hobart Town Courier*, 26 November 1831.

40   e.g. Story to Arthur, 25 October 1831, TAHO, CSO1/316, pp. 1015–22; Meredith to Arthur, 27 October 1831, TAHO, CSO1/316, pp. 1030–32.

41   Recollections of John Lyne, in E Stoddart, *The Freycinet Line, 1831: Tasmanian history and the Freycinet Peninsula*, Freycinet Experience, Coles Bay, 2003, p. 13.

42   Meredith to Arthur, 27 October 1831, TAHO, CSO1/316, pp. 1030–32.

43   *Colonial Times*, 11 January 1832.

44   *Hobart Town Courier*, 14 January 1832.

45   Meredith, *My home in Tasmania*, p. 78.

46   *Examiner*, 2 October 1847.

47   *Ibid.*

48   Fenton, *James Fenton of Forth*, pp. 201–2.

49   Calder, *Some accounts*, pp. 107–8.

50   Plomley, *Friendly mission*, pp. 148–49, 520, 604, 661–63, 800–2.

51   Plomley, *Friendly mission*, pp. 452–53.

52   Plomley, *Friendly mission*, pp. 517–98, 601–2.

53   Plomley, *Friendly mission*, p. 599.

54   Plomley, *Friendly mission*, p. 602.

55   Plomley, *Friendly mission*, p. 584.

56   Plomley, *Friendly mission*, pp. 248, 251; Calder, *Some accounts*, p. 86.

57   Calder, *Some accounts*, p. 86.

58   Nongoneepitta deposition, 24 September 1831, TAHO, CSO1/316, pp. 984–85; Plomley, *Weep in silence*, pp. 399–400.

59   Coronial report of Dr John Smith, 24 September 1831, TAHO, CSO1/316, pp. 976–79.

60   Nongoneepitta deposition, 24 September 1831, TAHO, CSO1/316, pp. 984–85.

61   Plomley, *Weep in silence*, pp. 399–400.

62   Clements, 'Frontier conflict', pp. 344, 346.

63   e.g. H Reynolds, 'Terra Nullius reborn', in R Manne (ed.) *Whitewash: on Keith Windschuttle's fabrication of Aboriginal history*, Black Inc., Melbourne, 2003, pp. 125–26.

64   West, *History of Tasmania*, pp. 57, 73.

65   Plomley, *Friendly mission*, p. 412.

66   Arthur to Murray, 15 April 1830, in Shaw, *Van Diemen's Land*, p. 17.

67   Robinson to CS, 5 January 1832, CSO1/318, p. 127.

68   *Colonial Times*, 11 January 1832.

69   Stokes, *Discoveries in Australia*, p. 466.

70   Robinson to Montague, 31 July 1835, in Reynolds, *Fate of a free people*, pp. 151–52.

71   Reynolds, *Fate of a free people*, p. 151.

72   Plomley, *Friendly mission*, p. 446.

73   e.g. Plomley, *Friendly mission*, pp. 427, 454, 457, 500, 599; Robinson to CS, TAHO, CSO1/318, pp. 45–51; Plomley, *Weep in silence*, pp. 747–48.

74   E Gover, 'Tasmania through Russian eyes (nineteenth and early twentieth centuries)', *THRA Papers & Proceedings*, vol. 37, no. 4, 1990, p. 157.

CHAPTER SEVEN: *The north-west frontier*

1   Jones, 'Tasmanian tribes', pp. 331–52.

2   McFarlane, *Beyond awakening*, p. 78.

3   McFarlane, *Beyond awakening*, pp. 81, 89.

4   Jorgenson memorial, 8 January 1828, in G Lennox, 'The Van Diemen's Land Company and the Tasmanian Aborigines: a re-appraisal', unpublished draft, STL, TL.Q 994.60049915 LEN, 1991, appendix.

5   Plomley, *Friendly mission*, p. 244.

6   Stokes, *Discoveries in Australia*, p. 459.

7   Plomley, *Friendly mission*, p. 215.

8   McFarlane, *Beyond awakening*, p. 90.

9   McFarlane, *Beyond awakening*, p. 91.

10   Hare, *Voyage of the Caroline*, p. 41.

11   *Ibid.*

12   Plomley, *Friendly mission*, p. 230; Windschuttle, *Fabrication*, pp. 249–94; I McFarlane, 'Cape Grim', in R Manne (ed.) *Whitewash: on Keith Windschuttle's fabrication of Aboriginal history*, Black Inc., Melbourne, 2003, pp. 277–98.

13   Plomley, *Friendly mission*, p. 230.

14   Curr to Directors, 17 January 1829, in McFarlane, *Beyond awakening*, p. 105.

15   Curr to Directors, 7 October 1830, in McFarlane, *Beyond awakening*, pp. 112–23.

16   Goldie to Arthur, 5 October 1829, in G Lennox, 'The Van Diemen's Land Company and the Tasmanian Aborigines: a re-appraisal', *THRA Papers & Proceedings*, vol. 37, no. 4, 1990, p. 185.

17   McFarlane, *Beyond awakening*, pp. 109–12.

18   Stephen to Arthur, n.d., in Reynolds, *Fate of a free people*, p. 112.

19   McFarlane, *Beyond awakening*, p. 112.

20   Plomley, *Friendly mission*, p. 230.

21   Plomley, *Friendly mission*, p. 229.

22   Curr to Schayer, 6 December 1841, in McFarlane, 'Cape Grim', p. 293.

23   Curr to Archer, 10 August 1841, in McFarlane, *Beyond awakening*, p. 117. Spring guns were designed to fire on persons who triggered a hidden switch. Mantraps (which were also used in the east) were large spring-loaded metal jaws.

24   McFarlane, *Beyond awakening*, pp. 169–80.

25   Hare, *Voyage of the Caroline*, p. 41.

26   Curr to Arthur, 6 January 1830, in Reynolds, *Fate of a free people*, p. 56.

27   Clements, 'Frontier conflict', p. 349.

28   Plomley, *Friendly mission*, pp. 236–37, 871.

29   Expeditions by James Kelly (1815–16, 1819); Cunningham and King (1819); Charles Hardwicke (1823); James Hobbs (1824).

30   Bowden, *James Kelly*, p. 31.

31   Plomley, *Friendly mission*, p. 696.

32   See Thomas, *Henry Hellyer's observations*, pp. 12–77.

33   Plomley, *Friendly mission*, p. 215.

34   Plomley, *Friendly mission*, p. 244.

35   Plomley, *Friendly mission*, pp. 806–16.

36   Plomley, *Friendly mission*, p. 215.

37   Plomley, *Friendly mission*, p. 645.

38   Plomley, *Friendly mission*, p. 230.

39   Plomley, *Friendly mission*, p. 225; McFarlane, *Beyond awakening*, pp. 111–12.

40   Plomley, *Friendly mission*, pp. 837–38.

41   e.g. Plomley, *Friendly mission*, pp. 220, 637, 881, 945.

42   Windschuttle, *Fabrication*, pp. 108–9.

43   Plomley, *Friendly mission*, p. 951.

CHAPTER EIGHT: *The sea frontier*

1   'Sea frontier' was coined by Patsy Cameron in *Grease and Ochre: The Blending of Two Cultures at the Colonial Sea Frontier,* Fullers, Launceston, 2011.

2   Not all men in Bass Strait were sealers, but most were, and the collective label was contemporaneous.

3   My estimate. See Plomley & Henley, *Sealers of Bass Strait*, pp. 18–19, 71–73.

4   K Merry, 'The cross-cultural relationships between the sealers and the Tasmanian Aboriginal women at Bass Strait and Kangaroo Island in the early nineteenth century', *The Flinders University Online Journal of Interdisciplinary Conference Papers*, vol. 3, no. 1, 2003, p. 80.

5   Stewart to Campbell, 28 September 1815, *HRA*, ser. 3, vol. 2, pp. 575–76; AC Begg & NC Begg, *The world of John Boultbee*, Whitecoulls, Christchurch, 1979, pp. 53, 59; Balfour report, 5 May 1826, TAHO, CSO1/36, pp. 180–96; Plomley, *Friendly mission*, pp. 86–87; *Hobart Town Gazette*, 10 June 1826.

6   *Hobart Town Gazette*, 25 March 1826.

7   *Hobart Town Gazette*, 18 February, 25 March, 10 June 1826; *Australian*, 9 March 1826; Balfour report, 5 May 1826, TAHO, CSO1/36, pp. 180–96.

8   Balfour report, 5 May 1826, TAHO, CSO1/36, pp. 180–96.

9   Plomley, *Friendly mission*, p. 162. Munro, an ex-convict, lived on Preservation Island from about 1820 until his death in 1845. Appointed the straits' first constable in 1825, he was a charismatic, but often unscrupulous man.

10   Plomley, *Friendly mission*, pp. 336–38.

11   Hobbs to AC, 9 March 1830, in Shaw, *Van Diemen's Land*, p. 50.

12   Backhouse, *A narrative*, pp. 88–89; Plomley, *Friendly mission*, 1047–48.

13   Stewart to Campbell, 28 September 1815, *HRA*, ser. 3, vol. 2, pp. 575–76.

14   Plomley, *Friendly mission*, pp. 212–15, 284–85, 345.

15   Plomley, *Friendly mission*, pp. 305–7.

16   Plomley & Henley, *Sealers of Bass Strait*, pp. 36, 48, 51, 54, 60, 70; Plomley, *Friendly mission*, pp. 284–85, 328–31, 340–42; Plomley, *Weep in silence*, pp. 443–44. Ages are observers' conjectures.

17   Plomley, *Friendly mission*, p. 91.

18   Kelly to AC, 10 March 1830, in Shaw, *Van Diemen's Land*, p. 51; Bowden, *Captain James Kelly*, p. 37.

19   Plomley & Henley, *Sealers of Bass Strait*, pp. 27–28.

20   Kelly to AC, 10 March 1830, in Shaw, *Van Diemen's Land*, p. 51.

21   Plomley & Henley, *Sealers of Bass Strait*, pp. 49–64.

22   Plomley & Henley, *Sealers of Bass Strait*, pp. 34, 50–58, 64–65, 70; Plomley, *Friendly mission*, p. 414.

23   Plomley, *Friendly mission*, pp. 333–34.

24   Plomley, *Friendly mission*, p. 294.

25   Stewart to Campbell, 28 September 1815, *HRA*, ser. 3, vol. 2, pp. 575–76.

26   Plomley, *Weep in silence*, pp. 445–46.

27   Plomley, *Friendly mission*, pp. 389–90.

28   Kelly to AC, 10 March 1830, in Shaw, *Van Diemen's Land*, p. 51.

29   Plomley & Henley, *Sealers of Bass Strait*, p. 25.

30   Kelly to AC, 10 March 1830, in Shaw, *Van Diemen's Land*, p. 51.

31   Plomley, *Friendly mission*, pp. 281, 284–85, 372, 625.

32   Plomley, *Friendly mission*, pp. 374–75.

33   e.g. Begg & Begg, *John Boultbee*, pp. 60–61; Plomley, *Weep in silence*, pp. 445–46.

34   Begg & Begg, *John Boultbee*, pp. 21–24.

35   Lockyer's journal, 17 January 1827, *HRA*, ser. 3, vol. 6, p. 472.

36   Plomley, *Friendly mission*, pp. 338–39.

37   Plomley, *Friendly mission*, pp. 291–92; Plomley & Henley, *Sealers of Bass Strait*, pp. 33–70.

38   Plomley & Henley, *Sealers of Bass Strait*, p. 65.

39   e.g. Plomley & Henley, *Sealers of Bass Strait*, p. 50.

40   West, *History of Tasmania*, p. 24.

41   Kelly used the name 'Lamanbunganah', but this was almost certainly Mannalargenna.

42   Bowden, *Captain James Kelly*, pp. 36–42.

43   Plomley, *Friendly mission*, p. 289.

44   Plomley, *Friendly mission*, p. 91.

45   Bowden, *Captain James Kelly*, pp. 36–40. Briggs eventually betrayed Mannalargenna, selling his daughter, and abandoning or selling their three female children (Plomley & Henley, *Sealers of Bass Strait*, pp. 27, 65).

46   e.g. Calder, *Some accounts*, p. 91; Balfour report, 30 May 1826, TAHO, CSO1/36, pp. 180–96; AC report, 19 March 1830, in Shaw, *Van Diemen's Land*, pp. 35–55.

47   Plomley, *Friendly mission*, pp. 291–92.

48   Backhouse, *A narrative*, pp. 88–89.

49   *Hobart Town Gazette*, 26 August 1826.

50   Plomley, *Friendly mission*, pp. 328–31.

51   Backhouse, *A narrative*, pp. 88–89.

52   e.g. Plomley, *Friendly mission*, pp. 328–31, 333–34.

53   e.g. Plomley, *Friendly mission*, pp. 305, 328–31, 428; Backhouse, *A narrative*, pp. 88–89.

54   Plomley, *Friendly mission*, p. 309.

55   Plomley, *Friendly mission*, pp. 336–38.

56   e.g. Plomley, *Friendly mission*, pp. 323–24, 427, 490–493; Backhouse, *A narrative*, pp. 88–89; Walker, *Life and labours*, pp. 108–9.

57   e.g. Plomley, *Friendly mission*, p. 356.

58   Walker, *Life and labours*, p. 119.

59   McFarlane, *Beyond awakening*, p. 56.

60   Plomley, *Friendly mission*, pp. 444–45.

61   Plomley, *Friendly mission*, p. 226.

62   e.g. Plomley, *Friendly mission*, p. 345; Robertson to Lascelles, 17 November 1828, TAHO, CSO1/331, pp. 171–72.

63   Robinson to CS, 11 October 1831, in Plomley, *Friendly mission*, p. 504.

64   Plomley, *Friendly mission*, pp. 287–88.

65   Calder, *Some accounts*, pp. 92–101; Plomley, *Friendly mission*, pp. 226, 284–89, 427–45, 871; Clark to CS, 29 October 1830, TAHO, CSO1/316, p. 709.

66   Plomley, *Friendly mission*, p. 300.

67   Plomley, *Friendly mission*, pp. 309–12.

68   Plomley, *Friendly mission*, pp. 489–93.

69   Plomley, *Friendly mission*, pp. 432–33.

70   Plomley, *Friendly mission*, p. 428.

71   Mannalargenna was shot by the sealer David Kelly at Ringarooma Bay (Plomley, *Friendly mission*, p. 646).

72   Robinson to Arthur, 20 November 1830, TAHO, CSO1/317, pp. 231–32; Campbell, *John Batman and the Aborigines*, 1987, p. 39.

73   Plomley & Henley, *Sealers of Bass Strait*, pp. 18, 71–90.

CONCLUSION

1   Plomley, *Friendly mission*, p. 524.

2   Windschuttle, *Fabrication*, p. 356.

ACKNOWLEDGMENTS

There are many fine PhDs that never get published. For an unknown writer like myself to get a contract requires a hearty measure of good patronage and good luck. First and foremost, I want to thank Henry Reynolds. As outstanding a person as he is a scholar, Henry has been an invaluable guide and inspiration, nourishing but never dictating the development of my ideas. I was further aided and abetted by scholars such as Alan Atkinson, Tom Dunning, Bill Gammage, Rex Hesline, Murray Johnson, Ian McFarlane and Phyllis Pitchford.

I am indebted to the Order of Australia Association Foundation for their encouragement and generous financial support during my undergraduate degree.

My gratitude is also extended to Debbie McGowan and Clive Tilsley, who were instrumental in putting me in contact with publishers. Numerous librarians, archivists and enthusiasts – those unsung heroes of historical research – have also been of incalculable assistance, as has Margaret Muir, Edwina and Michael Powell, Ben Thorp and Rohan Wilson, all of whom read early drafts. Topping it all off, the team at University of Queensland Press has been an absolute pleasure to work with. It is a singular thing to have such people believe in you, and I am grateful to them all, especially Jacqueline Blanchard, Madonna Duffy, Sybil Kesteven and John Hunter.

I especially want to thank my family and friends, splendid humans such as Joel, Sally, Nate, Marli, Betty, Hughie, Pat, Alma, David, Cathy, Kally, Dane, Simon, Caroline, Chris, Madeline, Stella, Rowan, Lauren, James, Marian, Alex, Dana, Ben, John, Nic, Anjie, Danny, Natalie, Sweeney and Mr Ris. Above all though, I am beholden to my wife, Kristy, and my parents, Lindy and Paul, for their unwavering love and support.

INDEX

Note: photographs (**FIG**), graphs (**g**), and maps (**map**) are in bold